CHAPLAIN DAVIS AND HOOD'S TEXAS BRIGADE

CHAPLAIN DAVIS AND HOOD'S TEXAS BRIGADE

Being an Expanded Edition of the Reverend Nicholas A. Davis's
The Campaign from Texas to Maryland, with the Battle of Fredericksburg
(Richmond, 1863)

Edited, with an Introduction, by

DONALD E. EVERETT

With a New Foreword by

ROBERT K. KRICK

Louisiana State University Press
Baton Rouge

Manufactured in the United States of America

Louisiana Paperback Edition, 1999
08 07 06 05 04 03 02 01 00 99
5 4 3 2 1

Library of Congress Cataloging-in-Publication Data

Davis, Nicholas A., 1824–1894.
Chaplain Davis and Hood's Texas Brigade : being an expanded edition of the Reverend Nicholas A. Davis's The campaign from Texas to Maryland, with the battle of Fredericksburg (Richmond, 1863) / edited, with an introduction, by Donald E. Everett ; with a new foreword by Robert K. Krick. — Louisiana pbk. ed.
p. cm.
Originally published: San Antonio : Principia Press of Trinity University, 1962.
Includes index.
ISBN 0-8071-2392-7 (pbk. : alk. paper)
1. Confederate States of America. Army. Texas Brigade. 2. Davis, Nicholas A., 1824–1894. 3. Hood, John Bell, 1831–1879. 4. United States—History—Civil War, 1861–1865—Regimental histories. 5. Texas—History—Civil War, 1861–1865—Regimental histories. 6. United States—History—Civil War, 1861–1865—Personal narratives, Confederate. 7. Texas—History—Civil War, 1861–1865—Personal narratives. 8. United States—History—Civil War, 1861–1865—Campaigns. 9. Fredericksburg (Va.), Battle of, 1862. I. Everett, Donald E. II. Title.
E580.4.T4D38 1999
973.7'464—dc21 98-50887
CIP

The paper in this book meets the guidelines for permanence and durability of the Committee on Production Guidelines for Book Longevity of the Council on Library Resources. ♾

For my son John and his friend Frank, great-grandson of the Chaplain.

ACKNOWLEDGMENTS

Grateful acknowledgment of their assistance is less than the deserved recognition due the following persons: Frank C. Davis Jr. and Miss Marjorie McGown, of San Antonio, and Mrs. L. R. Bryan, jr., of Houston, grandchildren of the chaplain; Dr. John C. Abbott, former librarian, and Mrs. Avis F. Bunton of the George Storch Memorial Library, Trinity University; Professor Paul R. Busch, Dr. H. T. Davis, Edgar Watkins, Miss Ann Hetherington, and Dale A. Somers of Trinity University; Dr. Llerena Friend, Barker Texas History Center, University of Texas; Miss Laura Armitage of Richmond, Va.; and Mrs. James F. Bartlett, James R. Nowlin, and Frank R. Prassel of San Antonio. The editor also wishes to express his appreciation to Trinity University for funds which made this research and publication possible. In particular he wishes to thank his wife, Mary Lou, for her forbearance.

CONTENTS

FOREWORD

The storied history of the Texas Brigade is buttressed by a bumper crop of primary narratives. Southwesterners who carried the brigade's muskets left enough strong eyewitness accounts to help us understand significant aspects of their war experience. Two fine books by J. B. Polley of the 4th Texas fit comfortably on any shelf of key Confederate books. John W. Stevens's *Reminiscences* deserves favorable notice as a standard; so too does John C. West's *A Texan in Search of a Fight.*

Good books by veterans J. M. Polk, Val Giles, Decimus et Ultimus Barziza, George T. Todd, D. H. Hamilton, M. V. Smith, and O. T. Hanks all contribute useful evidence about the Texas Brigade at war. The best Civil War novel ever written, John W. Thomason's *Lone Star Preacher,* chronicles the story of the brigade, focusing on the 5th Texas. The splendid published memoir of Samuel Henry Emerson (Malvern, Arkansas, 1918), unrecorded and unknown until recently, affords fresh information and insights.

Nothing in that impressive array of Texas Brigade literature—not even Emerson's rare gem—is as important as the work by Nicholas A. Davis.

Chaplain Davis wrote at firsthand, fresh from the battlefront, and went into print during the war. His perspicacious approach, his intelligent analysis, and his frontline vantage combine to give Davis's account tremendous value. The volume's salient defect is its scope: as the title suggests, the narrative ends halfway through the conflict. Thus the immediacy that is Davis's great strength is also the one drawback. The story he vividly launched was not yet completed at the time of publication.

Chaplain Davis and Hood's Texas Brigade affords a bayonet-level perspective on the first victory for Lee and his army, at the Battle of Gaines' Mill. The brigade played a pivotal role in that desperate encounter, charging headlong into a powerful, daunting Federal position that had withstood Confederate efforts for endless hours. The Texans performed magnificently at the storm center of the largest combined assault that Lee ever launched—perhaps four times as strong as the famous charge by Pickett's division and allied units at Gettysburg. Davis's writing breathes the drama and terror of that violent onset: "with a wild, mad shout . . ."; "one grand rush . . ."; and "threw themselves upon the enemy—charging over the mirey branch & over the breastworks."

The narrative also features a number of energetic harangues against the "deception and fraud . . . lying and stealing . . . and diabolical history" of northerners. In a single deep breath, the chaplain defines "Yankee" as synonymous with "meddlesome, impudent, insolent, pompous, boastful, unkind, ungrateful, unjust, knavish, false, deceitful, cowardly, swindling, thieving, robbing, brutal and murderous." Even those modern readers who are inalterably convinced that Yankees are, in fact, noblemen pure and simple will find interesting Chaplain Davis's eloquent exposition of the prevailing southern view on that subject, vintage 1863.

For a century, students of the war had little access to Davis's work. Secondary accounts of the brigade's role sometimes did not even cite it. Confederate-imprint first editions of Davis have always been expensive, and they command immense prices today. The 1863 Richmond printing, complete with its wraps, fetches a mid-four-figure price. The 1863 Houston imprint is even dearer. No Texas Brigade book is as scarce, collectible, and costly.

During the Civil War Centennial, Professor Donald E. Everett produced a first-rate new edition of the book published a century earlier. His skillfully expanded, edited, introduced, and indexed version constituted a major improvement on the 1863 printings—antiquarian collectibility aside. Everett's adroit additions about Davis and the brigade nicely augment the original material. It is that excellent edition that is reprinted here and thus made accessible to a new generation of readers.

The importance and fame of Nicholas Davis's book arise in considerable degree out of the towering reputation of the unit it describes. General R. E. Lee's Army of Northern Virginia counted a number of fabled military formations on its rolls. No brigade survived two defensive stands as desperate as those of the South Carolinians under Maxcy Gregg and Samuel McGowan at Second Manassas and Spotsylvania's Bloody Angle. The early war achievements of the Stonewall Brigade made that unit a legend. It would be difficult to argue against the prowess of S. D. Ramseur's North Carolinians, John B. Gordon's Georgians, and the Louisianians who followed Richard Taylor and then Harry Hays.

Of all that renowned roster, it seems to me that the Texas Brigade stands tallest in the Army of Northern Virginia pantheon. So subjective a judgment is of course impossible to prove. The precise final hierarchy is in any case not of profound meaning. Almost anyone examining the matter would readily assign the brigade a ranking at least very high among the army's most distinguished organizations. Chaplain Davis's classic book, accordingly, is the best primary source about a brigade unexcelled on the war's most famous battlefield.

FOREWORD

Reviewers readily recognized the importance of Davis's narrative and the value of Everett's additions. Dayton Kelley, author of a fine monograph on the brigade at the Wilderness, called the 1962 edition "one of the finest" books of its kind. Harold B. Simpson, the most prolific modern author about the Texans, declared that Davis ("a good writer" and "keen observer") and Everett (who did "an admirable job" and "so ably edited") had produced a volume "of particular interest and value." Other reviewers supplied a steady stream of superlatives: "masterfully," "epic," "vividly and movingly" (Fort Worth *Star Telegram*); "fine history," "vivid accounts" (San Antonio *Express and News*); "excellent," "wonderful," "a fine study" (Lincoln *Herald*); "rousing account," "priceless historical reference," "a good yarn" (Houston *Chronicle*).

The leading scholarly journal in operation at the time of the new edition called the 1863 book "one of the most sought-after Confederate imprints," lauded the "vast improvement" resulting from the revisions, and accurately prophesied that the Everett version would "win much popularity."

More than one-third of a century has passed since the release of Everett's fine work, itself now difficult to find and expensive to buy. Renewed publication of this great Confederate classic will introduce modern students of the war to the sturdy Texans and their fellow southerners who made the "Texas Brigade" the shock troops of Lee's Army of Northern Virginia.

ROBERT K. KRICK

Fredericksburg, Virginia

PREFACE

Chaplain Nicholas A. Davis had intended to expand his *Campaign from Texas to Maryland* (Richmond, 1863) after the war, but he was not a man to reminisce. Indeed, according to his children, he permitted no discussion of the war in his presence; perhaps it is well that he restricted himself to the slight revision published in Houston in August of the same year. Other members of Hood's Texas Brigade, including the General himself, wrote or contributed to memoirs published over a span of fifty years. Clouded by faulty memory, some composed their accounts in light of later events. Only the "Chaplain of Hood's Texas Brigade," as he came to be known even though he officially served only the 4th Regiment, left such an extensive contemporary account. Had he revised the *Campaign* after the war, it too might have become just another memoir.

When a book has become so rare as to be found in no more than a dozen depositories, when the asking price of the few available copies has moved into the three-figure bracket, and when the volume has remained uncited in major publications involving the principal subject, the historian ponders the problems of a new edition. Inasmuch as the writer had at his disposal both editions published in 1863, the manuscript diary kept by the chaplain during the first two war years, several hundred papers left by Davis, and the services of his generous grandson, Frank C. Davis, Jr., who provided these source materials, it seemed propitious to expedite a ninety-nine year old resolution: "When circumstances will permit, he designs publishing a more extended and complete narrative. . . THE AUTHOR."

What the present editor has in mind, of course, is hardly that which the author intended. This publication is an expanded version of the Richmond edition, with added interpolations from the Houston edition and the diary. It also includes an Introduction based largely on the diary and other materials found in the Davis papers, augmented by information from Richmond and Houston newspapers (1861-1862), the indispensable *Official Records,* memoirs of other members of the Brigade, and select secondary sources which deal with these Texans in Virginia. Editorial interpretation is restricted to a minimum to permit the chaplain and, occasionally, his contemporaries to speak for themselves.

Although an account by a participant, the reader must remember that Davis was not always on the scene of action. Absent from the regiment from February 13 to May 23, 1862, on a recruiting mission to Texas, Davis was not with his regiment in the Yorktown Peninsula. After the battle at Gaines' Farm his duties required attendance upon the sick and wounded Texans in hospitals in and about Richmond. Descriptions of subsequent battles are not from personal observations even though the chaplain recorded them in his diary. Davis nowhere stated it, but the information must have been obtained from Captain W. C. Walsh and R. A. Davidge, to whom the author wrote in the Introduction of the Richmond edition, "thanks are already due."

A faithful reproduction of the manuscript material has been attempted, the exceptions being in punctuation, capitalization, and the spelling of proper names. The absence of punctuation could easily confuse the reader and a minimum of marks have been added to improve readability. For the same reason, the expected [*sic*] does not appear to correct the numerous inconsistencies in capitalization and spelling. Diary entries inscribed in small pocket notebooks of varying sizes did not lend themselves to proper sentence structure. Other papers of Davis indicate that he had more respect for the teachings of grammarians, although he would have satisfied few. With the *Campaign* the editor has taken the liberty to correct obvious typographical errors and to omit photographs of Hood, Warwick, and a battle flag, each too poorly defined to be reproduced. Interpolations from the diary are indicated by italics and those from the Houston edition are indicated by brackets. These additions may correct factual statements (especially dates), present an interpretation sometimes at variance with the first edition, or present material which does not appear at all in the original work. Thus, the Richmond edition has been expanded by approximately 12,000 words.

The Houston edition, while deleting material, added some valuable biographical information. Unpublished diary entries included descriptive battle scenes not found in either publication, and more forthright comments on hospital conditions than the chaplain would have thought feasible to publish at the time. Diary entries which do not contribute to an understanding of the *Campaign* have not been interpolated, others which are of relevant but indirect connections to the story have been incorporated in the Introduction, while those of no significance have not been put to print.

PREFACE

In reading the *Campaign*, it must be remembered that Davis intended "to keep an account of the 4th alone." He did not presume to write a history of the entire Brigade, although he included information on the 1st and 5th regiments, especially in the Houston edition to meet their requests for further recognition. Furthermore, Davis published the volume because he believed that Hood's Texas Brigade had received insufficient praise. This motivation induced the chaplain to write less of his particular duties, of considerable interest to present day students, and more eulogistically of the Brigade. Notice of their superb fighting had been ignored generally in the Richmond press except in "letters to the editor" written by irate Texas soldiers. This was not enough for the men who filled the ranks of what Douglas Southall Freeman has called "the most renowned Brigade of the entire Army."

CHAPLAIN DAVIS AND HOOD'S TEXAS BRIGADE

INTRODUCTION

Richmond was an exciting place to reach on September 12, 1861, after the exhausting journey of nearly four weeks which the 4th Texas Regiment made by foot, wagon, carriage, steamer, and rail car. Like soldiers of a later day, Chaplain Nicholas A. Davis made the rounds seeking old friends. At the Hermitage Fair Grounds he found two companies from his native North Alabama; at the war department he renewed acquaintanceships and called upon Leroy P. Walker, secretary of war. A trip to the post office was less rewarding as he "got nothing."[1]

Rumors of Yankee troop movements floated about the city, according to Davis, but there was "nothing reliable, except the conformation of the fall of Hatteras [N.C.] & surrender of 600 or 800 of our men." Meanwhile, the chaplain concerned himself with the spiritual welfare of Texans far from home. The first evening in Richmond found him at his calling.

> At candle lighting we [had] divine service in the camp. It was well attended & the men participated as if they were glad of an opportunity to return their gratitude to high heaven for the care taken of them thro. all their perilous journey. We had passed wreck after wreck on the road where cars were smashed, & lives wer[e] lost.—We had not met with a single accident in the whole journey of 1600 ms. And I do know that my own heart did feel thankful.

Within the next few days, Chaplain Davis made "arrangements to get some religious papers & tracts for the men to read during their leisure hours—got 100 tracts for which I payed $1." He was pleased that "the boys seemed anxious to get them." Religious pamphlets were also forthcoming from the editor of the *Central Presbyterian*, William Brown, D.D.,[2] who was to aid the chaplain throughout his stay in Virginia.

Although on his first Sabbath in camp "everybody seem[ed] to be going to the city," Davis preached a sermon from Isaiah 63:1-3 to a small audience.

> We occupied the stand arranged by the 14th Reg. Lo[uisiana] Vol. A few of them were present. This reg. is a part of the celebrated Polish Brig. a no. of whom were killed by their officers on their way to this place on account of their insubordination.[3]—Tho' the no. was not great yet I hope some good impressions were made for I could see that the men wer[e] not only attentive but interested & a few were feeling. Their

> behavior was unexceptionable. The evening I spent in reading & talking on religious subjects with those who visited my tent. At 5 o'clk an Episcopal Clergyman said prayers & recited a sermon for the La. 14th. large attendance. He had on his white robe—looked like he needed some *Hoops* &c. principal portion of the audience were from the city—very few of the soldiers present. At night the Rep. of St. Peter conducted services for the Catholics of the same Reg. at the same place.

Davis spent considerable time in theological study and the diary entries during his first weeks in Virginia usually cited his Biblical reading for the day, ranging from three or four up to twenty chapters. He received a number of visiting ministers and chaplains at his tent, including the Methodist Reverend William H. Seat of Huntsville, Texas. Young men "who seem to be serious & love to talk about religious matters" were also attracted to the Presbyterian chaplain. Yet his whole attentions were not directed toward the righteous.

> A young man Johnson came & entered into a pleasant conversation & made many inquiries about old acquaintances in Ala. said he was the son of a minister—talked freely about the dissipation of the camp. asked me to pray for him & manifested a great concern for religious services—gave me a dollar to buy candles & bade me good night. May God give him that Spiritual light that will guide him to the throne of God. Riley Hammond a wicked boy called & conversed in same way. Oh Lord be merciful to him.

Waywardness in a faraway place presented a particular problem for Davis, just as it has for men of the cloth in uniform in other wars. Perhaps it is conventional that chaplains have attempted an amalgamation of Christian and national pride as a formula for keeping young soldiers within the narrow path. And certainly many of these Texans had not yet reached manhood. Davis' appeal, in one of his earlier Virginia sermons, also included the special reminder that they represented the Lone Star state.

> Read the 121 Ps.—talked about 20ms. good order & attention—poor singing. My object was to show the importance of an upright walk & especially to the young men, that they hereafter be judged by their conduct in the camp. They are the representatives of Texas and should keep an eye to the honor of our State. And they should also remember that they are the Repr[esentatives] of a christian nation, and if they would have God to preserve their 'going out & their coming in' they should 'look to the hill wherest cometh our help.'

> I feel to enjoy a great deal of the comforts of the religion of the Lord Jesus Christ notwithstanding I am in the midst [of] very wicked & vulgarly profane men. Oh my God, in life or death I am thine.

Spiritual ministrations to the soldiers, later extremely difficult under battle conditions, met with obstacles in a settled camp situation. In one instance the chaplain complained that he "had to contend with the disadvantage of natural as well as spiritual darkness. For the light was so dim that I could but see outlines of about one half of the men present." On occasions he did not preach planned sermons "because of other services near at hand" or "in consequence of misunderstanding at roll call." In other instances there were no divine services because "of the gen[eral] confusion of settling a new camp," of "a great want of discipline," or "the men had scattered off." Cold weather and rain also frequently canceled gatherings.

Scheduled services sometimes proved vexatious to the minister. "My Scripture lesson was not so interesting this evening owing [to] constant interruptions." On another occasion he "preached about midway of the camp at the south end of the street. About 100, only attended, had tolerable liberty in speaking." Lack of candles annoyed him also. "Stated to the men that the commisary Gen. refused to grant me candles for the purpose of holding Divine Service in the camp. Upon which $3.25 was contributed to buy candles."

Within a few weeks after his arrival in Richmond, Davis' reputation as a preacher became more generally known. It pleased him to note in his diary on October 4 the "increasing interest in the Services—about 200 present—sung well." A week later he reported "Sacred Sabbath Sun Shine—Preached at 10-1/2 o'clk. The largest cong. that has ever attended yet—From indications the discourse was very well Recd." By the following Sunday he ministered to his own regiment in the morning with "quite a number of Citizens" in the audience, and walked two miles in the afternoon to deliver a sermon to the 5th Texas Regiment with four hundred in attendance. The "good order" and a return invitation pleased him, but after candle lighting back in his own camp he found himself "quite fatigued."

Baptisms, attendance upon the sick, and funeral services were also routine for Chaplain Davis. Presbyterian though he was, he "immersed Charles Barhan, of Capt. Martins comp." on an October Sunday. Earlier that day he had performed his "first funeral Service over the remains of one of our Solders, Sloan of Capt. Martins comp. It was quite a solemn scene." Two days later the busy tempo continued as he "visited all the Sick in the hospital twice thro' the day—all are doing well—About 50 are in the camp. About 350 in the City.—learn that one in the City is dieing." Colonel John B. Hood, at the Spotswood Hotel with the "flux," the chaplain found "convalescent—but . . . quite feeble." Dissatisfied that so many of the ill soldiers were sent from camp to hospitals in the city, Davis obtained permission to move into Richmond the first Sunday in November so that he could more readily attend to their needs. Although provided for in various hospitals of the city, about fifty Texans received attention in the Barracks Chimborazo.[4] For several days the solicitous chaplain walked from one hospital to another, but by week's end Davis and many of the recuperative men returned to camp.

The chaplain's first experience with the wounded came during a visit to a prisoners' hospital just north of Richmond. En route he stopped on a hilltop to enjoy the view of the city and to visit an old cemetery where he was fascinated by an unmarked tomb where "*a* sweet little rose tree stood smiling up into the open face of heaven; while twining about its little armes below the meadow grass was still sparkling with the morning dew." His page-long escape from reality as he wrote of the "living tree that blooms along the river of heaven" ceased when he entered "the house of suffering."

> And here were objects of pity all around. Here is a poor emaciated creature from Mass. feeble and sinking from a wound recd. at the Battle of Manassas, his leg amputated. And theres another of two wounds from Me. Yonder is one in the corner who recd. a ball just under his heart from Hartford. There is a poor boy of about 19 summers whose right leg was gone . . . I spoke with several of the propriety of regarding this as a warning to prepare for another & Higher State of being. They all took it kindly & all but one seemed anxious that I remain longer & when my time was out some of them insisted that I return & visit them again. Poor fellows, here they are a long ways from home & some of them verry near the grave. Their homes on earth they never will see. One of them said he had a religious Mother—read his bible some but had not prayed. I asked if his Mother had not taught him while he was a little boy, to pray. He could not speek—said when I left he would pray. . . . As I left the hospital I really felt the truth of Solomans declaration 'It is better to go to the

> house of mouring than to go to the house of feasting.' And I felt like weaping over their misfortunes altho', they had come with manacles to fetter my brethren & subjugate my country —to overrun & burn & bleed those of my own community & household. But I humbly hope God will forgive them, both for what they have done & what they intended doing.

Religious duties did not prevent the chaplain from enjoying some social distractions during his Richmond stay. Visitors from Texas appeared in the camp on occasion, Governor Francis R. Lubbock on his way to Manassas, and Congressman Caleb C. Herbert who brought "supplies for the boys." The chaplain often combined pleasure with business when he went into the city and visited Richmond friends, both lay and clerical. Widower Davis often called in the home of Miss Mattie Brackston, "an interesting girl and fond of talking," toward whom he revealed no romantic attachment. At the Brackston's he found a generous family who received him frequently and informally, sometimes in the company of other Texas officers. "At the request of Capt Key I accompanied him to Mr. Brackstons to spend the night there. At 8 o.c. the boys, Surenade the family—the old host [Brackston] took us by surprise—Jumped in the floor & went to dancing. He says he is a member of the Baptist church. At bed time he requested family worship.—I complied—he seemed verry devotional.—had a pleasant nights rest with Dr Hill of the Tom Green Rifles." Mrs. Brackston gave Davis meals from time to time and saw to it that his clothes were "done up." Miss Mattie contributed to his comfort on occasion: "She hemmed my hand towels." Only an unidentified "Miss Maggie," among the young Richmond ladies he met, attracted the widower's attention briefly. On an October evening he had planned to "walk over [to visit her] after supper but a Gent. came in & prevented—I wish he had gone some where else."

Richmond offered much in the way of sightseeing for the small-town Texan. On one occasion he visited the Capitol "& after several efforts worked my way up to the top of the building and standing on a plank on the comb I had a magnificent view of almost the entire City." Descending, he made his way to the war department "& took a peep at Mr. [Judah P.] Benjamin, the Sec. of war protem. From his appearance I would guess him a business man, but not of a high order of talents."

On a horseback trip on which he set out to "examine the defences of the city" on an October morning, he had planned to draw a sketch.

The penned lines in his diary do not contribute to one's understanding of the defences of Richmond.

> Well I had thought I would make a drawing of the 7 forts on the east of the city but I make such a poor out at it & think I would do well to give the outline in words instead of lines. To the N. E. a fort commands the road leading to the city. About 2ms. from the Capitol where about 1000 may be worked. 1m. south of this fort another with an enclosed retreat in which the same no. may be employed. So. bearing west about 1/2m. are the barracks where about 30000 men can be wintered. S. E. & on a line with the other two is a little fort where about 200 can be worked. S.E. of this one that will employ 1500. S. of this 1m. another for 1000 and SWest of the latter one for 1000. North of the last about 1/2m. one for 500. None are mounted but may be in a few days. Some of the guns are at the place.

At this point the diarist digressed from the purpose of his mission to retell one of the oldest of American folk tales. The nineteenth century version may be of some interest.

> I visited Powhattan, the place where the great Indian chief whose life makes up a part of the history of the Old Dominion once lived. I saw the stone which is said to overly his grave . . . It is nicely inclosed by a little arbor of lattice work which stands west of Mr. Mayo's residence by which family it has been owned & settled about 100 years. From this point due south of the residence refered to are the two ancient Elms, between which the wigwam of Powhattan stood. Both of which are now dead & their stately arms are now falling & returning to the dust as did the strong arms of the Indian warrior . . . . The trees stand about 30 ft apart & an arbor marks the place where the Indian rested his weary limbs both from the battle & the chase. And around which the Indian girl amused her self in her native sports & gathered the blossoms from natures garden. Passing from the Wigwam S.E. about 50 paces I beheld the granite upon which once lay the head of Smith sentenced to death, but as the war club was swung into the air to make the fatal blow, Pocahontas threw herself upon the sentenced man & prevailed with the stern warrior—her Father, to stay the stroke & let his prisoner go. Wonderful girl, her history will be read with interest as long as the granite rock shall mark the spot, upon which her name became immortal.

The chaplain whose imagination could permit him to see "two marks" which "look as if made by a Broad axe one hundred & fifty years ago," was also blessed with a sense of humor. His military reconnaissance resulted in an episode which proved that the minister could enjoy a joke at his expense—on a week-day.

> In the evening about 4 o'clk I noticed two Cavaliers ride up to the gard line & heared the guard call out for Lieutenant [S. H.] Darden. I could hear a word occasionally & learned that they were describing some one whome they supposed to be a spy. But I paid but little attention until I heard one of them say he was riding a Bay horse with one eye—was dressed in black with slouch hat & slippers on. Sandy whiskers large & fine looking—And after he took a diagram of the Battery he inquired the way to the Tex camp & then turned in the other direction & rode off—towards another Battery. When this came out I called the Lt. & said to him that I thought I could find the man. And as soon as I put on my hat & walked up—all agreed that I was the spye, But no Yankee. The persuers were satisfied & returned. But the boys enjoyed the joke well. The man who saw me & reported must be *non compus* or he never would have supposed me a Yankee. The news ran over the camp in a few minutes & then to Col. Hoods tent & the superior officers enjoyed the joke at my expence. But as they did not get to see me this evening I will be ready for them in the morning. And it being Sunday I will tell them they must not talk about such things on that good day.

Davis was indeed a "fine looking" man and especially so in his new chaplain's uniform in which he had "three ambrotipes" taken for members of his family in Alabama and Texas. Upon cashing his first paymaster's check, he had gone to the "taylor to take my measure for a coat ($30.00) & pants at $13.00. The only difference between a chaplains uniform & a citizens dress is, the coat is straight breasted with two rows of brass buttons of seven each." His wardrobe also included a pair of pants ($8.00), a vest ($5.00), a pair of boots ($9.00), a flannel shirt ($3.00), and two pairs of flannel drawers. Within the week he was back in town to get his uniform. "I had it altered a little, fits well. Coat & pants 45.50 which is a little more than contracted for, but the coat was trimmed which was not anticipated at the time —verry much admired."

In a "little communication" to the Richmond *Enquirer* Davis objected to the "exorbitant charges of Tailors" even though he must have been pleased with the following published letter from a minister to the editor of the same newspaper.

> I observed a Chaplain (Rev. Nicholas A. Davis, of Texas) in uniform on yesterday, which uniform I admired above anything I have yet seen. A suit of black clothing strait breasted, with one row of brass buttons, and simple pointed cuff with a small *olive branch* about six inches long, running up the sleeve. We learn that it was made by C. Wendlinger No. 146, Main st. No stripes on the pants.[5]

Davis complained from time to time of the cost of other items and wrote another letter to the *Enquirer* on the salaries paid chaplains. As in the previous instance, a search did not reveal this communication; it may not have been published. Although the *Enquirer* had mentioned the subject previously in a September issue, it had little to say on this topic at a time when the *Dispatch* carried several comments on chaplains' pay.[6] Many ministers had difficulty living on the monthly salary of $50, but Davis had a stock farm back in Texas which apparently brought an income sufficient for his family's needs.

He revealed more personal than financial concern for his children. "I have not heard a word from my sweet little Elonora & Nannie since I heared them weeping as if their hearts would break, because their Papa was leaving to go to the war & it may be to see them no more on earth. Oh God, I commit them to thee." News of their good health did not reach him for more than two weeks after his arrival in the Confederate capital. In this instance the letter was seventeen days in the mails. Within the year, with the Yankees in control of New Orleans and the lower Mississippi, his letters arrived by a more circuitous route.

Mail from home supplied relief from the dull monotony of camp life which was noted in a number of the entries. These Texans had come to fight the Yankees and seemed overly anxious for activity. "Rather a lively day with the boys policing. Burning brush &c." was certainly not the type of excitement which the chaplain envisaged when he began his diary. Punishment meted out to wayward soldiers occasionally disrupted the wearisome routine.

> Quite a stir in the camp a little after dark this evening [October 25] in consequence of Frank Rogers being brought in by a guard from the Potomac—He had procured a furlow for *9* days, which he altered to *29*.
>
> Everything passed off pleasantly thro' the day except the drumming out of Butler for stealing money from a comrad—Capt Martin's company. It was a Sad Spectacle. He was marched under crossed Bayonets followed by drum & fife—On his knap

> sack in large letters the word *Thief* was written.—The whole Reg. almost to a man gathered round him & cheered him on & finally the boys ordered him to a double quick & fired several guns after him.

A more pleasant pastime attracted the 4th Regiment on the following evening when Daniel Collins' Brass Band "performed its first piece —The boys met & sung an hour in the harmony." Less innocent diversions have been recorded in the memoirs of other members of the 4th Texas; but if the chaplain participated in these, which is doubtful, he made no mention in the diary. His conscientiousness was reflected in such recorded transgressions as "I feel ashamed of the way in which I have spent the evening, layed down & slept for two hours" and "I did not rise until the sun was rising."

Early rising was not unusual for Texans, but Davis noted time and again one activity uncommon to these men—walking. Vicissitudes in the recruitment of infantrymen in Texas emanated from the "predilection of Texans for cavalry service, founded as it is upon their peerless horsemanship."[7] Once in the infantry, not only privates and chaplains traveled afoot. "Dined with Col. [R. T. P.] Allen of Bastrop who walked with me to the camp." Only on a few occasions did Davis indicate his good fortune to borrow a horse. Many errands of mercy involved distances of several miles and often he walked in the company of Texas officers. "Started to the city with Col. Darden at 1 o'clock. The walk fatigued me very much."

Confederate chaplains enjoyed no particular status. To judge the position of these ministers by a Confederate congressional act which stated that "chaplains in the Army be, and they are hereby, allowed the same rations as privates,"[8] would be misleading. As the army hierarchy did not provide a set role and position for these men, individual merit undoubtedly had much to do with the chaplain's acceptance in the social coterie of the officers. Newspaper accounts of the period certainly reflected the variable talents of these churchmen in uniform. In comparing criticisms made of the chaplaincy in general and the comments regarding this particular chaplain, Davis displayed qualities superior to the ordinary minister in Confederate service.

Upon his arrival in Richmond and for a month thereafter Davis' diary indicated, however, that his living accommodations approximated those of the common soldiers. He erected his own tent. Failing in an effort to obtain flooring for it, Davis reported that he "walked about a mile & gave 5cts. for what straw I could carry to the camp. I guess I got the worth of my money, but by the time I got to the camp I had paid well for my straw." On October 10 he commented that "the weather has been so bad I have not moved my tent yet, tho' assigned my position in the line with the field officers some days since." A week later Lieutenant Colonel "John Marshall wanted to know if I had recd. orders to move up on the officers line—I told him I had declined for the present. He looked rather puzzled." Two days later the chaplain complied when he moved his "tent on the staff line." By November 10 Davis moved his "Quarters from Capt Key's Comp. & by invitation of the Col. [Hood] I will mess with him in time to come."

Meanwhile there had been more than ordinary excitement in the Texas encampment. Rumors of their removal to a new site (Manassas being the most often suggested) circulated on October 30, the day before the troops were ordered to "pack up every thing that we would not need for the winter & deposit them with the Capts." Rain began to fall as preparations for movement were made.

> Rained & blew all night. Had to get up twice in the night to reset the stakes to keep my tent from blowing over—A great many blew down . . . . our whole camp is in a mess . . . . Rained all [the next] days. I do pray & believe that our God will wreck the Grand Fleet on its way to the South to bombard & burn our homes.

Two days later the chaplain "learned that Several of the Ships of the grand armada were stranded. Tha[n]k God, for this demonstration of his love."[9] Two weeks of confused preparation continued before the Texans departed to meet the Yankees. On November 11 Davis noted: "Today was my first Sight of contending armies. The roar of the cannon was terrific. Oh what a pity that a nation once so proud & happy must now be torn & rend from one end to the other, & overrun with fire & sword."

Dumfries, within earshot of the enemy base on the Potomac, was the destination of the 4th Texas, a movement accompanied by an inordinate amount of confusion due in large part to a threatened attack from the enemy. Changes in orders made "everybody mad," the cold and windy weather contributed to the discomfort of the men, and sufficient provisions had not been brought along. "Lt. Wade & myself were sent out with 18 men to press some waggons, corn, potatoes." Women and children cried as the Texans "pressed" three homes.

Cannon at Cock Pit Point, overlooking the Potomac, were mounted by a detail of one hundred men. General Louis T. Wigfall "with all his Colonels" came to inspect the camp, pickets were out, and the Texans daily anticipated a Yankee assault. Expectation of enemy attack and exchange of gunfire alternating with inactivity were to be the routine of the Texans in their winter camp for the next three months. "Yankees shooting at our batteries & at every hill & hollow & thicket to try the strength of our guns & find our position." Confederate guns meanwhile were able to cripple some of the enemy's shipping on the river.

During December, Davis, upon his return from a journey to Richmond for medicine, preached and visited in the Dumfries hospitals. While the sick improved, he seemed less satisfied with his spiritual ministrations. On Sunday, December 22, he "visited the 5th. Tex. agreeable to appointment but it was thought to be too cold for Service & at 2 O'clk. the bugle call was made but none turned out, and I think from the reason that no preparations had been made for seats. Col. Hood said it should [be] attended to and seats should be prepared." Year's end brought reflections of home and heaven to the Texas minister.

> CHRISTMAS day. The day celebrated for the nativity of my Lord & Savior, Jesus Christ. Twelve months ago I was at home with my little ones & the nation was at peace. Today I am 2,000 ms. from home & we are convulsed with war. Oh God what will another year bring forth. 'Thy will Be done.' I went to Dumfries. The officers & ladies making merry over a big 'Nog.' Returned & found a number gentlemanly tight—quite annoying at night. Oh God what will another year bring forth?
>
> * * * * * * * * * * * * *
>
> This is the last day of the year 1861. How Serious the thought—will I live to see another begin? Will I live to see it close? If so, will I be a better man than I now am? God being my helper I will. This day has been a busy one—Mustering the Reg. & I suppose it has been a busy day through out both armies N & S . . . . Oh my Father in Heaven forgive all that I have done & said & thought amiss thro' the year that is now past & almost gone. And if I live to see the close of another may I have done more to promote the Kingdom & thy glory than ever before. Amen. Bless & take care of my little

ones at home & if I see them no more on earth may I meet them in heaven. Amen.

* * * * * * * * * * * * *

This date [January 1] causes me to feel sad & yet greatful, because it reminds me of many events of the past & that I am hastening to the grave. Thankful because of his mercies & blessings which have preserved my health & perpetuated my being so amazingly [well] while so many have been sick & so many have died. From my verry Soul I will praise him for his loving kindness to me. I have seen the close of the year 1861 and God has permitted me to see the first day of the year 1862. Oh God help me to fear thee & keep thy commandments.

Several references during the Dumfries stay, "Col. Hood handed me the N. York Sun at bed time" and "our house" which had a "wall of logs and roofed with a hospital tent with a good floor & chimney," could suggest that the chaplain occupied the same lodgings as Colonel Hood.[10] A notation on the first Sunday night in the New Year indicated a close relationship between the chaplain and some of the senior officers; it also bespoke the religious interests of the unbaptized Hood.[11]

What a day or an hour may bring forth the God omniscient only knows. Before another Sabbath shall have come and gone the storm may burst upon us, and hundreds of our brave men may be torn & bleeding on the field. But into thy hand Oh God we commit us with all our cares both public & private—the care of loved ones at home as well as the affairs of our bleeding country.—Col. Hood picked up the Bible & opened it as we sat quietly by our fire tonight & the first sentence that his eye rested upon reads, I shall not die but live (Ps. 118:17), which he read aloud. And then read the remainder of the Ps. Hood then proposed that each of us open & read in like manner. And as I was near him I opened & read. Then Col. Marshall. Then Capt. Ryan. Next Dr. Ester. And last Adj. Bassett. The inferences & applications were made & we will see what will be our destiny. Believing that the Lord is our refuge & strength.

Snow covered the ground at Dumfries for several days in early January and the inactivity continued. J. B. Polley, a young private in Company F, recalled in his memoirs fifty years later that after building each "mess" the men had little to do other than fatigue and guard duty and maintain the pickets at Cockpit Point. Weather permitting, both Colonels Archer and Hood insisted on drill, guard mounting, and dress parades as a means of maintaining discipline. The one-time private recalled "cards, checkers, backgammon, and chess, and, with the cards, more or less gambling for small stakes" as pastimes, while conversation centered around news in the Richmond papers. "The one monotony was the staying in one place—the grievous lack was feminine society."[12] Chaplain Davis' notation of January 6 reflected their impatience. "The boys have spent the day in making fires & sitting around them—burning shins & breeches legs. Quite a number of which have to [be] stuffed in the boot legs to hide them. A cheerful spirit pervades all the camp. And all are looking for the northern mercenaries & anxious for them to come."

Packages from the outside offered something in the way of a diversion. Through the good offices of Dr. Brown in Richmond, the chaplain received thirty pairs of socks, two pairs of gloves, fifty-two Testaments, and a bundle of tracts from the "kind hearted people of Richmond." Davis enjoyed distributing these gifts to the appreciative men. "I offer my thank[s] to the kind donors & the warmest gratitude to God. And I pray that they may all be bless[ed] of him to the comfort—both Spiritual & temporal, of those for whom they are sent. And may a kind heaven smile upon the homes & hearts of those who are mindful for our good while in the field."[13]

Less pleasant tasks during the winter involved the chaplain's attendance upon soldiers on their deathbed. Prayers of supplication were offered and sometimes hymns were sung.

> Sent for after supper to see Mr. Harrison about to die of Capt Key's Co. Talked, read, sung & prayed with him but reason seemed ruling on her throne—Called to see him again at 10 O'clk. but he had expired. And it was a sad scene—his mess had moved him out in the moon light and there he lay unclad in the cold slumbers of death. Oh death thou pitiless tyrant! But thanks be to God who giveth us the victory. But this poor man did not gain the victory.

A week later a more tragic death involved the brother-in-law of General Wigfall.

> Dr. [G. W.] Cross, Brig. Surgeon, died this morning at 4 O'clk. from intemperance—He had got up and was sitting in his chair & supposing no one in the room exclaimed, 'Great God Almighty, am I left here all alone in the dark to die & go to Hell.' But Dr. Randall who was lying in the room got up

> & on approaching him found him holding to the chair to keep from falling. [Randall] took him up & laid him on his bed, but his fears were soon realized. He [Cross] expired in a few minutes. Oh what horrors hung round that awful moment. He has got his discharge. But oh the disgrace [that] hangs round that awful discharge.

Rain, sleet, or snow fell as routine hospital visits and several funerals each week occupied the chaplain until, on February 12, Colonel Hood received telegraphic orders from Richmond for his chaplain to return to Texas on a recruiting mission. Davis had requested this assignment on December 20, his application being "seconded by Col. Hood & Lt. Col. Marshall."

He entrained for Richmond on the day following receipt of the communication. Remaining the next five days in the capital he attended to business, visited with friends, and witnessed two memorable scenes. "Saw the procession from the Capitol of O. Jennings Wise[14]—a great concourse," and two days later "the confederate congress assembled & organized both branches. And so this is the first day of our permanent government—long desired come at last."

Davis departed for the "far west" on February 20, but "at the junction the Iron horse broke down & it took us until night to get to Lynchburg." Travelers to Lynchburg turned westward at the Burkville junction, some fifty miles south of Richmond. Davis could have been less fortunate; on the next day a freight train ran off the track on the Richmond side of the Junction, delaying traffic for four hours while the track was cleared.[15]

Poor train connections, a landslide, a stopover visit with Alabama relatives, and a sick slave resulted in a journey which required one month. Davis made the trip by train, steamboat, stage coach, and a few miles by foot before he arrived at his home on March 20. Following a route through Lynchburg, Bristol, Knoxville, Chattanooga, Huntsville, Jackson, and Berwick Bay to Houston, Davis encountered considerable inconvenience in Louisiana, where he was forced to wait two days in New Iberia for a stage. Once he boarded the stage he went "all day without anything [to] eat & all night without a place to sleep." Robbin, his servant who had accompanied him from his father's home in Alabama, became painfully ill prior to their arrival at Niblett's Bluff. Finding that their boat had departed two hours earlier, Davis spent several days here to enable Robbin to recuperate under the care of a physician. Although the boat which the chaplain and the slave traveled on to Beaumont went "ashore frequently," the remainder of the trip to his Bastrop home was relatively uneventful.

During the month which Davis spent in Texas he made trips to Webberville and Austin. Specifically, he busied himself with recruiting from March 27 to April 14, but he did not keep his diary in this period. No later comments attested to the success or failure of this venture, but the muster roll included in the Appendix lists forty-three recruits in March and April for the 4th Regiment. This enlistment effort did raise the ire of Texas Governor Francis R. Lubbock who complained in a letter to Judah P. Benjamin, Confederate secretary of war, that persons had been authorized to come into the state and recruit 1,500 men for infantry service to fill the regiments serving in Virginia without the Texas officials receiving any knowledge of their action. "I most respectfully demur and protest against the Government taking the men out of the State except by call through the State authorities."[16]

Meanwhile, Samuel A. Roberts, who had obtained this authority from Jefferson Davis in Richmond, was confronted with the problem of competing with still other individuals who had been authorized to recruit for shorter terms in the cavalry.[17] To this Lubbock likewise raised objections. The governor insisted that Roberts, whose area of recruitment was north and east of the Trinity river, had been "placed on a much more favorable footing to raise men than the Executive of the State" in that Roberts' enlistees would be permitted "to transport themselves on horses and mules to be ultimately purchased by the Government."[18]

Diary entries did not reflect these controversies and on April 14, Davis simply recorded that he "started back to the Potomac." Two weeks intervened before he actually departed from Houston, following closely the route he had traversed on his southward journey, detouring somewhat in Louisiana "as the Yankees have N. Orleans." A month later he rejoined the 4th Texas at Pine Island, three miles east of Richmond.

In the chaplain's absence the Texans had moved to the Yorktown peninsula, but by his return they had fought a retreat up the James river to the vicinity of Richmond. Davis later included in his diary regimental activities of this four-month interval recorded by unidentified persons, but as suggested in the Preface, probably by Captain

W. C. Walsh and R. A. Davidge.[19] However, the diary contributed little information not published in one of the editions of the *Campaign* on the trip to Yorktown, the skirmishes thereabouts, the return to Richmond, and the fighting during the remainder of 1862. Entries become more detailed beginning with the seven-days fighting around Richmond. In most details the published work follows closely the diary material; and in other instances the relevant diary material has been interpolated in the published work.

One additional accomplishment of the chaplain mentioned in both editions, the building of the Texas Hospital, merits further explanation. Dissatisfied with the dispersion of wounded Texas soldiers in hospitals in all parts of the city following the battles around Richmond, Davis on July 27 "had a consultation with the officers as to the propriety of establishing a State hospital—Agreed to & I was appointed to purchase the lumber & other material to erect a ward at the infirmary St. Francis De Sales." After two days of searching he found no proper materials. "I felt our project must fail." But he renewed his efforts and on the third day "as I passed over the bridge to Manchester I discovered a Saw Mill on the Island & went & fortunately found what I desired. So I immediately made the purchas[e]—returned to the camp & made requisition for waggons to haul it to the place." Lack of tools then delayed the project, but with the necessary materials purchased by Sergeant C. W. McAnnelly the work neared completion within two weeks. The Texas Hospital was as unpretentious as the chaplain's bookkeeping; including the building materials, expenditures for carpenter and negro hire, cartage, dishes, a stove pipe, a broom, and shirts and drawers for the patients, the expenses amounted to $758.47.

Extraneous undertakings of the chaplain included alms and loans proffered to needy men. Personal items of some soldiers found their way into the chaplain's care—pocket books, rings, a knife, and a daguerrotype among others. From time to time he made purchases of foodstuffs for the hospital and his own mess, recording the sums paid for eggs, matches, fruit, and candles. He also paid for such services as "removing patients" and employing carpenters and porters. Elsewhere inside the back covers of the small notebooks in which he kept his diary there are dozens of notations which are meaningless to the present-day reader, with the exception of one: "(K) David

Green dead, refused to give Hood the flag, but said, 'Tell me where & I will take it.' "

A later estimate of the chaplain of the 4th Texas Regiment, by Mrs. Angelina V. Smith Winkler, a Richmond girl who married Captain C. M. Winkler, Co. I, 4th Texas, ably summarized his role.

> It would be unjust to the work of a noble man if no mention was made of Rev. Nicholas Davis, Chaplain of the 4th Texas Regiment. He went with them from Texas, shared their camp life, ministered to them whether sick or well. Every man respected him for his many superior qualities, and to him they went with all their vexations and annoyances, always sure of the sympathy of a generous heart, filled with love and forebearance towards his fellow men. Soldiers, ever ready to make sport on all occasions, facetiously asserted that if their officers were not considered *au fait* on the military, their doctors were not wise enough to dose them, the authorities never meddled with their chaplain, as he was good enough to attend to their spiritual condition, if he had come all the way from Texas.[20]

Conceivably the great faith which these men had in their spiritual leader enabled the chaplain turned author to enjoy a "sell-out" within a few months of his only publication. When Edward Hopkins Cushing, editor of the Houston *Telegraph* published the second edition of *The Campaign from Texas to Maryland*, it received considerable notice in the press. Cushing's widely circulated *Telegraph* provided the chief source of information from the theater of war for such newspapers as David Richardson's Austin *State Gazette*.[21] An ardent supporter of the Southern cause, Cushing published his *Telegraph* throughout the war even though some issues were printed on butcher's paper and one on wall paper.[22] Davis, a sometime "letter to the editor" contributor to the Houston paper, found a logical publisher in fellow Presbyterian Cushing.

> THE CAMPAIGN FROM TEXAS TO MARYLAND IS NOW REPUBLISHED.—It embraces a history, particularly of the Fourth Texas Regiment, from the first enlistment in Texas down to the great battle of Fredericksburg last winter, including many notices of the 1st and 5th Texas, biographical sketches of nearly every officer of the Brigade who has distinguished himself, etc., etc. It is a book of thrilling interest.
> At the solicitation of many persons the book has been republished in Houston, the first edition published in Richmond having been exhausted, comparatively few copies ever having

> reached this State. The present edition is considerably amended by the author, and many new biographies introduced.[23]

Testimonials which the chaplain received following publication of the earlier edition, and reproduced in the Houston paper of August 17, supported the sale of the book. Colonel William Preston Johnston, aide-de-camp to President Jefferson Davis, wrote that he had been "directed by the President to return to you his thanks for a copy . . . commemorating the gallant deeds of the glorious 4th Texas Regiment and its commanders. This pious record furnishes an example for imitation, that the exploits of the heroes of this struggle may not pass from the memory of men."

Fellow Texan and by this time the commander of the 4th Regiment, Lieutenant Colonel Benjamin F. Carter, read the book with the "greatest of pleasure."

> Within the contracted limits of a work like this, it is impossible to embrace every incident of interest in the remarkable campaign of the Texas Brigade, but you have succeeded in grouping together the most important of them, and delineating them with great truthfulness and fidelity.—Your little book embraces valuable statistical information of enduring interest, and will prove invaluable to the future historian.
>
> I trust your enterprise and energy will place within the reach of all our friends at home this record of our toils, our sufferings, and our triumphs.[24]

Richmond newspapers had not ignored the Texan's first edition. The *News* described the volume as "a neat little work" and noted that the chaplain detailed "the adventures of the brave Texans, without indulging in fulsome praise." According to the *Enquirer*, the book would be "read with delight by all the people of the Confederacy. It will inspire fresh ardor, and rivet the conviction, that a cause, upheld by such men cannot fail." The *Enquirer* noted that the book, in relating the sufferings and triumphs of the Texans, recorded "many of the most stirring incidents of the war. No troops in the service have more distinguished themselves than those from Texas." A reviewer in the *Dispatch* found the *Campaign* "well written . . . amusing as well as entertaining." Comments in a Richmond publication, the *Central Presbyterian*, were undoubtedly by its editor and Davis' benefactor, Dr. William Brown.

> We have been much entertained in reading this Campaign, and all the more from having a personal acquaintance with its esteemed author, a minister of the Cumberland Presbyterian Church, and one of the most faithful, useful chaplains in our army. There is a sterling honesty and good sense pervading this production; the whole account is lively, and many of the incidents of thrilling interest. It is a valuable contribution to the history of the war, and Mr. Davis is to be much commended for the industry with which he has collected, arranged and presented so much valuable matter. If some one could have done the same for every regiment, the value of such contributions, as materials for general history, would be invaluable.[25]

Published in 87 pages (16 mo.), the Houston edition sold at the same $4.00 price as the Richmond publication of 168 pages (12 mo.). Obvious omissions in the Houston edition included the appendix listing the casualities of each regiment in Hood's Texas Brigade (comprising the 18th Georgia, but only a summary for the Hampton Legion of South Carolina) and a detailed muster roll of the 4th Regiment of Texas Volunteers. Not only did it list the participation of each man in each of the major engagements of the regiment in 1861-1862, but it included relevant remarks as to the status of many individuals. Davis explained this omission in the Houston edition (p. 83).

> In consequence of the many errors which were found to exist in the list of casualties and muster rolls as published in the first edition, I have determined to omit them, for I would not do one of the brave men of our command injustice in these reports under any consideration, and although great pains were taken by the officers to make the reports correct, and much care on my part to print them exactly as furnished to me, yet there are numbers of errors, and we feel that it were better that ninety and nine delinquents go unpunished rather than one innocent man suffer wrongfully; we, therefore, drop the roll for the present, and will not republish it unless it be perfected by the officers. And as so many mistakes have been made, I here take occasion to say that those absent without leave may not merit such a charge.

Inasmuch as the present editor does not have to answer to the thirty-seven men listed as absent without leave in one battle or another, he believes it of value to reproduce the muster roll. Furthermore, most of these Texans were not consistently absent from battle duty;

the percentage of men AWOL was certainly far less than in other Confederate units. In many instances it had been difficult to make one's way back to the unit after a battle; even the chaplain was lost on occasion. Finally, the editor's decision to reproduce the roster is based on Davis' letter to the Houston *Telegraph* reporting corrections of duty status which removed the AWOL stigma from approximately one-third of those previously listed in that category.

> In making out the muster roll of the 4th Texas, as per order of B. F. Carter, commanding, and published in the Campaign, the officers reported the following as being absent without leave; since the work was published they were either on duty, or unable to march.
>
> And this publication instead of doing them an injury, has called their attention to the fact that they were so reported on their muster rolls, and given them the opportunity to have the roll corrected, which has been done.
>
> R. A. Davidge, C. L. Freeman, A. J. Hathorn, C. M. McPhall, C. L. Morrison, W. E. Puryer, W. H. Marshal, A. Barry, W. Barry, R. W. Crawford, J. T. Green, H. H. Harrison, G. W. Jackson.
>
> The following noted absent with leave were present: J. T. Price, J. Callahan, G. H. Crozier, G. R. Nichols, S. T. C. Stone, J. B. Boyd, J. H. Griffin, J. D. Miller, A. R. Jones, D. Silverbough, H. F. Williams, G. W. Dale, J. C. Hopkins, Ed Savage, E. G. Sessions, H. E. Walker, D. N. Green, J. Forester.[26]

While muster rolls were printed in later works, it is the intention in this edition to publish *verbatim* contemporary material. The editor does not believe that a more accurate roster of this period has ever been published, although he is aware that some brigade veterans wasted valuable reunion time forty years later in attempts to "prove" that they were present at a given battle.

An introduction to the *Campaign* would be incomplete without a biographical sketch of the author. Many facets of his character revealed in his diary and book were reflected in other episodes of his life, both before and after the war.

Nicholas A. Davis' family pattern was not unlike that of many who lived in Texas at the outbreak of the Civil War. His father was born in Tennessee (1797); he was born in Alabama (1824); two of his children were born in his native state, a third by his first wife in Texas, and four by a second marriage in Texas. Chaplain

Davis' roots were in the north Alabama county of Limestone where he was born August 8, 1824, into a reputable and public-minded farm family of moderate means living near Huntsville.[27] His father, Nathaniel, who served in both houses of the state legislature from 1840 to 1851, lacked pretensions and formal education, but was endowed with "superior natural powers of observation and reflection."[28]

Religion became a dominant force in the son's early life; he joined the Cumberland Presbyterian Church at Shoalford, Limestone county. At about the age of twenty the young Alabaman felt "the call of God" to devote his life to the ministry, but his father protested briefly. Parental objections were withdrawn and the young man was received by the Tennessee Presbytery as a ministerial candidate. After studying theology with the Reverend Robert Donnell, Davis received his licensure, a license to preach but not to hold a pastorate. Until he became a full-fledged minister he preached on Sundays and taught school during the week in Benton (now Calhoun) county. After ordination Davis spent a decade in full time ministry in various north Alabama communities: Talladega, Gadsden, Gaylesville, and White Plains among others. At the last town, on November 2, 1852, he married Miss Nancy Isabella (Nannie) Worthington.

Years after his Alabama ministry, Davis was still remembered by north Alabama Presbyterians according to his protégé, the Reverend Dr. S. L. Russell, in a letter written on the seventieth birthday of the one-time army chaplain.

> Your name is still a benediction in this section of the country. I well remember your presence and efficient labors at the old Pleasant Vale campground. I remember your sermon on the 'Pale Horse and His Rider, Death.' I remember you as a very welcome guest at my father's old home. . . . It has been nearly forty years since you used to attend our camp meetings in this section and yet there are many whose hearts are stirred and whose faces beam with the radiance of old and hallowed recollections at the mention of the name of N. A. Davis. There is music in that name to me. May God's richest blessings rest upon my venerable father in the ministry.[29]

Mr. and Mrs. Davis, with their small daughters Eleanora and Nancy, moved in November, 1857, to Texas, where he continued his Presbyterian ministry at Bastrop. A son, Nathaniel, was born in 1858, but the child and Mrs. Davis died prior to the chaplain's departure for Virginia in 1861. During his absence in Virginia, the Davis household in Bastrop was managed by his widowed sister, Louisa Davis Bullard. Besides the minister's two daughters, Mrs. Bullard cared for her son, Draper, and daughter, Mary. In addition, six slaves, ranging in age from four to twenty-three, lived with the family.[30]

Other than the home in town, Davis owned property which he referred to as "my ranch." During his recruiting trip to Texas in the spring of 1862, Davis spent several days on the ranch. While in Texas Davis carried a little notebook with the inscription, "The Agent of Army Missions presents you this opportunity to aid us in sending missionaries to preach to the soldiers of our Army." Among the most generous donors ($100), there appeared the name Eliza E. Radford. Returning to Texas before the end of the war, Davis married Mrs. Eliza E. Coley Radford, widow of Robert W. Radford, on February 7, 1865. The Radfords had migrated to Texas from Georgia and he had acquired considerable property in Sabine county. Besides his land, assets at the time of his death on July 14, 1862, included some $8,000 in notes payable due him in his native state; this estate was not settled for some years. Particular difficulties arose between Davis and George W. West of Cedartown, Polk county, Georgia, and the good offices of General John B. Hood, who after the war became a New Orleans business man, were sought by West.

Shortly after the marriage, the Davis family moved to property known as the old John Smith (the original grantee) plantation of more than two thousand acres in Sabine county which was part of the Radford estate. West held notes against the Texas property signed by Radford and one David B. Bush, both deceased, to the amount of $4100. Davis was to redeem these notes by sending cotton to the firm of J. B. Hood & Co. in New Orleans. Documents in the Davis papers do not indicate the final settlement, but the family continued to reside on the property for several years and retained ownership a decade later.[31]

Before the enumeration of the 1870 census, the family had moved to Milam, in the same county. Davis' sizeable landholdings made demands upon his time when he was not preaching in that town, San

Augustine, and other nearby communities. Considerable changes had taken place in the family pattern since the previous census and the household now included fourteen, white and black. Besides the two daughters of the first marriage, there were Mary Eliza, age three, and the two-year-old twins, John Hood (named for the general) and Franklin Coley. Mrs. Bullard, the sister, had died and her daughter had married, but the seventeen-year-old nephew, Draper, remained. Two laborers, one white and one Negro, and four Negro servants completed the household.[32] Davis' seventh child, Nicholas, died in childhood.

Shortly thereafter the family moved to Rusk, in Cherokee county, but Davis continued to own land in Sabine county. Tax collection receipts in the Davis papers record 3102 acres in three tracts in 1874 and 3503 acres in four tracts in 1881.

Davis' attachment to the land was only second to that of his interest in religion. In 1868, as secretary of the Southeast Texas Agriculture Society, he ordered a cane mill from Blymyer, North & Co. of Cincinnati. On his Sabine county cotton plantation, however, he had difficulty in growing the staple because of worms. In 1873 "for a valuable consideration" he was authorized to use "G. F. Whisenants Pattent Worm, or Catterpillar destroyer," but apparently it did not work because in the following summer he paid forty dollars for "the Right to prepare and use ROYALL'S COTTON WORM DESTROYER" on the same property.[33] Attention to his peach orchards and the nurseries he established at Rusk and later at Jacksonville required some of the minister's energies. He "established the first commercial orchard at Jacksonville and started the development which has made the Jacksonville country the most noted in Texas for fruit growing."[34] Another outside interest involved Davis as president of the Rusk Transportation Company in 1874; he attempted to obtain a railroad for the area.[35]

Farming and business ventures, however, did not indicate neglect of his religious responsibilities. Presbyterianism was at its nadir in Rusk upon the planter-minister's arrival, but under his leadership the number of communicants increased and a new church was built largely out of Davis' own contributions. From this county seat town, he preached in Jacksonville, Larissa, and nearby communities, his activities being curtailed only during a two-month period in 1877 after he had broken his hip in a train accident. Two years later the family moved to nearby Jacksonville, and while continuing to serve churches at Larissa and Rusk, Davis again built a new church with the pastor "giving for this purpose a large part of the money." Organized at the Cobb Hotel as the New Hope congregation, within a five-year period it became a strong and influential church under Davis' leadership before he began to suffer from heart trouble. Even then, "with his medicines in his pocket, on his crutches, he went from place to place, preaching and doing other church work."[36]

Especially dedicated to the idea of Christian education, the former chaplain served intermittently nearly twenty years on the Board of Trustees of Trinity University. On a number of issues he found himself in the minority, and on one occasion so hopelessly so that he resigned from the Board. Davis sought unity among Texas Presbyterians.

Cumberland Presbyterians in Texas had been divided between three synods; each had supported ante-bellum schools, Larissa, Chapel Hill, and Ewing colleges which had become, indirectly, Civil War casualties. Davis believed that the Cumberland Presbyterian synods in Texas should be united so that they could support a single institution of higher learning, Trinity University, founded in 1869 in the town of Tehuacana. Once the synods of Texas consolidated, Davis again became a trustee of Trinity. In a *Cumberland Presbyterian* obituary, Trinity Professor L. A. Johnson stated that much of the progress of the college had been due to Davis' "clear head and warm heart." Trustee Davis led in the movement to obtain the "appointment of young men to membership in the faculty of the university," to reorganize the faculty, and to establish a policy "of allowing professors leaves of absence on full salary to pursue special lines of study." In addition, Davis served the institution in the Synod of Texas as chairman of the Committee of Education. His leadership proved to be an important factor in the progress of the institution to which he sent his three youngest children, who were "graduates in the classical course."

The leadership which he demonstrated in connection with Trinity, and earlier in his concern for wounded Texans in Virginia, was reflected in other areas. Young ministers sought his counsel and guidance, and "in our church courts he was regarded as one of our wisest legislators and soundest judges." His influence also extended beyond church and school. One is not surprised to learn of this landed minister that "prosperous business men, according to their own confession, owe their success to following his advice."[37]

His acumen seems to have met with the admiration of all, save one. George W. West, the Georgia note holder, complained self righteously to their mutual friend, General Hood, that in business dealings "Mr. Davis has not been as generous to me as I have been to him."[38]

Discounting the florid language of the nineteenth century, the estimate in Dr. Johnson's obituary of the one-time chaplain, who died in San Antonio while on a visit to his daughter, Mrs. Floyd McGown, on November 19, 1894,[39] accurately reflected the findings of the editor's research.

> In his personal character he was pure hearted, thoroughly devout and trustful in God; he was clear headed and courageous; he never lost the courage of his convictions in any presence. He was progressive. Youth is proverbially the age of expansion and aspiration, yet though his body became enfeebled and his head silvered with the frost of years, he never became old in heart; he always lived in the present, and the future which to him was full of happy realizations of the noblest ideals of life. He was aggressive; he would fight for the right as he saw it on any field, and he always went in to conquer. In friendships he was strong and enduring; he grasped his friends to him with hoods of steel. It is safe to say he never lost a warm personal friend who was worthy of his esteem.[40]

These facets of his character were revealed in the pages of his diary and *Campaign*. Chaplain Davis in his justifiable indignation of the treatment of wounded Texans did not turn to his diary and complain in self-righteous passivity. He acted. Only this manner of man could have assumed the religious leadership of a regiment of soldiers who, in their campaign from Texas to Maryland, could advance when others were in retreat.

THE CAMPAIGN FROM TEXAS TO MARYLAND WITH THE BATTLE OF FREDERICKSBURG

By REV. NICHOLAS A. DAVIS
Chaplain, Fourth Texas Regiment, C.S.A.

RICHMOND

Printed at the office of the Presbyterian Committee
of Publication of the Confederate States.

1863.

INTRODUCTION.

To the Reader.

In view of the many difficulties by which the Author has been surrounded, both while collecting the material and preparing his Journal for the press, if he has left sufficient room for criticism, no one will feel surprised. For it has been amid the confusion of the camp, trials of the march, and attentions to the wounded on the field and in the different hospitals, scattered all over Richmond, and at every intervening point from this city to Winchester, Va., that he has succeeded in gathering the items of the History of the Campaign, which are thus published for two purposes: First. To preserve and place in the hand of each soldier a correct account of all his trials; and, secondly. To enable each one to send home to his friends the history of the stirring events of which he has made a part.

When circumstances will permit, he designs publishing a more extended and complete narrative. And, in order to which, he solicits the assistance in the collection of facts, of all who feel an interest in these pages. His thanks are already due to Capt. W. C. Walsh and R. A. Davidge.

THE AUTHOR

THE CAMPAIGN FROM TEXAS TO MARYLAND

The spring of 1861 forms a memorable epoch in the history of America. To those who were living at that day, either active participants in the stirring occurrences of the time, or passive spectators of the drama being enacted before them—the period which ensued from the election of Abraham Lincoln, on the 2d of November, 1860, down to the commencement of open acts of war between the Northern and Southern sections of the people of the United States—will ever be looked upon with a degree of interest fully equal to that which marks any other stage of our Continental career.

True is it, that the time alluded to is not full of startling event or tragic consequence as some that have succeeded—events which have clothed a land, but yesterday, as it were, robed in the bright garments of a bride, in the sable habiliments of mourning, and spread a pall of sorrow and dismal woe from one extremity of the country to the other—but at the same time, the changes taking place, at the time of which we speak, are such as must ever mark it memorable in the history of the American people.

The spectacle of a people, at a time of unexampled prosperity and plenty, blessed with a system of government acknowledged by the world to confer the largest liberality of personal freedom known among organized communities; whose facilities for the attainment of knowledge or wealth were unexampled among nations; where ambition was unrestricted, progress unfettered, religion untrammeled, and liberty of speech, unquestioned and unlimited—whose books and periodicals were, but yesterday, filled with songs of rejoicing and peans of self-gratulation, on account of these manifold blessings—a people, the wonder of the world, and the admiration of mankind, all at once stopped in their onward career. Peace gives way to discord, and chaos takes the place of system. Law and order disappear as if by magic, and anarchy and confusion prevail.

Such were the results of that excited period of time on which we now dwell.

It is not our province to speak of the causes leading to these results. The historian, who shall write of these things, will, doubtless, dive through the dusty and time-worn labyrinth of the past, and uncover hidden causes which had long been at work to bring these evil days upon us; and he will establish, by a system of logical argument, that it was necessary that these things should come to pass, which now "overcome us to our special wonder."—Our task is less difficult. We only propose taking a glimpse of a band of heroes, who lived in these days, and whose deeds have formed a portion of the history of the times. To trace the career of a body of men who, whatever part they may have taken in bringing on or keeping off the days of peril, have shown themselves able and willing to breast the storm, and to meet the whirlwind in its course.

As early as the month of April, 1861, the State of Texas had undergone this transformation, from a State of peace to a State of armed hostility to the Federal Government. South Carolina and several of the Southern States had seceded, and the Ordinance of Secession had passed in the Convention of Delegates of Texas, on the 2d of March.[1] Argument had been estopped, and the people were preparing for war. Camps of instruction for the training of troops were established at different points in the State—militiamen, armed and unarmed, were marching back and forth through the State—towns and villages, but late so quiet, were filled with country people, who left their farms neglected to come to town to get the news; a crowd could be seen at every post-office, and on every corner—churches at night, instead of sending forth the voice of prayer or song of thanksgiving, were filled with the shouts of excited men, as they were harrangued by some friend to revolution—in a word, on every side could be heard the din of warlike preparation.

Among other camps of instruction, established by order of Gov. [Edward] Clark, then Governor of Texas, one was established on the San Marcos river, in Hays county, in which were placed some twelve or fifteen companies, who had gone there for the purpose of organization, and when organized, to offer their services to the Government for twelve months.[2] About the time that the organization was to have been perfected by the election of Regimental officers, it was made known officially that no twelve months' men would be received from Texas. This announcement caused considerable disaffection among the men, who had assembled at the camp by virtue of a proclamation from the Governor, more especially, as the announcement was accompanied by the declaration that two regiments for service *during the war* would be received.

It was given out that Colonel John Marshall, editor of the State Gazette, at Austin, a prominent politician, had just arrived in Texas from Richmond, Virginia, where the newly formed Confederate Government had affixed its Capital, and that through influences brought to bear on the President or Secretary of War, had obtained the privilege that Texas should, as a matter of favor, be allowed a representation in the programme about to be enacted on the soil of Virginia. The companies were to be formed by the enrollment of men, and the election of company officers, and the organization of the regiments to be completed after their arrival in Virginia—the President reserving to himself the authority to appoint regimental officers. This course of arrangement, so different from what the men had expected, disorganized the camp of instruction; but so eager were the men to enter into the service of the country, that four companies *for the war* were immediately formed upon the ground, and reported themselves to the Governor. The companies formed at that time were the Tom Green Rifles, of Travis county, Capt. B. F. Carter; Guadalupe Rangers, Capt. J. P. Bane, of Guadalupe county; Hardeman Rifles, Capt. J. C. G. Key, of Gonzales county; Mustang Greys, Captain Ed. Cunningham, of Bexar county; and on the 11th day of July, these companies were ordered to break up camps and rendezvous at Harrisburg, near the city of Houston. The companies had a day or two given them in order to make preparations for the journey, and those of them who did not live at too remote a point, visited their homes. The citizens of Texas were full of enthusiasm, and offered every facility in the way of wagons and conveyances, in order to expedite the departure of these first troops to leave the State, and who were going to represent the ancient valor of Texas on a distant theatre.[3] The companies arrived at the place of rendezvous in the latter part of July, and in a few days after the first arrival, twenty companies were in camp. [The companies of Captains Robertson, Turner, Cleveland, and J. C. Rogers were received afterward and sent forward.][4]

Brigadier Gen. Earl Van Dorn was at this time in command of the Department of Texas, by authority of the Confederate Government. He had signalized his advent into Texas by the rapid transaction or dispatch of business entrusted to his superintendence, and had impressed all classes most favorably with his character as a man of energy and ability. Gen. Van Dorn had been ordered to dispatch these volunteers as speedily as they were raised, to arm and equip them, and to send them to Virginia by the quickest practical route. Gen. Van Dorn however on this occasion, chose to be in no great hurry to send the troops off. Under one pretence or another, the men were kept in the camp, at Buffalo Bayou, for weeks, and until the General could send a messenger to Richmond, remonstrating against the orders which he had received. The messenger at length arrived with a verbal dispatch, (as was understood at the time,) for "General Van Dorn to obey his orders."

It was midsummer when the troops were taken to the camp, on Buffalo Bayou. The camp was in a low miasmatic, unhealthy region, and many of the men here contracted disease, from which they never recovered.

So exhaustive was the climate and the place on the constitution of the men, that very little was done towards drilling them, and at the expiration of the time spent at that place, little or no improvement was discernible. The time spent there was spent most disagreeably, and many were the anathemas indulged in by the men at the cause of delay. While in this camp much kindness was shown the troops by the citizens of the neighborhood, and by those in the city of Houston. One instance is deserving of mention here. Dr. [L. A.] Bryan, of Houston, had a commodious house fitted up as a hospital, which was filled to the utmost capacity with our sick. He gave his medical attention to all that were sent, and on our departure would receive no compensation whatever for his services, or reimbursement for his expenses. Such patriotism is in marked contrast with the course of many who, during the war, have been able to do something for the soldier, but who have failed, through their sordidness of soul, to do so, and it is proper that we should here notice this friend to the soldier.

DEPARTURE FROM TEXAS.[5]

On the 16th day of August, 1861, orders having been issued by General Van Dorn, the first detachment of troops broke up their camp at Harrisburg, and came into Houston on the cars. The troops were dispatched in divisions of five companies each, in order to meet the exigencies of transportation—the companies comprising the first division being A, B, C, D and E, all under the command of Captain J. C. G. Key, of Company A. On that night the companies were quartered in a large ware-house in the suburbs of the city, and the next morning, at an early hour, started for Beaumont, on the Neches, where they embarked per steamer Florilda for Nibletts Bluff, on the Sabine.

The hour of departure was hailed with rejoicings by the men, and all countenances were beaming with animation; all hearts were high with hope and confidence, and every bosom seemed warmed by enthusiasm;—the last greetings among friends were interchanged, the last good-byes were said, and away we sped over the flowery prairies, with colors fluttering in the breeze, each hoarse whistle of the locomotive placing distance between us and our loves at home.

At this, the beginning of our travels, which ere we are done with them, will be found to possess more of interest than the gay and lightsome spirit here portrayed would seem to foreshadow, it may not be amiss to take a glance at the *personelle* of our friends, with whom for a time we are to be so intimately connected, as to be their biographers.

The men of whom we are now writing had come together from the hills and valleys of Texas, at the first sound of the tocsin of war. The first harsh blast of the bugle found them at their homes, in the quiet employment of the arts and avocations of peace. It is a singular fact, but no less singular than true, that those men who, at home, were distinguished among their fellows as peculiarly endowed to adorn and enrich society by their lives and conversation, who were first in the paths of social communion, whose places when they left were unfilled, and until they return again must be as deserted shrines, should be the first to leap from their sequestered seats, the first to flash the rusty steel from its scabbard, and to flash it in the first shock of battle. But so it is, and we venture to assert, that of all those whom this war has drawn to the field, and torn away from the domestic fireside, there will be none so much missed at home as those who left with the first troops for Virginia. They were representative men from all portions of the State—young, impetuous and fresh, full of energy, enterprise, and fire—men of action—men who, when they first heard the shrill shriek of battle, as it came from the far-off coast of South Carolina, at once ceased to argue with themselves or with their neighbors, as to the why-fores or the where-fores—it was enough to know the struggle had commenced, and that they were Southrons.

Where companies had not been formed in their own counties, they hastened to adjoining counties, and there joined in with strangers. Some came in from the far-off frontier. Some came down from the hills of the North, and some came up from the savannahs of the South —all imbued with one self-same purpose, to fight for "Dixie."

Among them could be found men of all trades and professions—attorneys, doctors, merchants, farmers, mechanics, editors, scholastics, &c., &c.—all animated and actuated by the self-same spirit of patriotism, and all for the time being willing to lay aside their plans of personal ambition, and to place themselves on the altar of their country, and to put themselves under the leveling discipline of the army.

On the evening of the 17th [16th], we were embarked at Beaumont on the steamer Florilda, a large and comfortable steamer, upon which we glided off from the landing, and set sail for the Bluff, the terminus of navigation, and from whence our journey had to be made by land. The trip was unattended by any feature of particular interest, and all arrived at Nibletts Bluff, on the morning of the 18th [17th] at an early hour, and after debarking and getting all the baggage ashore, the men went into camp in the edge of the town.

BAD TREATMENT

Here we had the first realization of the fact, that we were *actual soldiers*, and had the first lesson illustrated to us, that a soldier must be patient under wrong, and that he is remediless under injustice—that he, although the self-constituted and acknowledged champion of liberty, has, nevertheless, for the time being, parted with that boon, and, that he is but the victim of all official miscreants who choose to subject him to imposition.

The poor soldier receives many such lessons, and his fortitude and patriotism is often taxed to bear them without open rebellion, but as this was the first instance in which we had an opportunity of seeing and feeling such lessons experimentally, we here chronicle the circumstance for the benefit of all concerned. Gen. Van Dorn had entered into a contract with one J. T. Ward to transport these troops from Texas across to Louisiana, and Ward had undertaken as per agreement to furnish transportation in wagons across the country. He had been going back and forth for weeks, looking at the different roads, preparing the means of transportation; had delayed us in getting off from Texas until all his vast arrangements were systematized, and until all his immense resources could be deployed into proper order, and concentrated at Niblett's Bluff for this grand exodus of two thousand soldiers, who were but awaiting his movements to begin their onward pilgrimage to the great Mecca of their hopes, the "Old Dominion." To hear this man, Ward, spout and splutter among the streets of Houston about his teams and his teamsters, his wagons and his mules, one would have thought that the weight of the whole Quartermaster's Department of the Confederate Army rested upon his shoulders, and that his overburdened head was taxed with the superintendence of trains from California to the Potomac. Be this as it may, on arriving at the Bluff, whatever may have been the resources of our quartermaster, Ward, on this especial occasion he fell short of an approximation to our necessities. We had started on the trip with clothing, camp-equipage, medical stores, and commissary supplies, all complete. The citizens of Texas had left nothing undone on their part to send their sons into the field well supplied with everything essential for their comfort, and, in addition, many things had just been drawn from the agent of the Government, at Houston, which it was important should be carried with us. The troops were new to service, and unaccustomed to marching. It could not be expected that they could make the tedious trip through the swamps of Louisiana, unaided by liberal transportation. Van Dorn had unwisely and unjustly kept them in the sickly miasma of Buffalo Bayou until disease had already fallen in the veins of many, and all of them were suffering more or less from the enervating effects of that confinement. Such was the condition of the men now thrown into a thin and sparsely settled region of Louisiana, dependent alone upon others for every necessity to their new condition.

Under this state of affairs we found *seven wagons*, with indifferent teams, which Ward had procured for the purpose of transporting five hundred men, with the equipments and outfit mentioned. Ward had come to the Bluff with us on the steamer, but had gone immediately back, after leaving assurances that his preparations for our conveyance were ample. It is said that the wagons that he did furnish, were gathered up in that immediate vicinity, and that he engaged some of them even at so late an hour as our arrival at the Bluff.

The consequences were, that the officers in command had to rely upon themselves for the means of prosecuting the march. Tents, cooking utensils, clothing, medical stores, &c., to a large amount, were stowed away with whosoever would promise to take care of them for us until they could be sent on. Our sick men were left behind, and our journey commenced with what few things could be carried in these wagons.

Such an inauspicious introduction to the service, was far from being encouraging to patriotic ardor, and many vented their curses against Ward, Van Dorn, and all concerned; but so earnest were the men in their devotion to the cause in which they had engaged, and so deep their confidence that all things would work right when we once got fairly under the protecting aegis of our new Government; that soon all mutinous mutterings or complainings were suppressed, and the men set about relieving themselves of their difficulties as soon as possible.

On Sunday, the 19th [18th] of August, the line of march was taken up. The morning was wet and rainy, and the roads soft. The column halted in the evening at Cole's Station, about six miles distant, and bivouacked for the night. Wagons were sent back to bring up our sick, and details were made to go out into the neighboring country, and to try and secure additional transportation.

On Monday, the 20th [19th], the troops remained in camp at Cole's Station. It was a bright sunshiny day, the only one of the kind which was experienced on the entire trip. Men from each of the companies were out hunting up wagons, and every hour or two during the day, the agreeable fact was made known by a cheer from boys that an ambulance had been captured. Some eight or ten were procured during the day, and our means of locomotion considerably increased thereby. Some of the "ambulances" thus impressed into the service were of a most interesting and unique fashion. Some were drawn by oxen, some by horses, and some by mules. Some rejoiced in four wheels, and some in two—some had wagon-beds, and some had none—some showed the handicraft of modern mechanism; while here and there a creaking set of trucks would lead us back to antedeluvian times, before men had discovered the uses of iron, or learned the arts of the blacksmith. This mode of improvement was a harsh method of introducing ourselves to the inhabitants of the Calcasieu, and fell upon many of them with inconvenience, but it was our only recourse, and most all of the victims resigned themselves to the tyranny with patriotic composure; but from the vain attempts made in some cases to conceal their stock from our inquisitive detectives, it was evident that their virtue was the resort of necessity.

The next day the journey was resumed over a flat and piney region, and about sundown we arrived at Escobar's store, on the Calcasieu river. Here we had an illustration of Calcasieu as it is—Calcasieu as it was—and Calcasieu as it must ever be in our recollections in future days. The march had been ardous and fatigueing, and scarcely had the train halted, and while the men were engaged in pitching a few tents for the accommodation of the sick, when the windows of Heaven were opened, and the floods descended. The sky had given no premonitory warnings of a *storm*—it had been drizzling rain during the day, and the boys were all dripping when they arrived at camp; but no hoarse mutterings of far-off thunder, no fitful gleamings of lightning had prepared us for this copious visitation of Heaven's bounteous showers.

It seemed now as if all the arteries and springs which feed the rivers of Heaven were swollen to high water-mark, and that the rivers had burst their channels in aereal space, and bounding over the limitless expanse, were pouring themselves on that devoted spot of Confederate domain, known as Calcasieu. The rain continued all the night through, and we had no respite from its peltings until sunrise the next morning.

The morning came and brought rest from the merciless peltings of the rain. The bright god of day again showed his face, and again we were travelers.

A day's journey of 12 or 15 miles brought us to Clendening's Ferry, on the Calcasieu. This stream is wide and deep at this point, and navigable for vessels of respectable tonnage. The troops were crossed over without difficulty in a schooner, owned by Captain Goos, a resident of the place, who not only in this, but in all other transactions with the soldiers, acquitted himself as a clever man and a true patriot. His house was thrown open to the reception of as many as could be entertained, and his open-hearted and hospitable lady set to work with her whole retinue of servants, preparing food for the weary and hungry soldiers. They set no price upon their labors, and would receive no compensation for their bounteous outlay of provisions, and seemed to be only desirous of learning our necessities in order to minister to them. The troops having crossed over, the wagons were next in order, and here came the tug of war. The banks on the east side of the stream were very steep, and the continued rains had made them so slippery that our animals could not hold their footing, and the men had to perform the labor of getting them up the bank themselves. A rope was attached to the tongue of a wagon, and the boys having formed a line on top of the hill, thus drew them up. The labor was severe; a continuous rain falling all the time, added to the discomfort. All the night long was thus spent, and daylight found them still at the work—but at last it was accomplished, and once more we are ready to proceed.

Leaving the Calcasieu, our march was continued through a constant rain, through swamps and marshes, lagoons, wrecks, and every imaginable species of watery element, many of them over waist-deep, until we at length came to a halt, after a day's journey of 10 or 12 miles. We were halted in a prairie, immediately on a stream, whose waters were running out of its banks, and still rising. The wagons could not be crossed, and we went into camp to await the developments of the night. The next morning a rude bridge was constructed, over which the wagons were hauled by hand, while the animals swam across. The teams were then hitched up, and we proceeded eight miles to a stage stand, at a point called Pine Island, when we encamped late in the evening, the weather still continuing rainy.

On the 25th [24th] we had the same sort of road, and similar weather for about 12 miles, to Welsh's Station. Here we crossed the stream on trees which we felled across it, and with some difficulty got our wagons over.

26th [25th]. Came to the Mermenteau river. This day's march was, perhaps, the most severe on the trip. The distance traveled was not so great as on some other days, but at every step the toiling and wearied pedestrian encountered what appeared to be a *little deeper* and a *little softer* spot. It was on this day that we made the crossing of the "Grand Marias," or more aptly termed by the boys the "Grand *Miry*." In many places the men waded up to the neck through the swamps, where the alligators lay basking in the tall grass, as if disputing the passage, and seemed reluctant to give way without a stern admonition in the way of a bayonet thrust, to impress them with a proper respect for the characters of the newcomers. Many were bayoneted by the soldiers, and held up in triumph as they went on plunging through the dangerous waters.

Leaving this stream on the 27th, a long march of 26 miles was made, diversified by the same series of watery trials, and on the next day, the 28th, we arrived at Lafayette, a nice little town in Lafayette Parish, Louisiana. The troops bivouacked that night about two miles distant from the town, on Vermillion Bayou, in grounds owned by ex-Governor Mouton.

The Governor not only offered his grounds and timbers adjacent for our use, but called in his neighbors and gathered together all the vehicles that were serviceable in the community to forward us on to New Iberia, distant twenty-five miles.

Hitherto our journey had been made through a country almost destitute of civilization. No smiling towns or villages had dotted the watery waste—no sight of groaning barns, or fields of waving grain had delighted our visions as tramp, tramp, splash, splash, we threaded the uncertain depths of swamp and morass. What few settlers we had passed were a poor class of citizens, chiefly engaged in the business of shipping lumber out of the numerous lakes and bayous, or now and then a herdsman with a band of cattle or sheep in charge. Now we had again arrived in the white settlement, and were once more among a generous and hospitable people. The next day we made an early start, our largely increased transportation enabling by far the greater number of the men to ride; and as we continued our day's journey, other wagons, carriages, and horses were kindly placed at our disposal, until by the time we reached New Iberia, almost every one had some sort of conveyance to ride upon. The advance part of our train arrived at Iberia about 12 o'clock, M., and by 4 or 5 P.M., the whole party were up and ready for embarkation on the steamer.

Col. Wm. H. Stewart, of Gonzales, had preceeded us in order to engage a steamer to convey us to Brashear city, and on our arrival we found the steamer at the wharf, ready to bear us on our journey.

As a matter of course, great joy was manifested on our arrival at the terminus of our long pilgrimage. We had now travelled a distance of one hundred and fifty-five miles in a period of about twelve days.[6] During this entire period we had seen but one dry day, and the men had not known what it was to have dry clothing or dry blankets. On the march, during the day, they were wholly unprotected from the peltings of the elements, and at night threw themselves on the wet ground, very frequently without fires, where they shivered the night through. In order to travel better, the men divested themselves of all heavy articles of apparel, even to their coats, pants and shoes; and it was a common spectacle on the road to see a manly specimen of human nature trudging along, singing Dixie as he went, minus everything in the shape of clothes except a shirt. Such was the appearance of our men when they entered the lively little town of New Iberia. But the generous and whole-souled denizens of the town soon gave us assurances that we were among friends, and that they appreciated the patriotism and devotion that had thrown us in this plight among them. Provisions, eatables, drinkables, &c., were furnished us in abundance, the beautiful ladies greeted us with the witchery of their smiles, and fathers and mothers cheered us with approval as we came, and sent us away with their best wishes and prayers. Evening found us gliding down the waters of the last Louisiana Bayou [Teche] which we were for a time to know, and in the morning without accident we lay at the wharf at Brashear city. From hence we took the cars for the Crescent city, where we arrived at night, crossed the river and were quartered in an old cotton ware-house for the night.

We tarried in New Orleans but one day, and left on the evening of Sept. 1st, on the cars for Richmond. While the trip possessed an interest as showing the mighty revolution going on in the country, it was unattended by any feature of particular adventure.

The journey was slow and tedious. The roads were thronged with soldiers from New Orleans to Richmond, and the whole country presented the appearance of a vast camp. We were the first Texans that had passed in a large body, and on this account were more or less the objects of attention. We were delayed at several points, and laid over at Knoxville, Tenn., four days, awaiting transportation. *Having arrived in Manchester on the 11th day of Sept. at 12, o'clk P. M. At sunrise the next morning I started on foot across the bridge on James R. to get a cup of coffee & to see the city for which I had been travelling so long & for which had suffered so many privations & inconveniences. And as the cars had to wait until the mail train passed out I concluded to go over to see what was to be seen & found to eat. A few minutes were all, that were necessary to bring me to the Capitol*

& find me stationed on this side of a table in a Restaurant discussing the good qualities of a bad cup of poor coffee. But the good qualities of a fine beef stake were & more numerous as they were sustained by a peace of good corn bread, which we have found to be very rare thro' our rout, & especially in the land of good families; I directed my most interested argument to that subject. After spending about 25 minutes in this way I lost my appetite. Consequently I payed the man 30¢ & started for the Depot. Here I met Gen Sidney Johnson who was leaving to enter upon his duties on the Miss. R. He seemed much interested in the Texas solders & made many enquiries—the cars whistle & he bade me goodbye. At 9 o'clk the train arrived & I went aboard & changed my clothing while they were transferring our baggage from the cars to the waggons.[7]

We arrived at Richmond on the 12th day of September, and were placed in camp at Rocketts *which I found to be 1-1/2 ms. out.*[8] In a few days the remaining companies arrived, *seven more companies Tex. Vol. arrived yesterday* [*16th*] . . . *They are now coming in*[9] and the whole body of Texans were removed out of the city about three miles, to await our organization into regiments.

CAMP TEXAS ORGANIZATION.

Our new camp was situated in convenient proximity to the city, in a healthy locality, and was styled "Camp Texas," in honor of our Lone Star State. Here the drill was again resumed, and our company officers set to work in earnest in preparing the men for the field.

The great topic of conversation, and the all-absorbing question was, "Who will be our Regimental Officers?" "Who will command us?" It has been seen that the two regiments had come on to Virginia without organization—this matter having been deferred to the Confederate authorities in Richmond—and now that the time was approaching, the question became one of interest to all Texans at the Capital, whether belonging to the army or not.

It had been represented in Texas that the President and the War Department had taken this matter of military appointments especially in charge—that their wisdom had grasped the subject, and considered it in all its details, and were resolved no mishap should befall our arms by reason of neglect in this particular matter—the appointment of leaders to show our brave boys the nearest and easiest paths to victory and glory.

It was said that the lives of soldiers were too precious, and the interests of freedom too dear, to permit incompetent men to have places in the army as officers.

It was intimated that at Richmond there would be found sitting in imperial state, an imposing board of military Savants, deeply skilled in all the mysteries of military science, and so deeply inbued with occult lore, that no one but a man of military requirements and personal ability might hope to pass the ordeal of their examination. Under such an apprehension, several gentlemen of ability and experience in the field had abandoned their association with us in Texas, through fear of submitting their humble pretensions to so severe a system of anylization, and we had come on in calm trust of these flattering promises of the Government, and were here ready to undergo the transmutation from a state of provincial rusticity and greenness to a state of military system and perfection, by some legerdemain of the West Point tactician. But alas! for the deceitfulness of human hopes, and the mutability of human calculations, it did not appear that we were so likely to get as competent officers over us by the appointment of the authorities as we had left behind us in Texas, or brought with us to Virginia. The first attempt at giving a Colonel to the 4th Regiment, was the appointment of R. T. P. Allen, a citizen of Bastrop, Texas, and the President of the Military Institute at that place. This gentleman, although a man of thorough military education, was not acceptable to either men or officers. He had been in command of the Camp of Instruction, at Camp Clark, Texas, and the men had there with remarkable unanimity, come to the conclusion that he did not suit their views of a commander. A protest against this appointment was made by the officers—*the Capts are figuring about to get the President to recall the appointment of Allen & as I think to get some position themselves*[10]—of the Regiment, and Colonel Allen returned to Texas. [The Secretary of War then offered him a Captaincy of Artillery, which he respectfully declined].[11]

John B. Hood was then appointed Colonel of the 4th, and as his name will appear interwoven through many pages of this narrative, it is not necessary to speak of him here.

John Marshall, of Austin, received the appointment of Lieutenant Colonel, and Bradfute Warwick, of Virginia, that of Major.

These two latter appointments were, at the time, matter of severe animadversion among the men. Neither appointment was acceptable to the command.

Colonel Marshall was esteemed as a brave man, and admired as an eminent civilian—an able editor, and a good Democrat—a friend to Secession, and devoted to the cause of the South. But it was not deemed that he came up to the standard as a military man, and his selection over the heads of others who were qualified, was looked upon as savoring too much of a spirit of political favoritism.—*Lt. Col. John Marshall brought out his camp chattles & left again in a few minutes. This is his debu[t]. And I suppose he is aware of the fact that the men receive him in the same manner that he has put himself off on the reg.—By force.*[12]

Major Warwick was altogether unknown, and being a Virginian, in nowise connected or identified with Texas or Texans, his appointment was looked upon as unjust to the men and to the State of Texas. No steps were taken, however, in opposition to the appointments. J. D. Wade, [Co. F], Quartermaster, with the rank of Captain—Lieutenant Burroughs [Burress], of Co. K., Commissary, which he resigned in favor of Tom Owens [Co. H], who assumed the position—R. H. Bassett, of Co. G, was appointed Adjutant, and Tom Cunningham, of Co. F, was appointed Sergeant-Major. Thus was the 4th Texas organized, and with these officers the Regiment entered the field.

The 5th Texas Regiment was being organized at the same time, and a similar policy was pursued in the appointment of officers for it. The first individual who presented himself with his credentials as Colonel, was a representative of the Tribe of Benjamin, whose name is now forgotten [Shaller.][13] I do not know that I ever heard it, and how he came to be put forward, where he came from or whither he went after his untoward reception, is altogether unknown. He was a veritable Jew, and his career with us was of short duration. He came out to the camp in all the pomp and circumstance befitting his high position, splendidly mounted on a steed as splendidly caparisoned—glittering with the tinsel of gold, and bearing about him all the symbols of his rank, in a manner quite unexceptionable. He rode among and examined his new command, and expressed himself satisfied with the material turned over to his care. In fact, after looking over the tall forms of our boys, their intrepid bearing and speaking force, he thought they would do for him, and had as little doubt that he would do for them. In the exuberance of his satisfaction at the prospect before him, he exclaimed—"I *tinks* I can manage *te* Texas poys, and I tinks *pofe togetter* we can clean out *te*—Yankees."

The boys gathered around him and manifested their wonder at the liberality of the appointing power, by divers and sundry remarks, which to be appreciated properly should have been heard.

"What," says one, "*What is it?* Is it a man, a fish, or a bird?" "Of course it is a man," says another, "Don't you see his legs?"

"Well," says another, "*that thing* may be a man, but we don't call them men in Texas."

With such polite remarks were the ears of our Israelitish friend greeted on every side, and while he was at a loss somewhat to comprehend the conduct of *te poys* in its full significance, he saw enough to give him some uneasiness and misgivings as to the task he had assumed.

The next morning, on ordering his horse to take a ride, our Colonel discovered that instead of the sweeping air of his proud charger as hitherto displayed, that he came out dejected in gait, and with downcast looks. An examination proved that he had been entirely divested of his great ornament. His tail had been cut off during the night.

Without a remark of any kind, without a solitary good-bye, without one last sign of farewell, Colonel [Shaller] left, and was never heard of by the 5th Texas again. The Regiment was then organized by the appointment of J. J. Archer, Colonel; J. B. Robertson, Lieutenant Colonel; and Q. J. Quattlebaum, Major—Lieut. Col. Robertson the only Texan among them. [And although somewhat dissatisfied with their Colonel at first, they soon learnt to esteem and love him.][14]

The time was improved by a daily system of drilling, the men and officers all entering into the exercises with a spirit and zest worthy of the cause to which they had consecrated themselves.

We were now organized, and new life and vigor diffused itself through every department, and into all our exercises. The question of "Who shall be our officers?" gave place to speculations as to the ability and relative qualifications of those who had been appointed to command. The measles had thinned our ranks, but we still had quite a respectable line, save in one thing. On dress parade there were so many of the convalescents coughing at the same time, that it was difficult sometimes to hear the command of the Colonel. But when the Colonel himself—with whom the men were not sufficiently acquainted to take liberties—was absent, the noise made by one hundred and one men coughing, with the interesting style and unique, orders given by the commanding officer afforded opportunity to the boys for the exercise of their risibles, which they improved to great advantage. And many of them were so delighted at the displays as to be heard even until a late hour of the night going through the manual of arms.

REMOVAL TO THE POTOMAC

The winter coming on, all felt anxious to know to what part of the field—whether to the Peninsula, Western Virginia, or Potomac—we would be ordered; or if we were to go into winter quarters at this place. *Recd orders at 3 o'clk from the war department to hold ourselves in readiness to move at a minutes warning.. Lt. Col. Marshall was on dress parade this evening—Ordered to "Order arms" from a present & then, "Shoulder arms" "fix Bayonets," the bayonets being already fixed—the men all burst into a hearty laugh. He ordered the Adj to dismiss the parade and when he recd. the officers salute he said. We may make some mistakes But we had better make them here than some where else. For we are ordered to hold ourselves in readiness for a minutes warning & we may be in a battle on the Potomac in a day or two—"Double Quick" by the orderlies & a grand hurray was kicked up & away they went. "Shoulder arms," "Fix Bayonets" shouted all over the camp. Marshall never drew his Sabre.*[15] Orders were received on the 4th of November, to send away all surplus baggage, and prepare for the march, and not until the 7th did we know where we were going. At last it was announced that we were to become a part of the "ARMY OF THE POTOMAC." All were satisfied. This was the place to which we wished to be assigned. For it was believed that that would be the scene of active operations, and as the boys were spoiling for a fight, they were delighted with the prospect; *Orders to decamp—"Forward to the Potomac," has come at last. The men are in a grand glee.*[16] [The camp was illuminated by bonfires, while the brass band delighted the ear with patriotic sentiments of Dixie.][17] On the 8th we marched in and took the cars for Brooks' Station, where we arrived in the evening, and pitched our tents for the night. Next morning, while making arrangements to march, we received orders from General [Theophilus] Holmes to remain. It was rumored that the enemy were making demonstrations on the Maryland shore, as if they intended crossing. [Here at the mouth of Aquia creek we first witnessed the firing of those tremendous engines of death—the batteries were shooting at the federal schooners on the Potomac.][18] No further evidences were given of such a design up to the 12th instant, when we received a telegram from Gen. [Louis T.] Wigfall to move forward on the next morning to Dumfries. In a short time another message by the wires came for us to move up without delay, for the enemy was threatening his position. In a few minutes every tent on the field dropped, the wagons were packed and piled—and now it became apparent that our baggage was much beyond the capacity of transportation, and a large quantity had to be stored and left—and a little before sunset the line was formed and wheeled off for a long, muddy, tiresome tramp. It was an interesting march. *A general bustle, every one working for himself and every one doing his own talking. Here comes the teams [of] horses in a long trot the waggons rattling—chains jingling, drivers hollowing & whips poping . . . Now for a nights march. Supposing the boys might get into a fuss by moving towards Yankeedom. I procured a rifle & 40 rounds in my cartridge box & a six shooter with 50 rounds & took up the line of march with the boys—having no supper, about 9 o'clk. I began to have a strong warm feeling for the coffee pot. but I supposed it was no use to have & to cultivate so much feeling for any individual unless there would be a reciprocity. But halting at the roadside where a waggoner was camped for the night I found him at supper & he offered me a cup with bread & fresh butter which I accepted readily & with much "respect" in company with the "Pill Staff." After which we struck out to overtake the moving column which we did, at Aquia Creek. They had halted & were gathered around blazing fires.*[19] We had traversed the swamps of Louisiana when they stood at high water-mark, but we had day light to travel in. Now we had to sight for the course, and guess at the bottom. And, if I were allowed to guess, judging from my own feeling, the "soundings" were not so amusing as when aboard the Florilda, crossing the Bay. We had been in the service just long enough for the company officers to feel considerable pride in keeping their lines well "dressed," and it is unnecessary for me to say that they had a good time of it that night, and especially towards daylight, about half an hour before which we reached the ancient city. We had moved 18 miles during the night, and were present, if not ready, for a fight. But as good luck would have it, the signs for a fight had disappeared, and we were allowed to sleep and rest during the day. Next morning we were ordered to move down and select a camp on the Potomac. But we had not gone far when a courier arriving in post-haste, said "the Yankees are coming." General Wigfall soon rode up and told us we must meet them. The boys said, "that is what we came for," and with a loud cheer moved off—now for a lively time. After a mile through the deep mud, the weight of gun, cartridge-box, big knife, six shooter, and tremendous knapsack, begun to steady the men down to a moderate gait—for they were packed like Mexican mules for market.[20] We were halted, and the surplus was piled, and on the line moved for about three miles. Here we met another courier who informed us that it was a mistake. There were no Yankees on this side of the river, and the cannonading which we heard was the batteries firing at some little schooners passing the river. All felt disappointed. *I don't know how the men felt, but I was very tired myself. And was verry glad to hear "Halt"—Rest."*[21] But in the absence of a chance to annoy the Yankees, the boys begun on each other, and there were some good jokes and hearty laughs passed along the line. One was accused of turning pale, another with breaking down to get to the rear. Somebody had taken the cholic, and one of the officers [Lt. M. Wade] had taken the ring off of his finger and given it to his servant saying, "Here, Charley, take this ring, and if I get killed, give it to . . . . ," &c., &c.

We then moved to the river [and witnessed an attempt by some of the men of the 1st Texas to burn a schooner, which had been abandoned by the Yankees on account of the fire of our battery. The boat was fired and they pulled off towards our side; but the Yankees showed themselves equally gallant by extinguishing the flames and pulling the schooner off under fire of our guns.][22] and camped for the night, and it was several days before we went into a permanent camp, on Powel's Run, where we remained during the winter. There was but little of interest in our quarters, except rain, sleet, snow and mud, with which we were blessed in great abundance. How often it rained, and how deep the mud got before spring, it would be needless to tell any one with the expectation that he would believe it, unless he had seen the Calcasieu.

We here met with the 1st Texas Regiment, commanded by Col. [Hugh] McLeod, and the three regiments, 1st, 4th and 5th, were organized into a Brigade, styled the Texas Brigade, under the command of Brigadier General Louis T. Wigfall. The 18th Georgia was afterwards added to the command, and at a later period Hampton's Legion, from South Carolina. The 1st Texas Regiment was composed of companies that had hurried to Virginia on the first breaking out of hostilities; they had come on without any regimental organization, and were at first formed into a Regiment and placed under the command of Col. Wigfall. When the Brigade was formed, Wigfall became Brigade Commander. Col. Wm. H. Stewart, on the organization of the Brigade, received the appointment of Commissary, with the rank of Major, and Moses B. George that of Quartermaster, with the same rank.

As soon as it was understood we were quartered for the winter, the men set about building cabins; and it would puzzle any artist in the world to give the style of architecture in the cantonment, consequently we will not attempt the task. For some of them were on the hill, and some under the hill; some were on top of the ground and others were under the ground. Some were large, while others were small. One was in this shape, and another in that shape. Mess No. 2 had a high house, while No. 5 had a short house. No. 3 had his chimney inside, and No. 7 had his on the outside. And the doors—where do you suppose they were? But I must here call to mind the important night alarm we had about the time these skillful builders were laying out their plans and laying off their buildings. For it was in the midst of their consultations as to whether they would have the door by the jam, or in the gable-end; the window under the bed, or in the chimney; the shelf on the floor, or out of doors; whether all should sleep in one bed, or each by himself—when at midnight, in the midst of a drenching rain, a picket came dashing in and reported the enemy crossing the river and marching upon us. All hands were called up, *I suppose in one hour 10,000 men were under arms,*[23] and the preliminaries for a night attack were hastily disposed of, and all were in readiness for a fight or a foot-race, as future development should indicate would be for the best. Over on the other side of the run Col. [William T.] Wofford had his men in line of battle awaiting the onset. And we heard Col. Hood tell General Wigfall that Colonel W., he thought, had taken his position down on the hill-side, in front of his Regiment, and was ready with his pistol cocked, to blow them up if they came. To the right we could hear that "same old drum" calling up the braves of the 5th to go after the disturbers of our dreams. And the ardor of Colonel [James J.] Archer being greater than that of the other commanders, *our Col. was not fool enough to pitch his men out in the dark & rain,*[24] he [Archer] marched his men out to meet them—half way—two miles from his camp. But as the rain continued to fall during their reconnoisance, we are of opinion—although we never heard from him on the subject—that he returned to camp considerably cooled down.[25] When morning came, it developed the fact that no troops had crossed, except about a dozen, whose object, from the tracks left on the beach, was to catch our pickets and introduce them to General [Daniel] Sickles, on the Maryland shore, but had failed.

During the greater portion of the winter there was a detail of about twenty men from each of the Texas Regiments, kept on the Occoquan, to watch the enemy's movements, and annoy them in their advances. They soon became a terror to scouts and pickets from the other side, and chances for a shot grew more unfrequent as the enemy became better acquainted with their style of manners. In the latter part of January, nine [ten] of these scouts [viz: C. Mills, S. W. Trowbridge, J. W. Webb, S. W. Webb, Willingham, Burk, Watrous and J. S. Spratling, (who was mortally wounded) of the 1st, and B. J. Burns and Templeman, of the 5th],[26] principally of the 1st, put up at a house near the Accotink Mills, on the other side of the river, to spend the night. At a late hour, being led by a citizen, Lieut. Col. Burk, 37th N.Y., with 90 men and a detachment of cavalry, surrounded the house and demanded a surrender. The boys were aroused from sleep, and gathering their guns, immediately opened fire, which was briskly returned. After three rounds one of the men shouted, "Hurra, boys, Hampton's coming, I hear him on the bridge;" at which they [the Yankees] took fright and left.—Next morning revealed the fact that they had killed as many as there were men of their own party, and through prisoners learned they had wounded as many more.[27]

About the 1st of March, 21 of the 18th Georgia were ordered to this party, who passed up to the Poheick church for the purpose of ambushing the enemy's scouts, but the enemy ambushed them; yet they [the Yankees] did not fire on them, fearing they might be their own men. After going half a mile, they [the Georgians] concealed themselves to await the coming of the enemy, but to their surprise they came in a different direction to the one anticipated. But when in proper distance, our men fired and brought down a Colonel, a Quartermaster, a Captain, and eleven privates, and then made their way back across to our side unhurt. After our men passed them [in their ambuscade], they sent off for four companies to surround them [the rebels],[28] but they were too late, but were in good time to bury those who had sent for them.

Early in February, a detail from each company of the different Regiments, of a commissioned and non-commissioned officer was made and sent to Texas for recruits, who left about the 10th inst.[29]

While at Richmond we had Divine Services regularly on [the] Sabbath, and each night when circumstances would permit. But after removing to the Potomac, for the want of a comfortable place for meeting, our opportunities were lessened. For while the weather was so unpleasant, we had the privilege of preaching only when the Sabbath was suitable for out-door services.

EVACUATION OF THE POTOMAC

Previous to 5th March, nothing of stirring interest occurred.—The same unvarying round of camp duties was performed; but little interest was felt either by officers or men. The weather was so disagreeable and the roads so muddy, that drills and even dress parades had to be dispensed with, and cooking, eating and sleeping constituted our chief employment.[30]

On the date above mentioned, a detail of 20 men was made from each of the three Texas Regiments, with orders to report to Col. Wade Hampton, then on the Occoquan. They did so, and formed a rear guard to his command, as it moved back via Manassas to Fredericksburg, where they arrived March 11, and were highly complimented by that excellent officer, in a written order, not only for the manner in which this duty had been performed, but for their services on former occasions.

Orders having previously been issued, the Brigade decamped on the afternoon of March 8th. After forming for the march, Colonel Hood addressed the 4th Texas as follows:

"Soldiers—I had hoped that when we left our winter-quarters, it would be to move forward; but those who have better opportunities of judging than we have, order otherwise. You must not regard it as a disgrace—it is never a disgrace to retreat when the welfare of your country requires such a movement. Ours is the last Brigade to leave the lines of the Potomac. Upon us devolves the duties of a rear guard, and in order to discharge them faithfully, every man must be in his place, at all times. You are now leaving your comfortable winter quarters to enter upon a stirring campaign—a campaign which will be filled with blood, and fraught with the destinies of our young Confederacy. Its success or failure rests upon the soldiers of the South. They are equal to the emergency. I feel no hesitation in predicting that you, at least, will discharge your duties, and when the struggle does come, that proud banner you bear, placed by the hand of beauty in the keeping of the brave, will ever be found in the thickest of the fray.—Fellow-soldiers—Texans—let us stand or fall together. I have done."

With three cheers for Colonel Hood, and a lingering look at the old camp—the scene of many a merry and idle hour—we took up the line of march, and camped that night on the south side of the Chapewamsic.

To prevent our movements being known to the enemy, whose camps could be seen on the Maryland shore, we left our tents and cabins standing, and, for want of transportation, were forced to abandon a portion of our personal baggage.[31] Of the small amount with which we started, the quartermaster threw away a great part, owing to the wretched condition of the roads, and by so doing bitterly disappointed many, both officers and men.

Moving next morning at daylight, we reached Austin's Run just before dark. This camp will long be remembered by every lover of the wild and beautiful who was there. Two hill-sides, facing each other, were occupied each by two regiments. The night was dark and cold, and fuel plenty. The countless fires, sparkling and crackling the dense shadow of the heavy forest, and the dusky forms of the soldiers moving to and fro, combined with the impenetrable darkness of the background, lent a wild grandeur to the scene, which fully explained the charms of a gipsy life. Started early next morning, and marching all day through the rain, camped about four P.M. on Potomac Run. On the 11th, Colonel Hood received notice of his appointment as Brigadier General.[32] This made Lieut. Col. Marshall our Colonel, and the other officers took rank accordingly. March 12. Left our camp on Potomac Run, and crossing the Rappahannock at Falmouth, took a position about two miles west of Fredericksburg.

March 13—A detail was made from each Texas Regiment of one Lieutenant and fifteen men, who were ordered to return to the vicinity of Dumfries, to watch the movements of the enemy. They captured prisoners daily, and on the 18th, at Glasscock's Hill, they saw a brigade cross the Potomac, pass up to Dumfries, back to Evansport, and recross the river. On the next day they captured a Yankee Chinaman, who being committed to the care of Barker, (of Co. G, 4th Texas,) and proving a little stubborn, that practical frontiersman quietly placed the *Celestial* across his lap, and with his leathern belt administered such a chastisement as that "ruthless invader" had probably not received since childhood.[33] March 20—McAnnelly, Norris, Gee and Barker visited our old camp and brought away a considerable quantity of baggage, and destroyed most of the tents. On the 27th, McAnnelly and Barker discovered a boat with what they thought but three men, land at Glasscock's Hill. Slipping up, under cover of a fish-house to within thirty steps of the river, they demanded surrender. Judge of their surprise, when instead of *three, fifteen* men made their appearance, and showed a disposition to fight. This was what "Old Abe" would call a "big job," and so thought the scouts; but it was too late "to rue," and they immediately opened the fight by shooting down the two nearest, and hastily repeating the fire, the Yankees "took water" and pushed out from shore. Before getting beyond range, however, six more had rolled from their seats, wounded if not killed. The crew briskly returned the fire, but the scouts with commendable prudence, *kept the house before them,* and the minnies whistled harmlessly. On the 2d April, Barker, Horn and Dickey, having discovered a regiment encamped near Evansport, attempted to cut off and capture four of their guard. But their motions were discovered and the squad broke for camps, yelling "*Rebels*" at every jump. Two of the scouts fired, wounding one Yankee, and Barker succeeded in capturing the Sergeant in charge, but that official showing a disposition to be troublesome, Barker shot him down and did what he could for "number one." On the 3d, Sickles' Brigade landed at Glasscock's Hill and Evansport, and moving in two columns, met at Acquia church, the head-quarters of the Texans.—The avowed object of this foray was the capture of these same scouts; but old rangers were not to be caught so easily. Dispatching a courier to Gen'l [William H. C.] Whiting, they quietly retreated before the baffled enemy, and taking advantage of every hill to pick off a straggler, they succeeded, according to Gen'l Sickles' own assertion, in killing and wounding eight of his men. Through some mishap, the courier did not reach head-quarters until after dark. The Texas Brigade was immediately ordered to meet the Yankees, and moved at 10

P.M. in the following order, 5th, 4th and 1st Texas, and 18th Georgia. When within about three miles of Stafford C.[ourt] H.[ouse], Col. [John] Marshall having fallen asleep on his horse while the men were resting a few minutes, the 5th Reg't moved off unawares, and when the Colonel was roused up, was out of sight. In a short distance the road forked and we took the wrong direction, and did not regain the right road until daylight, when we found the 5th Texas waiting for us. Here we learned that Gen'l Sickles, after pillaging most of the houses at Stafford, had taken the alarm and left the Court-House in retreat, just one hour before we left Fredericksburg in pursuit. As overtaking them was impossible, we remained in bivouac until the following morning, when we returned to camps. On the 6th, orders were issued to be ready to move in an hour, and severe punishment threatened all "stragglers" and "foragers" while on the march. On the following day, at noon, we started, the weather alternating with snow, sleet and rain, until we reached Milford's Station. General Hood pronounced this the severest weather he had ever experienced on a march. Here we were placed upon the cars, and arrived at Ashland about noon, where we remained for two or three days. Leaving here we took the road to Yorktown, where we arrived in tolerable condition, considering the rain and mud we had encountered. Here we were assigned the position of "1st Brigade of the 1st Division, Reserve Corps of the Army of the Potomac," and bivouacked about one mile in rear of the line of defences, on the ground occupied by the Rebel Army of the first revolution, just previous to the memorable battle of Yorktown. How many pleasing recollections crowd upon the mind of each soldier as he walks over these grounds, or sitting thoughtfully by his faggots, recalls the history of the past, and compares it with the scenes of the present. The patriots of the Revolution were struggling for liberty, and so are we. They had been oppressed with burdensome taxation—so were we. They remonstrated—so did we. They submitted until submission ceased to be a virtue—and so have we. They appealed to Parliament, but were unheard. Our Representatives in Congress pointed to the Maelstrom to which they were driving the ship, but they refused to see it. Our fathers asked for equality of rights and privileges, but it was refused. The South asked that their claim to territory, won by the common blood and treasure of the country be recognized, and that our domestic institutions, as guaranteed by the Constitution, be respected. These petitions were answered by *professed* ministers (?) of the Church of Jesus Christ, in raising contributions from the sacred pulpit, on the holy Sabbath, of Sharpe's Rifles, to shed Southern blood on common territory. Their Representatives declared upon the floors of Congress that they were "in favor of an anti-slavery Constitution, an anti-slavery Bible, and an anti-slavery God!!" What was now left us? Naught but the refuge our fathers ha'—the God of Justice, and the God of Battles. To Him have we appealed, and by his aid and our good right arms, we will pass through the ordeal of blood, and come out conquerors in the end. But to return. The spring here referred to is about two miles above the old city, and the battle ground about the same distance below. There are yet histories of that battle to be found in the houses, which were not written by the pen of the scribe, but with iron shot from British cannon. Who would then have believed that the Stars and Stripes, the emblem of liberty, would so soon become the ensign of oppression.

During our stay at Yorktown, details were made daily from the Texas Regiments to act as sharp-shooters in the trenches. Some of their skirmishes were brisk and interesting. Previous to our arrival, the sharp-shooters of the enemy had approached to within two hundred yards of our fortifications, and from tree tops and rifle pits easily picked off every man who thoughtlessly exposed his head. This they could do in comparative safety, as the troops in the trenches were armed with smooth-bored muskets. The Texans, however, were supplied with Minnie [Minié] and Enfield rifles, and what was still more to the purpose, knew how to use them. During the first day's shooting, several Yankees were picked out of trees and holes, evidently very much to their surprise, and after that confined themselves chiefly to their fortifications. The sport then consisted principally in watching for each others heads above the breast-works, and woe to the man who exposed himself for more than a few seconds. On one occasion a Mexican, becoming interested in some object outside the works, incautiously raised his head above the trenches, when crack went a rifle, and a minnie ball ploughed through his cheek. Exasperated by so severe a reminder of his duty, he sprang over the defences and in full view approached within a hundred yards of the enemy's lines, and dared any and all to come out like men and fight him. This they declined to do and commenced firing; but either he bore a charmed life or their nerves were unstrung, for not a ball touched him, although he walked back very deliberately and climbed inside our works. In these little affairs two Texans were killed and several wounded, all owing to some carelessness or bravado of their own.

While here the horse arrived which had been purchased by the privates of the 4th Texas as a present to General Hood. At dress parade on the 26th of April, 1st Sergeant J. M. Bookman, of Co. G, presented him in the following words:

"Sir: In behalf of the non-commissioned officers and privates of the 4th Texas Regiment, I present you this war-horse. He was selected and purchased by us for this purpose, not that we hoped by so doing to court your favor, but simply because we, as freemen and Texans, claim the ability to discern, and the right to reward, merit wherever it may be found. In you, sir, we recognize the soldier and the gentleman. In you we have found a leader whom we are proud to follow—a commander whom it is a pleasure to obey; and this horse we tender as a slight testimonial of our admiration. Take him, and when the hour of battle comes, when mighty hosts meet in the struggle of death, we will, as did the troops of old, who rallied around the white plume of Henry, look for your commanding form and this proud steed as our guide, and gathering there we will conquer or die. In a word, General, 'you stand by us and we will stand by you.' "

General Hood here advanced, and springing into the saddle, addressed the Regiment in a few feeling and eloquent words, expressing his gratitude at this mark of confidence, and promising we should not look in vain for a rallying point when the struggle came.[34]

Nothing further of interest occurred until the

EVACUATION OF THE PENINSULA.

This important movement, rendered necessary by the fact that we were confronted by a superior force, and flanked both right and left by navigable streams, occupied solely by enemy's fleet, was fixed for the 3d of May, but owing to the mismanagement of some commander along the lines, was delayed until the following morning. It might then have been accomplished in secrecy, had not the whiskey-drinking propensities of some of our cavalry led them into a trap which had been arranged for the reception of the Yankees. Secret mines had been placed in several houses, to explode on entrance. Ignorant of this fact, our enterprising troopers burst open a door, and though unsuccessful in their search for liquor, came out of the house considerably "elevated," though without any serious results to themselves. The explosion which followed started other matches, and soon it seemed as though a fierce battle was raging in the ancient little city. Many of the buildings caught fire, and just as the grey of morning began to tinge the eastern sky, a lurid glare was thrown upon the surrounding country, which gave a wild and exaggerated aspect to every object in sight. It was a grand scene. Our army had already passed up the road towards Williamsburg, leaving Whiting's Division, of which we were a part, as the rear guard.[35] We remained here in line of battle until sunrise, when we took up the line of march, the Texas Brigade in the rear and the 4th Texas in rear of that. [An atmospheric phenomenon occurred, which was to our men one of great interest. Two well defined suns made their appearance in the heavens. The Bay, from the reflection, looked like a sea of molten fire. Finally the lower sun disappeared, and the other moved westward through the heavens. They felt that the scene was an omen for good, and began their march in good spirits.][36] Why our men were so often used as the rear guard, not only to the army corps, to which they belong, but detailed for other portions, as in the case of Hampton's Legion in evacuating the Potomac, I never could imagine, unless it was for their superiority in woodcraft and skirmishing. After a tiresome day's march, during which we were several times thrown into line of battle, we reached Williamsburg, where the army had halted at about 5 P.M., and passing through, bivouacked about two miles above town. About an hour after we had passed through, the advance guard of the enemy appeared, and after exchanging a few artillery compliments, retired. On the following morning a field onset was made and continued until evening. In this battle the Federals were repulsed with a heavy loss, amounting in killed, wounded and prisoners to about 5,000. Our loss was also severe, and amounted to about 2,500. The courage and endurance of our troops were fearfully tried in this engagement, but they stood the test like true Southrons and patriots, battling for freedom. On the night previous to this battle, news reached our Generals that the enemy with gun-boats and transports was pushing up York river. It was now evident that by a rapid movement on our rear, they expected to retard our progress until they could debark troops at Eltham's Landing, opposite West Point, and by cutting our army in two, at least capture our artillery and wagon train.—Great energy and courage were now required to save the retreating army. If they were allowed time to select and occupy their positions, serious disaster must be the result. This enterprise was committed to proper hands. At 11 o'clock that night, General Whiting's Division, notwithstanding their hard day's march, were called up and put in motion. Through the rain and mud they marched until day, and on until night again, when a halt was ordered, and tired, hungry and wet, the men dropped where they stood and slept in spite of the storm. The next morning scouts were thrown out to feel for the position of the enemy, and the command was allowed a few hours rest. This being "ration day," and the commissary "missing," the men were informed that they could go across the road to a *corn-crib*[37] *and help themselves to some corn on the cob,* to be eaten raw; or roasted in the ashes as their different tastes might prompt. All were hungry enough to appreciate this *liberality,* and such corn-cracking as followed has seldom been heard outside a hog-pen, and a hearty laugh went round, when some wag, seated on a log, called imperiously for "*a bundle of fodder and bucket of salt and water.*" After night, two men of the 5th Texas got separated from their company, which was out on picket duty, and while searching for it came upon a squad of men in the woods, just as the order "Fall in—company" was delivered. Not being ceremonious they obeyed promptly and marched off. Judge of their surprise and chagrin when they, too late, discovered that they had joined a Yankee company, and being unable to "surround it" as the Irishman did the Hessians, they quietly surrendered their arms, and acknowledged themselves "taken in."

BATTLE OF ELTHAM'S LANDING.

The command was put in motion at daylight of May 7th, and about 7 o'clock A.M., came upon a picket of the enemy, who fired two shots at Gen. Hood, who was riding at the head of the 4th Texas, now in front. One shot struck Corporal Sapp, of Co. H, in the head, inflicting a severe but not dangerous wound. Private John Deal, of Co. A, whose gun was loaded, immediately fired upon the pickets as they ran, and struck the only one in sight, killing him instantly.[38] Some confusion was observed at first in consequence of empty guns, and Col. Marshall's order to "Fall back into the woods and load;" but Gen. Hood immediately called out to the men to "move up," which they did at double quick, and line of battle was immediately formed on the brow of a hill. Beyond this hill, which had a precipitous descent, was an open field of six or eight hundred yards width. On the opposite side were some four or five companies of the enemy, who immediately began falling back into the timber, but not until several random shots had been fired by our men, which we afterwards discovered had killed five and wounded as many more. Company B (Capt. Carter) was then ordered by Gen. Hood to deploy as skirmishers and "feel the enemy." They advanced across the open field, and entering the timber, began a "running fight." Co. G (Captain Hutcheson) was then ordered forward to support Co. B, if necessary; if not, to deploy on its right—the latter course was adopted. Co. K. (Capt. Martin) was next sent to support Co. B, and Co. E (Captain Ryan) to the support of Co. G. After retreating about half a mile, the Yankees made a stand behind an old mill-dam, and a spirited engagement ensued between them and the right platoon of Co. B, under Captain Carter, and Co. G, Capt. Hutcheson. Co. H (Capt. Porter) now arrived upon the ground, with orders to support the left platoon of Co. B, under Lieut. Walsh. The firing now became general, and the enemy, many of their guns missing fire, threw them down and fled. While pursuing them, the second platoon of Co. B came upon a large force (some two hundred,) protected by a heavy palisade. This was more than was bargained for, and the boys, some twenty-five in number, immediately "*treed,*" and answered their volleys, by picking off every one who showed his head. At this juncture Gen. Hood appeared, and ordered the Lieutenant in command to charge the works, and he would send support. Just as the command "charge" was given, and the boys with a yell, had started for the works, the first platoon of Co. B appeared upon the left flank of the palisade, and the Yankees fled in confusion, leaving seventeen killed and several wounded in the track of their flight. While Co. B was thus engaged, Co. G had also had its share of "fun." Discovering a company of about eighty Yankees, Capt. Hutcheson with his company and part of Co. E, attacked them so vigorously, that they dared not run, and were so unnerved, that they fired volley after volley into the tree-tops. Capt. Hutcheson, who was a Chesterfield in manner, did not for a moment forget himself during the fight. "Charge them, gentlemen, charge them." "Aim low, gentlemen, aim at their waistbands," were his constant exhortations, until a portion of the enemy cried for quarters. "Throw down your arms, gentlemen, you scoundrels, throw them down." Sixteen obeyed the order, and the remainder taking advantage of the momentary cessation of hostilities, turned and fled. Bewildered, however, they took the wrong direction, and coming upon the 5th Texas where it was lying down in line-of-battle, they were greeted by a volley, which left *not one* standing. The fruits of Capt. H's victory, were eleven killed, several wounded, and sixteen prisoners, together with several stand of arms. While these events were transpiring, the 1st, 5th, and remainder of the 4th Texas had entered the timber, leaving the 18th Georgia to support the artillery in the rear. A Yankee regiment now appeared upon the left and rear of the skirmishers, with the intention, doubtless, of cutting them off. Here we witnessed for the first time,

THE GALLANTRY OF THE FIRST TEXAS.

The regiment now advancing, 1st California, evidently *intended* to fight well, and advanced steadily to within eighty paces of the 1st Texas, when they halted, poured in a volley, and with three *huzzahs*, attempted to charge. This was expected, and "aim low, fire," was ordered by Colonel [A. T.] Rainey, and a discharge followed that seemed to mow down the whole front rank, and sent the remainder in confusion back again. A whole-souled hearty *yell* now went up from the Texans, such as only Southerners can give, and they in turn, charged. But the Californians were not yet ready to yield, and rallying, they made a stubborn resistance, and for about twenty minutes, the fire raged with terrible fury. The Texans charged again, and the enemy broke and fled, leaving about two hundred killed and wounded on the field, and several prisoners in our hands. The loss of the 1st Texas in this engagement, was eleven [six][39] killed and twenty-one wounded. Among the former, however, we regret to chronicle Lieutenant-Colonel [Harvey H.] Black and Captain Decatur, who were loved and mourned by all, as brave men.

After the rout of this regiment, the enemy did not again attack us, but contented themselves with shelling us from their gunboats, and sweeping the woods with grape, from a battery they had planted upon the river bank, without, however, doing us the slightest injury. While this was going on, the boys had a hearty laugh at the conduct of an

INDIAN WARRIOR,

who was attached to the 1st Texas Regiment. During the entire battle, with musketry, he had conducted himself in the most gallant manner, and had even succeeded in capturing a Yankee, whom he turned over to the proper officer, with the brief announcement, "Major, Yank yours, gun mine," and again participated in the struggle. When the first shell came tearing through the tree-tops, with its screaming inquiry, "where you, where you," he uttered a significant "ugh!" and listened until it burst. At that instant, another came, and exploded just over our heads, when he sprang to his feet exclaiming, "no good for Indian," and made for the rear with the agility of an antelope. The boys did not, however, reproach him, because it has long been understood that Indians won't stand to be shot at by wagons, more particularly when the projectile itself shoots so terribly. The entire loss of the brigade in this engagement was thirty-seven. Of that number, Captain Denny, Commissary of the 5th, was killed by a picket, and two men captured, as previously related. Corporal Sapp, of Co. H, and private Spencer, of Co. G, 4th Texas, were wounded, all the other casualties were of the 1st Texas, of which regiment, we cannot speak too highly.—These are the men who came from their distant homes, at their own expense, before the President had called upon Texas for troops, to assist in this great struggle. And, though their names have not occupied a place in the journals of the day, they have ever been at their posts, ready and willing to do and die for our common cause. They are a lively, merry set, and though often hungry and "ragged," they have shown in numberless instances, that they can march as far, and fight as hard, as any troops in the service.

THE ENEMY'S LOSS

in this engagement, as estimated by General Hood in his official report, was three hundred killed and wounded, and one hundred and twenty-six prisoners. McClellan's estimate is even greater, as he reported a loss of five hundred men and officers. This is probably correct, though a New York paper, which claims that the troops participating in this battle were chiefly from that section, viz: Albany, states the entire loss at twelve hundred. A correspondent of the New York "Herald," writing from West Point soon after the fight, gravely asserts that they *"were charged furiously by four regiments of negroes!"* This paragraph caused considerable sport among the boys, being regarded as a direct reflection upon the state of the brigade toilet. The writer, however, was in probability, more knave than fool, for just at that period, the question of enlisting slaves in the United States Army was being agitated, and such an assertion would not be without its effect on the unthinking masses of the North.

THE IMPORTANCE OF THIS BATTLE,

in reference to which, the Richmond papers have been silent, cannot be better illustrated than by reference to the language of some of our general officers. President Davis, in conversation with one of our Senators, said, in speaking of the Texas Brigade, "they saved the *rear* of our army, and the *whole* of our baggage train."

General Gustavus W. Smith, in a letter to Colonel Horace Randall, writes, "the Texans won immortal honor for themselves, their State, and for their commander, General Hood, at the battle of Eltham's Landing, near West Point. With forty thousand such men, I would not hesitate to invade the North, and would before winter, make them sue for peace upon our terms, or destroy their whole country. But in praise of the Texas Brigade of my Division, I could talk a week, and then not say half they deserve. If the regiments now organized in Texas, could be transported here, and armed to-morrow, properly led, they would end the war in three months."[40]

General Samuel W. Melton, also writes, "here we first had a fair sample of your Texans, under Hood. They are, incomparably, the best fighters in the confederacy; men upon whom one could depend under all circumstances—who seem to fight for the very love of it. * * * Oh! that we had more of them. Forty thousand such men could march through Yankeedom now, from one end to the other, and conquer a peace in a month."

THE BRIGADE "CUTS DIRT," WHILE THE YANKEES DIG.

The fighting ended at 2 o'clock, P. M., and the enemy showing no disposition to leave their gunboats again, the brigade was ordered back from the bottom, leaving only a sufficient force for observation. *Two reg. Andersons Brig. came up after the fight was over—Hood proffered the command to him, he declined & transfered his 2 Reg. to Hood. Gen. W[hiting] arriving Gen. H. said, "I am glad to see you. We expect some big fighting and will need a big Gen. No you made this fight & you are big enough Gen. to fight it out."*[41] Returning to the camp, from which we had started in the morning, we remained until 10 o'clock at night, when the whole army, baggage and all having passed up the road, we again assumed our position as the rear guard. Strict silence and quick time being enjoined, I am sure no troops ever marched more swiftly, or kept more obstinate silence than we did until daylight. How ludicrous the scene. What a hearty laugh a man could have had, had he been in a position to observe both armies that night. Ours, moving swiftly and stealthily along, casting many and anxious glances to the rear, fearing to discover the head of a pursuing column—theirs, digging, toiling and sweating, in preparing to receive the furious onslaught which they *knew* the "rebels" would make at daylight. Then to have watched the Yankees in the morning, feeling cautiously through the woods, listening every moment for the dreaded sound of the guns of troops, who were miles on their way to Richmond, and still going. Late in the afternoon of May 8th, the brigade was drawn up in line of battle, in the lawn, in front of Doctor Tyler's residence, five miles west of New Kent Court House, as the enemy were threatening to attack us. They did not, however, come up, and we remained here until the following evening, when we moved one mile up the road, and formed a new line of defence, to be held until our army could reach, and take its position in front of Richmond. About noon on ————————, we decamped, and, though constantly in motion, only reached the Chickahominy, *about six miles*, by 1 o'clock at night. This was owing to the fact, that the road was blocked up by the rear of our artillery and baggage train, and not daring to lie down or rest, we could only "mark time" in the rain and mud until the hour above mentioned, when all others having passed over, we reached the bridge. Here we found several Generals, with their attendant aids and couriers, all exhorting us to "close up," and for God's sake to hurry. This was more easily said, than done, for the roads had been cut by artillery and wagons, until a perfect mortar had been formed from one to three feet deep, and through this below, and a heavy soaking rain above, the men floundered on. At length, losing all patience, General Whiting dashed upon the bridge. "Hurry up, men, hurry up, don't mind a little mud." "D'ye call this a *little mud!* s'pose you git down and try it, stranger; I'll hold your horse." "Do you know whom you address, sir? I am General Whiting." "General ————————, don't you reckon I know a *General* from a long-tongued courier?" says the fellow, as he disappeared in the darkness. This, repeated with sundry variations several times, at length discouraged the General, and leaving the Texans, whose spirits he had threatened to subdue, to cross as best they might, he rode away. Finally all were safely landed on this side the Chickahominy, and without waiting to eat or build fires, the men threw themselves upon the muddy ground, and slept soundly until morning. We occupied this point until evening, and then moved back about two miles, and bivouacked until the command was relieved, and marching to the rear, we camped at "Pine Island," three miles east of the city.—Nothing of interest occurred here. The men gave their whole attention to *resting & greesing feet & rubbing up rusty guns,*[42] eating, sleeping, washing bodies and clothes, and watching the recruits who had recently arrived, attempting "balance and left." On Sunday [May 25], the Chaplain having just returned from Texas, where he had gone on recruiting service, we had Divine worship, which was remarkably well attended.

PREPARATIONS FOR THE MARCH—AGAIN.

May 26th.—Orders were issued to send off surplus baggage, which always accumulates with amazing facility when the camp is near a city or town. On the following evening at sunset we departed, and marching and "marking time" all night, we accomplished a distance of *seven miles,* and at dawn were halted one mile this side Chickahominy, on the Meadow Bridge road. Here we remained until the following day concealed in the woods, and then marched back and camped between the Mechanicsville Turnpike and Central railroad. On the next evening a most terrific thunderstorm, accompanied by torrents of rain, began and lasted through the night, thoroughly drenching the men. One man in the 4th Alabama Regiment, camped near us, was killed by lightning, and several were severely shocked. It was this storm which filled the Chickahominy, and suggested to General [Joseph E.] Johnston the movements which resulted in

THE BATTLE OF SEVEN PINES.

At six o'clock, May 31st, orders were received to march immediately, and in a few moments we were moving down the Nine-Mile road. Pursuing this road until within a mile and a half of the enemy, we halted, and until 2 o'clock, waited for the signal of battle, which was to be the roar of fire-arms on our right. It subsequently appeared that General [James] Longstreet had begun the attack at, or near 9 o'clock, A. M., but owing to some atmospherical phenomenon, the sound of battle was not heard until five hours after, when the enemy had been driven from his position, and had fallen back near the York River railroad. As our movements were dependent on General

[Benjamin] Huger, we waited until 4 o'clock, when despairing of his arrival, the Brigade was formed in line of battle, with its left resting on the road, and ordered forward. Following, at some distance, to render what aid I could to any who might be wounded, I soon discovered that I had lost my Regiment in the swamps, and, as I could be of but little use alone against so many, I immediately determined upon a "change of base," and started to the rear. *Passing out of the timber to the road I aimed to reach it again. But was ordered by Gen. Whiting to get out of the road. It was here that I heard the whistling of the first bullet, and was simple enough to look up a tree for it, thinking it a flying bird. The next I thought a bunch of pine leaves falling & looked again & while looking another passed just over my head & I immediately discovered my mistake & as I turned from the litter squad standing in the road I heard one strike & looking round found one man on the ground—shot in the foot—Hastning a few steps further & heared another & looking discovered that a man was shot in the head—killed instantly. These shot were thrown a distance of 1/2 M. Our men advancing soon drove them off. I hastened on to rejoin them—passing thro' several camps I finally stopped for a minute to take a view of a camp from which some 5000 Y[ankees] were driven. I was quite surprised at the report of about 12 guns an[d] a volly of musketry over the camp. The shell grap[e] & bullets flew all round.—I felt [it] is safe to Skedaddle a little & came out unhurt—next morning I found a hole in my coat. That looked a little suspicious. I concluded it would be well to defer my further inquiry for the Reg. until next morning.*[43] The battle had now become terrible. Regiment after regiment, and brigade after brigade were thrown against their batteries, which, protected front and flank by earth-works, palisades, fallen timber and swamps, were almost impregnable. *One reg. after another & one Brig. after another was brought up in double quick & thrown into the field cheering & Shouting as they went. To our left the attack was made principly upon Floods Battery supported by 2 other batteries & a heavy body of infantry. The Shout of victory was heared every few minutes by our advancing lines as they routed & drove the enemy before them. As the sun was setting a desperate struggle to take these batteries was made by our forces. And altho' they advanced right up to the cannons mouth several times, they were driven back by heavy infantry reserves. An attempt was then made to flank them but was unsuccessful in consequence of a marsh, pond & ditches of water.—We succeeded in taking all their artilery except this.*[44] In passing to the rear, I met Generals Lee and Johnston and President Davis, riding at speed, and going, not only upon the field, but directly under the fire of the enemy's guns, which I could not but regard as imprudent, knowing how much depended upon their safety. Soon after, General Johnston was wounded. In storming these batteries, Whiting's Brigade suffered severely, and the name of the 4th Alabama was again written in letters of blood. *The wounded were going to the rear by every road & in every possible way. I returned to the field infirmary & there assisted in attentions to the wounded the greater portion of the night.*[45] . . . *On the night of the 31st I witnessed some of the terrors of battle. The wounded were being brought in all night; quite a number reached the field infirmary before dark. Arms broken-off, legs shiveried, the body pierced in every part & every possible way. —face disfigured, skull fractured—nose gone, mouth disfigured. I spent a great portion of the night in assisting to dress & alleviate the suffering.*[46] All efforts however proved unavailing, and finally at 8 1/2 o'clock, P. M., the firing ceased, and the weary soldiers slept upon their arms. At daylight, June 1st, the engagement was renewed, and by 9 o'clock, A. M., had become almost as general as on the day previous. The enemy having, during the night, strongly reinforced, were endeavoring to regain their lost position, but were repulsed in every instance. At 10 o'clock the firing ceased, leaving us in possession of all their positions and batteries, except one, several hundred prisoners, a large quantity of camp equipage, small arms, ammunition, &c.

HOW THE REBELS FIGHT.

The Cincinnati "Commercial" publishes an extract from a private letter, written by a member of Battery A, New York Artillery, in Casey's Division, better known as the "Napoleon Battery," in which the unyielding and irresistible prowess of our troops is described as something wonderful. If the writer had only stood to his gun a little longer, he would have learned still more of the fierce and dauntless resolution of brave men fighting for liberty and home. He is speaking of the battle of The Seven Pines:

"Our spherical case shot were awful missiles, each of them consisting of a clotted mass of seventy-six musket balls, with a charge of powder in the centre, that is fired with a fuse, the same as a shell.

The missile first acts as a solid shot, ploughing its way through masses of men, and then exploding, hurls forward a shower of musket balls that mow down the foe in heaps. Our battery threw twenty-four of these a minute, and as we had the exact range of every part of the field, every shot told with frightful effect. But the enemy were not at all daunted—they marched steadily on, and hailed a perfect torrent of balls upon us. Why we, as well as our horses, were not every one shot down, will forever remain a mystery to me. We did not mind the leaden hail, however, but kept pouring our case-shot into the dense masses of the foe, who came on in prodigious and overwhelming force. And they fought splendidly, too. Our shot tore their ranks wide open, and shattered them asunder in a manner that was frightful to witness; but they closed up at once, and came on as steadily as English veterans. When they got within four hundred yards, we closed our case shot and opened on them with canister; and such destruction I never elsewhere witnessed. At each discharge, great gaps were made in their ranks—indeed, whole companies went down before that murderous fire; but they closed up with an order and discipline that was awe-inspiring. They seemed to be animated with the courage of despair, blended with the hope of a speedy victory, if they could by an overwhelming rush drive us from our position. It was awful to see their ranks torn and shattered by every discharge of canister that we poured right into their faces, and while their dead and dying lay in piles, closed up and still kept advancing right in the face of the fire. At one time, three lines, one behind the other, were steadily advancing, and three of their flags were brought in range of one of our guns, shotted with canister. "Fire!" shouted the gunner, and down went those three flags, and a gap was opened through those three lines as if a thunderbolt had torn through them, and the dead lay in swaths. But they at once closed up, and came steadily on, never halting or wavering, right through the woods, over the fence, through the field, right up to our guns, and, sweeping everything before them, captured every piece. When we delivered our last fire, they were within fifteen or twenty paces of us, and, as all of our horses were either killed or wounded, we could not carry off a gun. Our whole division was cut to pieces, with what loss I do not know. We fell back to a second line of entrenchments, and there held the enemy in check until reinforcements arrived, and then we kept our position til night put an end to the battle."

The Texas Brigade was not directly engaged during this battle, although under fire during a great part of both days. *In obedience to orders they continued along on the south side of the road to the York R. R. at which point it was expected they would meet the enemy driven by Gen. Longstreet from below; but instead of falling back in this direction luckily for them they fell back into the swamp & thereby avoided the trap. In moving down to this point the 4th became divided by Col. Marshall not properly understanding the orders of Gen. Hood.*[47] Much dissatisfaction was expressed by the men at having had so much "double quicking" through swamps and fallen timber, and no opportunity to vent their wrath upon the enemy. The Confederate loss in this battle was about four thousand five hundred in killed, wounded and missing. The enemy subsequently admitted a loss of nearly ten thousand. After occupying the field until the evening of June 2d, our forces fell back to their old line of defences, and the Yankees reoccupied their old ground. This afforded a fine scope for the lying talent of McClellan, and he immediately published a flaming report of a *three day's* battle, professing to have re-taken on the third day all he had previously lost, and stating that he had driven our routed and panic-stricken army into the very lines of the city; but neglects to state why he did not immediately perfect his "on to Richmond." Of this *third day's battle* our army was entirely ignorant as there were no guns fired, and no "brilliant bayonet charges" made. After this battle the Texas Brigade was thrown to the front, and detailed each day as scouts, sharp-shooters and spies—two hundred men and the requisite number of officers. These men operated beyond, and independently of the regular pickets, and soon became a terror to the enemy. On the morning of the 7th, a party of one hundred and fifty Texans, under command of Lieut. Jamison, of the 1st Texas, Lieut. Barziza, of the 4th, and Lieut. Nash, of the 5th, were ordered by Gen. Hood to drive in the enemy's pickets, and ascertain, as far as practical, what the main body were doing. They immediately proceeded to carry out his instructions, and attacked the Yankee outposts with such fury, that they fled, "pell mell," running over in their flight a Regiment of Infantry [71st Pennsylvania], which was supporting them.—The regiment, thinking from indications which they saw, that at least half the "rebels" were coming, also took to their heels, and for half a mile made regular "Bull Run time." Having at length discovered that they were flying from a mere squad, they rallied, formed and opened on our boys with a will, but were so promptly answered that they dared not advance. Here, securely protected by trees, the Texans poured an effective fire into their dense ranks, and would probably have given them another chase, had they not discovered a Yankee Regiment moving up on their left flank. This necessitated a retrograde movement, which they promptly executed, fighting front and flank, as they fell back to the cover of our batteries. The enemy afterwards confessed a loss of between forty-five and fifty in this skirmish, while ours was but six, in killed and wounded—none missing.[48] So successful was this foray, that Gen'l Hood issued an order complimenting the men and officers. Among our killed on this occasion was Mr. ____________ Davis, an *amateur*, who was widely known in Eastern Texas, as an editor of ability and promise. His fall was regretted by all who knew him, as his gallant conduct in the field and social qualities in camp had endeared him to all. A few days after this affair, some of our scouts penetrated the Yankee lines, by "*relieving*" one of their pickets, to see what they could "pick up." Just as the gray of dawn appeared, a Yankee Lieutenant Colonel, officer of the day, visiting his pickets, rode up to a member of the 18th Georgia, who promptly presented for his inspection the muzzle of his rifle, and at the same time enjoining silence. "You fool," exclaimed the indignant officer, "I am Lieut. Col. _________, of the _____ th New York Regiment." "Ah," said Georgia, "Well now, Colonel, that's just what I was thinking; and as it's rainin' a little, I think I'll take you in 'out of the wet.' Let's have your pistol and sword, if you please." No alternative was left the chargrined "Yank," and the elated Georgian marched him to Gen. Hood's headquarters, where he turned him over, and received his fine "Colt" for his trouble.

HO! FOR STONEWALL JACKSON

On the morning of June 11th, orders were received to be in readiness to move at 5 P. M., which we did, passing through Richmond and over James River to the Danville Depot, where we remained until 8 A. M., the following morning. We then took the cars, and in twenty-four hours arrived at Lynchburg. Here we remained until the 15th, when we were moved to Charlottesville, and thence, on the 18th, to Staunton. On the 19th, marching orders were issued, and the 20th we started back towards Charlottesville. "Where are we going?" now became the popular question; but, alas! no one could answer it. Some "guessed" to the Valley, some to Alexandria, some to flank McClellan, &c.; but no one knew.[49] That all possibility of our plan being discovered might be destroyed, orders were issued by General Jackson that if any one asked a question, to answer, "I don't know." After a few miles of our march had been accomplished, our Brigade was halted, and General Hood delivered General Jackson's orders to us verbally. "Now," said he, "you will often be asked, Where are you going? Where from? Who are you? &c.; and you must answer, 'I don't know.' In fact, you need not give a direct answer to any one."—This was just as much license as the men wanted, and they forthwith knew nothing of the past, present, or future. On the following day General Jackson noticed a "straggler" making for a cherry tree, near the road. Riding up, he asked, "Where are you going, sir?" "I don't know." "To what command do you belong?" "I don't know." "Well, what State are you from?" "I don't know." The General was evidently fast losing patience, when another "straggler" explained the matter. "Old Stonewall and General Hood issued orders yesterday that we were not to know anything until after the next fight, and we are not going to disobey orders." The General said no more, but rode on in silence, reflecting, no doubt, upon the perversity of human nature in general, and soldiers in particular, thinking it unnecessary to ask the soldier if he knew the way to the cherry tree.[50] As we neared Gordonsville, the problem of our destination grew intensely interesting. Would we turn to the left or the right—move on Washington or Richmond. Soon the enigma, which had roused up many a drowsy brain, was solved. The head of the iron-horse turned towards the South. The Chickahominy was the theatre of action. Leaving the railroad at Frederick Hall, we moved in as many columns as there were roads towards Ashland, and for the want of roads we sometimes marched through fields and woods, where we arrived on the evening of the 25th, and drove in the Yankee pickets. Orders were received that night to move at 3 A. M., which we did, taking the Hanover road. During the morning, the sound of cannon could be distinctly heard, and each discharge quickened the step of our men. Sharpshooters and skirmishers were in advance, and occasionally the clear crack of a rifle announced that some "Bucktail" [Pennsylvanian] had received his *quietus*, or saved himself by flight. At 3 P. M., we reached a small creek, on the opposite side of which our scouts reported two Regiments ambuscaded. The bridge, a wooden structure, was burning when we arrived, and the sound of axes could be plainly heard in the timber ahead, where the enemy were obstructing the road.—Riley's Battery was immediately thrown forward and shelled the timber, forcing the Yankees to save themselves by a precipitate flight, leaving a number of axes on the ground and sticking in the trees they had been chopping. Just then an amusing scene took place. A number of darkies, who understood the use of the hoe better than the fire-lock, were at work in the field a little to our rear. When the first shot was fired from the "big gun," they let all holts loose and started for the house, which was still further to the rear, screaming and running for dear life, as if they thought the old-boy was after them. And from our position, it was hard to tell which made the better time, they or the Yankees. [Here we had a slight exhibition of the generalship of Gen. Jackson. For Gen. Whiting had halted his command and sent forward the 4th Texas to protect the pioneers while they were reconstructing a bridge to cross the artillery. The position of the regiment was on this side the stream. The Yankees were on the other, and concealed from view by the underwood. Gen. Jackson came dashing up from the rear, and having ordered the rear regiment of the division forward to assist the pioneers, ordered the 4th to cross the creek and drive the enemy from the hill beyond. The other regiment immediately followed, and by the time the infantry had crossed the bridge was finished, and all moved on.][51] Having at length rebuilt the bridge and crossed the artillery, we proceeded cautiously for some two or three miles, and halted for the night in line of battle.

DESCRIPTION OF THE FIELD, AND PLAN OF ATTACK.

Before proceeding with the important events now ready for development, which are to change the entire aspect of the campaign, and send the "Young Napolcon" [McClellan] howling back to his patron, it becomes necessary to give the reader some idea of the position of the two opposing armies. That all may readily understand this, I transcribe from "The Seven Days Battles around Richmond," the following simple explanation: "Place your hand upon the table with the index finger pointing a little north of east. Spread your fingers so that the tips will form the arc of a circle. Imagine Richmond as situated on your wrist; the outer edge of your thumb as the Central

Railroad, the inner edge as the Mechanicsville Turnpike, first finger as the Nine Mile or New Bridge road, the second as the Williamsburg Pike, running nearly parallel with the York River railroad—the railroad running between the two fingers. The third as the Charles City Turnpike, (which runs to the southward of the White Oak Swamp,) and the fourth as the Darbytown road. The radius of this arc averaging about seven miles to Richmond.—Commanding these several avenues were the forces of McClellan. Our own troops, except those under Jackson [who were at Ashland twenty miles above the city],[52] occupied a similar position, but of course a smaller circle immediately around the city; the heaviest body being on the centre, south of the York River railroad.

BATTLE OF MECHANICSVILLE, THURSDAY, JUNE 27th [26th].

The morning dawned bright and beautiful. All arrangements being completed, Jackson's forces moved down between the Chickahominy and Pamunkey, driving the enemy before them, until the front of General [Lawrence O'B.] Branch was so far uncovered as to allow him to cross at Brooke Turnpike, and marching down the north side of the stream, uncovering the front of Gen'l A. P. Hill, as he attacked the enemy at Mechanicsville. This division crossed at the Meadow Bridge about 4 P. M., and uniting with the command of General Branch, immediately attacked the enemy and drove them from their strong positions. Here they had erected formidable earthworks, and mounted upon them were heavy siege guns, and the storming of these defences is justly reckoned among the most gallant and bloody scenes of the campaign. The indomitable valor of our troops soon sent the Yankees flying, and mounting their works, the Confederates turned their own guns upon them with terrible effect. The loss on both sides was heavy, but when we view the nature of the struggle, it is a matter of wonder how any of our troops escaped destruction. About a mile farther down was another formidable battery of sixteen guns, supported by heavy bodies of infantry, who were protected by rifle pits, abattis, and the bed of Beaver Dam Creek, which passed in front and to their left flank.—This position was attacked with a furious onset. The charge was made on the rifle pits, but the creek and abattis which still intervened rendered the capture impracticable. At this juncture the batteries took a commanding position, and over the heads of our troops poured into the infantry such a storm of shot and shell as almost to silence their fire, and to entirely distract the attention of their battery from our infantry. No further advance was, however, attempted that night, and, at 10 o'clock, P. M., both batteries ceased firing. Soon afterwards the enemy abandoned his position, leaving some of his disabled guns upon the field. During the night, General Longstreet crossed the Chickahominy, and formed a junction with the two Generals Hill.

OUR LINE OF BATTLE ON FRIDAY MORNING

was fully completed, and extended for miles over hills and plains, woods and valleys, the different commands taking positions as follows: Jackson on the extreme left, next D. H. Hill, then [General Richard Stoddert] Ewell, Whiting and A. P. Hill, while Longstreet moved down, with his right resting upon the swamps of the Chickahominy. Early in the afternoon, a scattering fire of skirmishers was heard on the right. About 2 P. M. several of our batteries were placed in position, and opened with a view to attract attention from Longstreet and A. P. Hill on the right; but they were soon overpowered and driven from the field. It was now discovered that McClellan had made a strong stand on Gaines' Farm, and was determined to hold it, if *possible.* His position was an awkward one. The left wing fronting Richmond westward, and his right at angles, and to the rear, facing north.

THE BATTLE OF GAINES' FARM, FRIDAY, JUNE 27th.[53]

At 4 o'clock, P. M., Longstreet commenced the fight, driving the enemy down the Chickahominy. This was the signal for a general assault, and in quick succession Hill, Whiting and Ewell took up the fire, and the work of death begun. This part of the day's work is correctly given in the [Richmond] "Whig" of the 30th, as follows:

"Gen'l A. P. Hill's Division, supported by Gen'l Pickett's Brigade from Longstreet's Division, made the first assault upon the enemy's works, which were of the most formidable character, and seemingly impregnable. Brigade after brigade advanced upon the fortification, and delivered their fire, but were compelled to fall back under the terrific fire of the Yankees, who were comparatively secure from danger behind their works, and poured volley after volley into our brave troops. After the fight had been prolonged for several hours, without results, Gen'l Whiting's Division, now of Jackson's *corps d'armee*, advanced to the assault, and after a desperate charge, succeeded in dislodging the Yankees. As they fled from their works, they had to pass through an open field, about two hundred yards in width, before reaching the woods. Several of our regiments fired at the fugitives and killed a very large number of them. The field was nearly covered with the dead and wounded Yankees. The regiments composing Whiting's Division are the 4th Alabama, 11th Mississippi, 6th North Carolina, 2d Mississippi, 1st, 4th and 5th Texas, 18th Georgia, and Hamptons' Legion. It was now nearly dark, and though the pursuit was continued for some time, it was deemed inexpedient to follow the wretches through the swamp, to which they fled, and, accordingly, our men were recalled."

In the [Richmond] "Examiner" of July 2d, appears the following article, which, in view of the many reports in circulation, I insert as an act of justice to those noble men who contributed so largely to the success of that memorable day.

THE FIGHT AT GAINES' FARM—AN OFFICER'S STATEMENT.

There have been many confused and contradictory statements of the forces engaged in the attacks of the enemy's works near Gaines' Farm on last Friday. We have received the following statement from an officer on the subject of this doubt:

"At about two o'clock on Friday evening last, I reached the lines of the enemy's entrenchments near Gaines' farm. A fierce struggle was then going on between A. P. Hill's Division and the garrison of the line of defence. Repeated charges were made by Hill's troops, but the formidable character of the works, and murderous volleys of grape and canister from the artillery covering them, kept our troops in check.

"It was about half-past four o'clock when [General George Edward] Pickett's Brigade came to Hill's support. Pickett's Regiments fought with the most determined valor. At five o'clock Whiting's Division, composed of the 'Old Third' and Texas Brigades, advanced at a 'double-quick,' charged them, routed them, and captured their artillery.

"The struggle was brief, but, perhaps, the most bitter of the war. *Fully one-fourth* of the entire division were cut down in this gallant charge.

"The brave Texans were led by Brigadier-General Hood, and the 'Old Third Brigade' by the dashing Colonel [E. McIver] Law, late commander, of the Fourth Alabama.

"The works carried by these noble troops would have been invincible to the bayonet had they been garrisoned by *men.*

"Whiting's Division is composed of Hood's Brigade—First, Fourth and Fifth Texas, and Hampton Legion and Eighteenth Georgia, and Colonel Law's Brigade—Fourth Alabama, Second and Eleventh Mississippi, and Sixth North Carolina.

"I mention these Regiments because their names will be historical."

That the reader may have an idea of the manner in which each Regiment of Whiting's Division acted, I transfer from the "Whig" a letter written by *Wauzee,* which, in its more prominent facts, is strictly correct:

Battle Field, Near Chickahominy,
June 28, 1862.

To the Editor of the Whig:

* * * * * * * * * * * * *

It was early in the evening when your correspondent reached the enemy's main line of defence. Their position skirted a strip of dense woods, while to their front extended a vast undulating plain, ploughed up, here and there, with deep gullies and wood-girt water courses. That they were entrenched we knew, but of the nature of their works, owing to the deep foliage that screened them from view, we knew but little. It was absolutely necessary, however, that we should carry their line, and to do this, regiment after regiment, and brigade after brigade, were successively led forward; still our repeated charges, gallant and dashing though they were, failed to accomplish the end, and our troops, still fighting, fell steadily back.

Thus, for more than two mortal hours, the momentous issue stood trembling in the balance. The sun was getting far in the west—darkness would soon be upon us, and that point *must* be carried.

At this juncture—it was now 5 o'clock—the division of the gallant Whiting hove in sight. This division is composed of the brave Texan Brigade, under Hood, and the old Third Brigade, commanded by the dashing Law, of Manassas memories.

On reaching the field these troops were rapidly deployed in line of battle, when Colonel Law detached Colonel Stone's regiment, the

2d Mississippi, and sent it some distance to the right, where it sucessfully resisted, with heavy loss, a flank attack from the enemy. The 6th North Carolina, (Major Webb) he held in reserve: then taking the 4th Alabama (Colonel McLemore) and 11th Mississippi (Colonel Liddell) he led a dashing charge upon the enemy's entrenched position.

This charge was made under the most galling fire that I ever witnessed—shot and shell, grape, canister and ball, swept through our lines like a storm of leaden hail, and our noble boys fell thick and fast; yet, still, with the irresistible determination of men who fight for all that men hold dear, our gallant boys rushed on.

Suddenly, a halt was made—there was a deep pause, and the line wavered from right to left. We now saw the character of the enemy's works. A ravine, deep and wide, yawned before us, while on the other side, at the crest of the almost perpendicular bank, a breastwork of logs was erected, from behind which the dastard invaders were pouring murderous volleys upon our troops.

This position was, perhaps, the most formidable of the kind that was ever built. Scaling ladders and boarding pikes would have been far better adapted to its reduction than bayonets, and had the wretched Hessians, who garrisoned it, done half their "duty," they might have held it until doomsday.

The pause made by our troops, however, was but a brief breathing space. The voice of Colonel Law was heard—"Forward, boys! Charge them!" and with a wild, mad shout, our impetuous soldiery dashed forward, flinging themselves into the trench, struggling up the precipitate bank, climbing over the breastworks, and driving the flying foe terror-stricken before them.

In this charge, the 6th North Carolina came up, and it, uniting with Law's other regiments, formed a junction with the 18th Georgia and the 4th Texas, of Hood's Brigade. These five regiments then made a brilliant charge on the plain beyond the works, capturing two batteries, and turning some of the guns on the enemy before he could make good his escape.

The rout was absolute, but night coming on deprived us of most of the fruits of the victory.

A little after dusk some apprehensions were entertained lest the enemy should make a night attack and attempt to retake the batteries we had captured, but to meet this emergency, General [Richard H.] Anderson, at the united request of Colonel Law and Colonel Jenkins, gave permission to Colonel Law to detach Jenkins' regiment, which he joined with one of his own, and successfully repulsed a flank assault. All the artillery we took is secured.

General Whiting has won imperishable fame—wherever the fight raged fiercest there was he, urging his gallant troops to victory.

All is quiet now. There is no demoralization among our men.— We are ready to renew the conflict at any moment.

They "paused and wavered" long enough for the 4th Texas to pass them. And but a few men of the 11th Mississippi, were all of the 3d Brigade, who were with the 4th Texas and 18th Georgia when they took the last battery.

The following letter from *"Chickahominie,"* [who gives the most correct account of the battle of any publication which has yet appeared from the press],[54] is introduced as an act of justice to the 18th Georgia, (better known in the brigade as the *"3rd Texas,"*) as gallant a regiment as ever fought beneath a Confederate flag:

THE EIGHTEENTH GEORGIA REGIMENT.

Camp 18th Georgia Regiment, Hood's Brigade,
Twenty-five Miles from Richmond.

To the Editor of the Whig:—For the Gratification of the relatives and friends of the members of this regiment, I desire to give a brief account of the particular part enacted by them on Friday, 27th June, in the engagement at Coal Harbor or Gaines' Mill. Having been with them through the whole action, and taken part in them, your correspondent had perhaps a better opportunity than any one else of knowing exactly what they did. It will be remembered that the fight began early in the afternoon and was raging with great fury while Hood's Brigade was yet a considerable distance from the scene. Marching rapidly through the woods and fields, apparently with a view to turn the enemy's extreme right, the whole brigade was halted about 4 o'clock and formed in line of battle in the following order, 18th Georgia, 1st Texas, 4th Texas, 5th Texas. The position of the 4th Texas was subsequently changed to the right of the 18th, in this order the brigade advanced through the woods, which being so very thick we soon lost sight of all except our own regiment. Advancing across a deep muddy swamp, and up a steep ascent, they were placed in position to support a battery and ordered to lay down. Here they were just in range of a heavy battery of the enemy, and the missiles fell so thick that our battery soon became disabled and had to withdraw. Another came up but was also compelled to retire after a few rounds. After which, the regiment was ordered to change position, moving by the right flank at double quick. They remained behind this battery about thirty minutes and lost some twenty or thirty men killed and wounded. After marching by the flank for about a half mile, they were halted in an open space to the right of a piece of woods and in rear of an apple orchard and formed in line of battle. Then advancing under a shower of shot and shell down a long slope which was completely commanded by a body of the enemy's infantry on their left, posted on a wooded eminence on the opposite side of the ravine at the foot of the slope. Here we lost many more men but passed on without returning the fire of the enemy poured into our ranks, and crossing the ravine at the point where the 4th Texas had so gallantly driven the enemy back, advanced up the steep hill on the opposite side, and here, for the first time, obtained a view of the terrible work that then remained for them to do.—Several regiments claim to have taken batteries, and no doubt justly too, for there was enough for all to have a showing. Several had been taken up to the moment the 18th reached the crest of the hill, but the main battery on the hill in the field, said to be the Hoboken Battery of fourteen splendid brass pieces, which was filling the air with its deadly missiles, and dealing destruction all around, whose position is said to have been chosen by McClellan himself, and whose guns, according to the account of numerous prisoners and wounded men, had been directed by him, was still playing with terrible effect. It was supported by a large body of infantry in the rear, and a detachment of the 2nd Regular Cavalry on the left, besides the approach to it was completely commanded by two other batteries. So admirable was this disposition of the forces and the natural conformation of the ground, that McClellan is said to have assured his men that it was impregnable.—In front of the 18th, at the moment it came in sight of the battery, lay a long sloping hill, at the foot of which, some three hundred yards distant, was a deep, and in some places, an impassable ditch, then a quick rise, that afforded some protection from the guns above. Preceding regiments had done their work well, and gallantly had they driven the enemy from some of its strongest works and taken several batteries. Some had even advanced on this battery, but found their forces so much scattered, after crossing the ditch, that they became powerless, and could do little else than seek protection under the crest of the hill from the guns above.—Down this first slope the 18th advanced in splendid order, at double quick, under a cross fire from two batteries on the right and left and a terrible direct fire from the battery in front. Shot after shot tore through the ranks, leaving wide gaps, which were quickly closed up; the clear, shrill voices of Major Griffis and Adjutant Patton could be distinctly heard amid the bursting of shells and whistling of shots, coolly commanding, "close up," "Dress to the right" or "left," while every other officer exerted himself to preserve the line unbroken. Dead and wounded men fell on every side, while the living pushed on to the work before them. Here Lieutenant L. A. McCullock, of Co. C, Jackson County Volunteers, fell terribly mangled with a shell. Lieutenant Sillman, who succeeded him in command of the company, was wounded a few steps farther on, Lieutenant Callahan taking command of the company.—Lieutenant John Grant, commanding Co. H, was also wounded and left, the command devolving on 1st Sergeant Cotton. On reaching the ditch, the line was necessarily broken, the men being compelled to get across as best they could. Advancing a short distance, they found themselves under cover of the hill in company with a detachment of various other regiments who were in a broken and disorganized condition. Some had lost their leaders, some their regiments, and all, for the time being, seemed, to have lost their organization. In front of all these the colors of the 18th was planted, and the men quickly rallied and formed. A short consultation among the officers was held to secure concert of action, after which, a small detachment of the 11th Misssissippi, under the command of Colonel Liddell, formed in support of the right, and another from the 4th Texas, under Captain Townsend, supported the left. Thus supported, at the command "forward," the 18th moved steadily up the hill in the very jaws of Death itself! As soon as they were discovered the enemy's cavalry made a desperate charge at the right wing, which might have broken and ruined the line, had they not been received with so much coolness and deliberation by the gallant men composing Companies A, B and C, commanded respectively by Captains O'Neal, Stewart and Lieutenant Callahan, who held their fire until the enemy were within good range, and then poured in a deadly volley, that broke their front, brought down their leader, and so discomforted them that they changed their direction and endeavored to make their escape, but before they succeeded in doing so, scores of their saddles were emptied and many a crippled steed left hobbling across the field. Just as this charge was made the left wing had come up within range of the guns, when one of them delivered a volley of grape full into the ranks of Co. K, instantly killing Lieutenant Dowten and a private, and wounding half a dozen others. The whole line halted to deliver their fire, which they did so effectually that for a moment the firing of the battery ceased, and the infantry began to fall back. Seizing the opportunity, Colonel Ruff ordered the charge, and rushing to the front, hat in hand, waved the boys onward, and, in less time than it takes to write it, nine pieces of the battery was theirs.—At this moment, the scene in front was indescribable. Cavalrymen, artillery limbers and caissons and infantry all rushed away in one wild sea of confusion, running for dear life. Some few cannoneers, however, stood to their guns and continued to load—one was shot at the piece while ramming down a cartridge—another, while adjusting a friction primer, was shot down by private Monroe Windsor, of Co. H, and his bag of friction primers captured by him. Lieutenant Lawes, of Co. D, with four men, rushed forward and shot the men at one piece while they were on the eve of firing it. Corporal Foster, of Co. F, deserves great credit for the gallantry with which he bore the battle flag to the front—ever foremost. When he reached the battery, he mounted one of the pieces and waved his flag in triumph, but as soon as the regiment was again ordered forward in pursuit of the enemy, he took his place and rushed on. At this point, Colonel Ruff, seeing that his regiment had pierced the enemy's lines to a considerable distance, left Major Griffis in command, and stopped to rally stragglers, who were constantly coming up, and turn their fire to the left, whence the enemy were pouring a hot fire on the men about the guns. The regiment followed and drove the enemy about four hundred yards into the woods, when it was thought advisable for them to fall back, as they were entirely unsupported, and had pierced the enemy's lines about a mile, and there was a considerable body of the enemy in the rear, both on the right and left. Fortunately, our forces drove these back about night, and the 18th held its position for the night, sleeping between the pieces and the enemy. The regiment was under fire for about three hours, and lost one hundred and forty-eight in killed and wounded. Two officers killed and six wounded. Carried into action five hundred and seven men. Every officer and man acted with great gallantry and coolness. Captain Armstrong, seeing one of the guns aimed at his company, saved them by an oblique movement to the right in double quick. Captain Maddox led his company through the fight, though so badly wounded as to have to retire to the rear immediately after the engagement was over. Lieutenant S. V. Smith, Co. K, led his company with great coolness, not withstanding his loss was very heavy. At the ditch in front of the battery, he found fugitive Yankees so thick that he had to make them get out of his way and allow his men to pass. Lieutenant Hardin, commanding Co. F, manoeuvered his company finely, and did splendid service. Orderly Ramsour, commanding Co. E, acted very gallantly. The regiment took about two hundred prisoners, among them one Colonel and several Captains and Lieutenants.—The commander of the cavalry that charged our lines and who fell into our hands a wounded prisoner, declared he had as leave charge a wall of fire.

"CHICKAHOMINIE."

The foregoing extracts sufficiently illustrate the part enacted by Whiting's command, and show, beyond question, that all did their duty unflinchingly; but I desire to speak now, more particularly of the conduct of the 4th Texas Regiment on that occasion.[55] While Hood's Brigade was formed in line of battle, the 4th Texas was held in partial reserve, and soon became separated from the other regiments of the brigade. After remaining in the rear, lying down, for perhaps half an hour, General Hood came for us, and moving by the right flank about half a mile, halted us in an open space to the right of some timber, and in rear of an apple orchard. The sight which we here beheld, beggars description. The ground was strewn with the dead and dying, while our ranks were broken at every instant by flying and panic stricken soldiers. In front of us was the "Old 3d Brigade," who, but a few moments before, had started with cheers to storm the fatal palisade. But the storm of iron and lead was too severe, they "wavered" for a moment, but remained upon the ground. At this instant, General Hood, who, had in person, taken command of our regiment, commanded in his clear ringing voice, "Forward, quick, march," and onward moved the little band of five hundred, with the coolness of veterans. Here Colonel Marshall fell dead from his horse, pierced by a minnie ball.—Volleys of musketry, and showers of grape, canister and shell ploughed through us, but were only answered by the stern "close up—close up to the colors," and onward they rushed over the dead and dying, and passing the *3d Brigade,* without a pause, until within about one hundred yards of the breastworks. We had reached the apex of the hill, and some of the men seeing the enemy just before them, commenced discharging their pieces. It was at this point, that preceding brigades had halted, and beyond which none had gone, in consequence of the terrible concentrated fire of the concealed enemy. At this critical juncture, the voice of General Hood was heard above the din of battle, "Forward, forward, charge right down on them, and drive them out with the bayonet." Fixing bayonets as they moved, they made one grand rush for the fort; down the hill, across the creek and fallen timber, and the next minute saw our battle flag planted upon the captured breastworks. The cowardly foe, frightened at the rapid approach of pointed steel, rose from behind their defences, and started up the hill at speed. One volley was poured into their backs, and it seemed as if every ball found a victim, so great was the slaughter. Their works were ours, and, as our flag moved from the first to the second tier of defences, a shout arose from the shattered remnant of that regiment, and which will long be remembered by those who heard it; a shout which announced that the wall of death was broken, and victory, which had hovered doubtfully for hours over that bloody field, had at length perched upon the battle flag of the 4th Texas. Right and left it was taken up and rang along the lines for miles; long after many of those who had started it, were in eternity. [Soon after the 4th Texas had passed the 3d Brigade, the 4th Alabama and 11th Mississippi came on bravely to the charge.][56]

No pause was made here, but onward and upward they pressed. At the summit of the hill, the gallant Lieutenant-Colonel, Warwick, fell mortally wounded, while grasping in his hand a Confederate battle flag, which had been deserted by some regiment near where we began the charge. No nobler death, no brighter destinies could have been asked by a soldier. Falling at the head of brave men, in the hour of victory, and in defence of his native city, his name will be forever cherished in its annals, and proudly written in the history of his country. [On the same spot also fell Captain Bryan and Lieutenant Lambert, cheering their men in the charge.][57] Just in front, and about four hundred yards distant, was a splendid battery of fifteen guns, and without halting, they made on in that direction. They had proceeded but a short distance, when General Hood discovered an attempt by the enemy on the right to flank and cut off the 4th.—Gathering up the stragglers near, he formed sufficient opposition to hold them in check until the regiment had time to reform its line, and then moved forward, having been joined by a portion of the 11th Mississippi. In a depression in the field about half way from this position to the battery, they halted, where they were joined by the 18th Georgia. Captain Townsend now led the 4th--Major Key, the last field officer, [who had shown himself a soldier and an officer in the fight],[58] retiring with a painful wound, left him in command. Forming on the left of the 18th—a squadron of about six hundred cavalry, at full speed, charged down the slope upon the right. A "look out for the cavalry," was sufficient to put them on the alert, and they received them in splendid style. Soon their horses were running wildly over the fields, many without riders, and others frantic from bayonet cuts and minnie balls. The line of retreat was well defended by fallen steeds and dead Yankees. But the boys felt more sympathy for the poor horse than for the degraded rider, who was left bleeding and mangled, to bite the dust. The charge upon the battery was continued, and the work was soon over—for rushing forward at a run, while the hill-tops blazed and thundered like a bursting mountain, and pouring a storm of grape and canister through their advancing ranks, they drove the enemy from their guns. The infantry, cavalry and cannoneers, with five guns, mixed and moving at their utmost speed, gave to the mind the idea of GRAND CONFUSION! as they moved off in search of the new "base," which McClellan had just gone in haste to select. Our Confederate battle flag now floated over the guns where the Stars and Stripes with the "Spread Eagle," had so recently hovered over the Young Napoleon's head.—But they rested only a few moments here. For the sight of the broken and flying columns of the enemy invited them forward, and they pressed the rear of the Grand Army in its "*On from Richmond*," as it makes its grand charge to the rear, where safety is to be won by a gallant run, until night puts an end to the slaughter. These two flags might have remained to guard the trophies won and cannon captured on this memorable hill, and would ever have been the pride of the States they represent, but they hastened to make their victory still more complete.

The Hampton Legion entered the fight on the left of the Brigade, on the crest of the hill in the woods. The 5th Texas next, then the

1st, and engaged the enemy from left to right in great fury, slowly pressing him back, and almost covering the ground with the dead from their ranks.

To decide the points of honor for our Brigade on that bloody ground, we have but to offer the testimony of General Whiting, who commanded the Division. He says: "Thc 1st Texas and Hampton Legion were sent in as hundreds were leaving in disorder.—Two regiments, one South Carolina and one Louisiana, were marching back from the field, and the 1st Texas was ordered to go through or over them, which they did. When the line was completed and advanced to the crest of the hill, a brigade was skulking and hiding from danger, and never advanced from the west side of the ravine. Fourteen pieces of artillery were taken and nearly a whole regiment of men were turned over by Col. [Jerome B.] Robertson, of the 5th Texas, to Brigadier General Prior or staff.

"Brigidier General Anderson supporting on the right. The troops on my immediate left I do not know, and am glad I don't. I have reason to believe that the greater part of them never left the cover of the woods, on the west side of the ravine.

"I take pleasure in calling special attention to the 4th Texas Regiment, which, led by Brig. Hood, was the first to break the enemy's line, and enter his works. Its brave old Colonel, Marshall, fell early in the charge, on the hither side of the ravine. The stubborn resistance maintained all day faltered from that moment, and the day was gained. Of the other Regiments of the Division, it would be invidious and unjust to mention one before another."

General Hood says, "directing in person the 4th Texas, they were the first to pierce the strong line of breast-works occupied by the enemy, which caused great confusion in their ranks. And here the 18th Georgia, commanded by Colonel Ruff, came to the support of the 4th, pressed over the hotly contested field, inclining from right to left, with the 5th Texas on their left, taking a large number of prisoners, and fourteen pieces of artillery. The guns were taken by the 4th Texas and 18th Georgia, and the prisoners by the 5th Texas."[59]

There were many regiments who claimed the honor of capturing these guns, but in justice to the men who did the work, both the Division and Brigade Commanders have settled the question. We may here remark, that five of the guns spoken of were captured by the 4th, at the time they stormed and took the first and second breast-works.

There were but few who failed to do their duty well. And as for those officers and men who "skulked and hid in ditches and in the woods from danger," we will leave them with their superiors, and on the historian will devolve the task of assigning them position in the back ground, and let their deeds screen them from the world's view.

The secret of our success is found, in a great measure, in the discretion exercised by Hood at the moment we reached the top of the hill, upon which so many had fallen before us. Where, instead of halting and making the fight, as others had done and been driven back, he gave the word, and our brave men rushed headlong from the hill, and at short range, and with cold steel drove the enemy from their hiding places below.

At 4:15 PM. we heared the first volly of musketry. we were halted—countermarched by regiment the order having been right in front & fronted in line of battle in the direction of the fireing (south) the 5th, 1st, 4th, 18th, Hampton Legion. At the counter marching the 4th became a little confused by order of Col. M. [arshall] in counter marching. When formed we advanced a short distance into a skirt of timber & remained for a short time—waded a slough, halted a short time while moving to the next. Here Col. M. sent his orderly to Lt. Col. W. [arwick] informing him that he was Col. of the Reg. & would comd. it. Lt. Col. W. had said to me 3 hours before that he would command, he also spoke of his serious reflections & said he never expected to survive the fight.

Gen. Lee & Whiting rode up inquiring for Gen. Hood—after a minutes interview with him Gen. Hood rode off in the direction of the fight but in a short time returned on foot, hat in one hand & sword in the other, he had been looking the situation of the enemy & nature of the ground over which he expected to move—and called out where is my old 4th. Tex.? They had layed down in consequence of their exposed situation & were concealed from view by the bushes & timbers fallen by the enemy—"here we are General," was the general response as they sprang to their feet ready to do and die at his command. "I want you to follow me." And then came a shout that mad[e] the forest ring. "Forward" was distinctly heared & recognized by every man as the battle shout of their old leader. They sprang forward as if by magic & passed up the hill & emerged into an open field; which when fully gained & then obeying the order "Left Wheel" they were confronting the enemy, yet at a distance of about 600 yds. "Forward." And their whole line struck off at a double quick—"Steady." "Steady" I don't want you to run. Move steadily. Then at a "Quick" steady march they swep[t] in solid line across the field. The General himself and on foot leading them like a champion to the charge. It would be a difficult task here to describe feelings of mutual confidence which existed between this regiment & their general. He had been relieved of the command of cavalry, his favorite service on the Peninsula & appointed to the command & to share the trials and destiny of this Reg. on the ______ of Oct. He had taught them the importance of discipline & drill, the manual at arms, in short the service of war. And on the Potomac at West Point & at the Seven Pines he had a sufficient test of their bravery & skill to inspire him with the highest confidence of their ability in an hour of the greatest peril. Consequently the 4th had been held in reserve to be hurled like a thunderbolt upon the enemy at the point where the fortunes of this awful day were to be determined. The time had come. 40000 men in combat had been struggling for two dreadful hours. Alternate hopes & fears contended with almost every moment of that time. At one time our troops advanced with firm & vigorous step. Again they wavered haulted & withdrew. The muskets roared the artilery thundered—Flying horseman & charging squadrons. Advancing legions & retreating divisions presented to the eye of the beholder a scene of wildest confusion. The day was growing dark with the smoke of burning powder & the ear deafened with the hideous thunder of a hundred cannon. The country around was full of wounded soldiers & the ground strewed with expiring warriors. It was 6 o'clock. the sun was fast sinking over the western hills. Light clouds had begun to veil his [God's] face as if to shut out his light from the misfortunes of the strugling heros & let the mantle of darkness cover the bleading wounds of expiring freemen. And veil the tears of the goddess of liberty as she wept over the departing hopes of the Sons of the South.

To allow a defeat at this point would give the enemy the power to throw his left wing into Richmond—which he confidently believed he could do as his message to that wing of the army plainly shows. "I have the 'Rebels' right where I want them. So soon as they are checked on the right I will throw the left across the Chickahomany and Richmond falls." This dispatch created the wildest enthusiasm through out that entire wing of the army. And their joy was to be equaled only by their subsequent mortification, at the final & utter defeat of the right wing.

The position against which the 4th. was to be led seemed to be the key of the whole field. It had been well selected. Naturally strong & the appointment well made—well entrenched & strongly garrisoned. It had resisted several attacks & broken & driven one line after another with its storm of iron hail from the field. And as we advanced to the charge we met two regiments in full retreat and soon after wheeling in the field we passed a branch the channel of which was filled with hiding men & sulking officers. One Reg. had left its battle flag on the field which was picked up by Lt. Col. Warwick & borne on by him as he cheered men towards the goal of his country['s] *glory until he was shot down & was covered with his flag—the warriors pride. As they move over the open field there were two lines of infantry & 3 batteries of 24 guns that had them in full sight & under direct range. The rifle's crack, the cannon's roar, the whistly bullets & screaming shells & bursting bombs. The howling balls & whizing grap*[e] *thinned & tore our ranks at every step. But steadily & right on they pressed for the enemies lines without haulting or delivering a single shot. Four hundred yds. brought them in full view of a third line of infantry which were concealed in a breastwork of logs on the opposite bank of the branch—of steep banks & mirey channel—who opened a deadly fire upon us at a distance of about seventy five yds. Col. Marshall was shot dead and fell from his horse soon after we entered the field and at about 555 yds. from the enemy—taking effect in his neck. Lt. Col. Warwick discovering our near approach to the enemy ordered the men to "Halt" & "Fire". Fortunately General Hood was still with the reg. and instantly cryed out "Don't Halt Here." "FORWARD" "FORWARD." And without waiting to reload the men moved at a double quick; loading as they ran, & threw themselves upon the enemy—charging over the mirey branch & over the breastwork put them to flight. and following up the advantage gained pressed the flying garrison upon the second entrenchment, which was so masked by their retreating, cowardly comrades as to protect us from their fire until we had gained near half the distance to the second position. And by the time they were unmasked, seeing Southern Steel advancing at rapid strides, they joined their frightened friends & made for the third line composed of U. S. infantry drawn up on the crest of the hill. The advantage gained at this point was also improved & soon the three lines were mixed in glorious confusion & hastning for shelter towards the heavy battery of 16 guns on the hill to the rear. This battery occupying an elevation above the one occupied by the advanced lines, had been operating fearfully upon us while passing over the first platoon before reaching their first position. And as soon as their retreating lines had passed into the second depression, they opened upon us with frightful terror; Throwing a fearful storm of grape & canister into our midst. Our line had become broken & our men were advancing in some disorder, occassioned by the number of men & officers that had fallen & the irregularity of the ground over which they had to pass & after passing the first breast work & before reaching the top of the hill Lt. Col. W. fell mortally wounded & by his side Capt. E. Ryan also fell, both shot thro' the lungs. Gen. Hood seeing the confusion & that the enemy were advancing up on his right to cut them off, gathered up the scattering men on the right & put them in position to keep them in check and ordered the 4th. to fall back to the edge of the timber & "re-form." And at the same time sent off for aid which soon arrived. Putting them in motion again after g[u]arding the prisoners who had been captured about the Yk. hospital, the barn & stable which were filled with sculking Scoundrels to the rear, they were soon protected by the depression in the field from the deadly fire of the last battery on the field. The others having been captured & silensed in the march. Here the 18 Ga. came up & forming with the 4th. advanced right in the mouth of their guns. Here as a last & dying struggle there dashed a heavy squadron of cavalry upon our line. But its charge was not more gallant than its retreat was magnificent. There were but few of them who had the courage to reach the sticking point. One man received a bayonet & another carried a musket off in his horses side. Many saddles were instantly emptied of their riders & many horses fell upon the ground. The line of their retreat was well defined by fallen men & slaughtered horses—And our battle flag was planted upon their guns & midst the shouts of our valient men. The day is won. The victory is ours and the brave Sons of the South are persuing the defeated far & capturing straggling squads, scattered Cos. & broken Regs. And night at last stops the chase. And with what mingled feeling of pride & sorrow do our brave boys lie dow[n] & rest—for but few can quiet themselves to sleep. Conscious that they have done their duty, and that they have kept the high trust committed to their care—foiled & defeated the invaders of our homes & sent his broken ranks in disorganized confusion flying across the Chickahominy in search of another "base" for future operation which McC[lellan] says he has been considering for some time. But I am persuaded, that had he succeeded in "checking" us at Gains mill & been able to throw his left across the Chick-[ahominy] he never would have divulged to the world his intention of "Changing his Base."*

Oh what a world of suffering and blood has this evening to record. The sun went down. But the work of slaughter continues. Night comes on. The enemy has fled. The whole field of battle from one end to the other is ours. Thirty six pieces of artilery are captured. Ten thousand stands of arm lie scattered on the field. Abandoned camps are full of supplies that add comfort to a soldiers privations. Quartermaster & commissary stores are found in great profusion & heaped & scattered in great confusion. Knapsacks, Haversack, canteens, overcoats, blankets, shoes, boots, knives, pistols, sabers, bayonets, shovels, picks, axs, pots, kettles, waggons of the ordinance, commissary, transportation & pontoon trains. Ambulances, single, double, Quadruple. Supplies of medicine, in short everything that will tend to fit up a grand invading army are seen in every direction in which the eye is turned. Books of every variety. Port foleos, papers, letters, journals, diaries, etc., help to make up the sum total of the grand picture of this field of death.

Night having put an end to the persuit of the flying foe, the long train of ambulances are crowding on the field to gather up the wounded & carry them to the field infirmary. Hundreds have already gone to the rear. But there are hundreds more not able to go. They lie scattered over the field and mark the line of our advancing army. All night long the soldiers who seemed so reckless of friends & of life wanders over the field in search of a dear Bro. or fallen friend. He entered the field with him but since then he has had no Knowledge of him and maybe morning has come before he gets the tidings that he fell as he advanced upon the breastwork or was grappling with the foe at the mouth of the cannon. Maybe his arm was shivered or body pierced with the sabre or a minnie ball & faint from loss of blood & exhausted & famishing for water & food he has fallen by the way & lies yonder in the field or in the woods & his life fast flowing out—he is found. He is dead. None but his God knows the

Sequal of his career. Whether he instantly expired or if he suffered long hours in excruciating pain. Whether he felt like he was prepared for that solumn change or not. Here lies the warrior upon the ground, Thy battle is fought, Thy victory is won, If my cause succeeds my countries free, My highest boon is to die for thee, My country Farewell.

After the battle was over Gen. Hood manifested that kind feeling for his men that a long & severe campaign together, is sure to beget. All night he rode & walked to have them gathered & sent to places of comfort—the hospitals where they could have their wounds clensed & dressed. And on the next morning when the line was formed & the roll was called it was found that out of 531 present & entered the fight 261 were missing. And of these 46 were left dead on the field. It was then that the strength of his attachment was seen developing itself in tears over his manly cheeks. And every soldier felt the same emotion. He rode up & inquired "Is this the 4th. Tex." Some one answered "this is all that remains." He turned his horse but not soon enough to prevent the regiment from witnessing how well he loved his men. They watched him as he rode using his handkerchief until out of sight. There was not a soldier in that line but what thought more of [him] now than ever before.

To the hospitals the wounded were carried all night & all the next day. The yards were soon filled & they were lying all round the yards in every shades & many lay a long time in the sun.

This was the most heart rending scene that I have ever witnessed. We worked on thro' the night & thro' the day & next night. And on Sunday morning all having been brought in I left with a train of 13 waggons loaded with the wounded for Richmond. And on arriving they were all sent to Chimborazo.[60]

[CONDUCT AND FATE OF OUR OFFICERS.

First Texas.—Colonel Rainey, a gallant officer, who was elected by his regiment after the death of Colonel McLeod, received a shot in the hand, which ranged up the arm, which had well nigh cost him his life. Captain Benton, Company K, and Lieutenant Shotwell, Company B, were killed while nobly doing their duty; and among the wounded were found Lieutenant Snow, Lieutenant Jamison, Lieutenant Sheridan, Lieutenant Wall and Lieutenant Waterhead. Sergeants Crawford, Giles, Armstrong, Smith, Foster and Autry were wounded, and Sergeants J. Crobert and J. A. Lawson were killed.

Fifth Texas.—Lieutenant J. E. Clute was the only commissioned officer killed. Colonel J. B. Robertson and Ensign J. Onderdonk were wounded; also, Captain Clay, Lieutenant Nash, and Sergeant Norwood.

Fourth Texas.—Of the field and staff, Colonel John Marshall fell soon after the charge began; Lieutenant-Colonel B[radfute] Warwick was mortally wounded and fell soon after storming the enemy's works; Major [J. C. G.] Key also received a dangerous wound, but his gallantry would not allow him to quit the field until exhausted from the loss of blood; Captain [Tom] Owens, Commissary, was mortally wounded.[61] And of the Captains, E.[D.] Ryan, J. W. Hutcheson and P. P. Porter were mortally wounded, and J.[ohn] P. Bane's arm fractured. Lieutenant W. C. Walsh, in command of Company B, severely wounded; and the wounds of Lieutenants R. J. Lambert, P. S. Wood, C. Reich and L. P. Lyons, all proved to be mortal; Lieutenant T. H. Holaman was killed on the field; Lieutenants Brandon, Brooks, Randolph, Loughridge, Beasley, Burress, Clanahan and Rounsevall were also painfully wounded. And of the Sergeants, D. L. Butts, N. A. Myer, R. L. Tyler and T. O. Wilkes were killed, and A. H. Rogers, Wilton, G. A. Wynne, J. L. Gould, Davis Roberts, Galloway, Simmons, J. T. Price and A. P. Brown were wounded.

After looking over the lists of killed and wounded of the Brigade, it is unnecessary to add a single syllable as to their behavior in the memorable fight. For the length of these lists will tell where each Regiment was, and that all were in their proper place.][62]

VIEW OF THE BATTLE-FIELD.

Our victory was complete. Hundreds of prisoners were sent to the rear, and thousands were left lying on the field and scattered through the woods, weltering in their blood, while hundreds more were left dead upon the soil their feet had polluted. And now we must give them graves in the very fields they have pillaged. Night has hung its dark curtains around and over the arena so recently lit with fire-arms, and the flash of the glittering sabre in the hands of valiant men. The roar and rush of armies has ceased. All is quiet as the grave, only when disturbed by busy trains of ambulances, and the heart-rending groans of the ten thousand sufferers, co-mingling their voices in piteous discord on every hand. No troopers are dashing headlong, and not a single roar of the cannon is to be heard. But low, deep murmurs rose upon the gloom of night, which lent to the surrounding scene the darkest shade to which earth-born sufferers are heir in their brief stay in a world of sin and woe. Nothing this side the regions of blackness of darkness is half so terrible as the theatre upon which the maddened armies of empires seek revenge, and settle their quarrels. The darkness of the night, intensified by the clouds of smoke now settling down upon the earth, with the cries of the suffering and groans of the dying, tend to deepen and blacken the pall that shrouds the mind of the wounded soldier. Thoughtful and suffering, on the cold ground where he fell, he longs for the coming morning. But he knows not that it shall dawn upon him. Exhausted, hungry, bleeding, famishing, and no one to fill his canteen, or bind up his broken arm or shattered leg. It is a long, long and dreary night; and beyond he knows not that he shall have another day. And, although hours are dark and the cannon's roar is not to be heard, yet every watch was disturbed, and the sentinel hears the groans of his suffering comrades all night long. Many tears were shed under the long shadows of each hour of that night, that will never be numbered on earth, and that too from eyes all unused to weeping. Oh! how sweet the comforts of religion in an hour like this. Friends walked and looked for friends, and brothers knew not the fate of each other, whether living or dead. Long trains of ambulances are passing to and fro nearly all night, gathering and carrying to the field Infirmary—to which place we will now go to see if there are any there we know. Yes, there is one, and yonder another, and another, but we will not call their names—the whole yard is filled with suffering friends, stretched upon the ground.—Nurses are washing and bathing their wounds, and surgeons are using the knife. Many arms and legs are amputated, and the poor boys are maimed for life.

The long-desired morning comes at last, and with it hundreds more are brought in. They are carried to the surrounding shades, in the orchard and field. These are some of the horrors of war, while the counterpart is found at the home of the soldier's mother, his wife and friends. But upon this sacred ground we will not tread. For we imagine we see them, when the letter with the black seal reaches their anxious and trembling hand, while the heart's deepest fountain is broken up and gushes forth in streams of such grief as none can portray. Oh God, how long shall such scenes as this afflict our unhappy land? How long till thou will put a stop to the shedding of human blood? Thus ends the battle of Gaines' Farm.

But we had not finished the strife when the sun went down on Friday. Each day for a week we must witness the re-enactment of this bloody drama. On Saturday, from the hill on which we captured the heavy battery of the enemy the evening before, we could see the consternation of McClellan's army. Clouds of rolling dust wound their serpentine course over hills and valleys, along every road leading away from the position he had occupied, towards the south and east; and they, together with the mountains of smoke which ascended from piles of commissiary and depots of quartermaster's stores, marked the line of his retreat, and wrote the nature of his defeat upon the skies. In the general conflagration which we could see for miles in different directions, they destroyed millions of dollars worth of property. And it is now that he [McClellan] announces to his government that he is performing "a strategic movement, and changing his base of operations from the White-house to the James river."

On the 28th, General [Robert] Toombs attacked the enemy near the Nine Mile road, but the advantage was apparently slight, yet it contributed to the general confusion and dismay of the enemy.

General [J. E. B.] Stuart with his Cavalry was doing good service in the direction of the White-house[63]—each day capturing and destroying property, and sending large bodies of prisoners to the rear.

General Hood received orders to advance at an early hour on Saturday morning. *He asked to be excused that he might have a little time to recruit his ranks—but Gen. Whiting answered that he could not do without him—and he would favor him all he could;*[64] but on reaching the Grape-Vine bridge he was compelled to halt and wait until the bridge, which had been destroyed by the enemy, could be repaired.

BATTLE AT SAVAGE'S STATION.

On Sunday morning, 29th, fierce picket firing was heard in the direction of the out-posts of the army, at an early hour. About noon the fight began under General Magruder's command—the slaughter was dreadful and our victory complete—and burning stores and scattered arms and clothing in every direction, gave evident signs of an unexpected retreat.

"The Railroad Merrimac," an ugly monster, moved down early in the morning and shelled the adjacent woods and fields, until the enemy fell back from the road. It was struck several times with heavy iron balls, but was uninjured. At this place also the destruction of property was immense.

Late in the evening the enemy was again overtaken; the rear of the retreating forces warmly engaged us, but night coming on we could not realize the advantage gained, as we were unable to follow it up.

During the day it had become apparent that McClellan had eluded us, and was in full retreat over a road which Gen. Huger had been intrusted to watch. The reason why he suffered the enemy to move undisturbed along the road leading under the protection of his gunboats remains still a mystery to all. While many believed him guilty of criminal favortism towards the enemy—which we do not believe—and, especially, as this was not the first time he had failed to come up with his men when ordered in to the fight.

BATTLE OF FRAZIER'S [FRAYSER'S] FARM.

Monday morning, June 30th, General Jackson crossed the Chickahominy in pursuit of the retreating foe. In the evening the advance came up with his rear at the bridge at White Oak Swamp, which they were defending with artillery. Scouts from the Texas Brigade were sent over and drove in their pickets. Their artillery was then turned upon our men, but sheltering behind a hill, no one was injured. But morning revealed the fact that we had directed our fire sufficiently well to kill several pickets before they retired. After dark the fire of their artillery was again turned upon the crossing, which they kept up until about midnight, when they withdrew, and our men commenced repairing the bridge, which, by sunrise the next morning was completed, and we crossed over, and had the pleasure of knowing that our powder had not been burnt in vain by our artillery the previous evening. For dead and wounded Yankees and artillery horses proved the fact that random shots are as deadly when they hit in the right place as any others.

Generals Longstreet, A. P. Hill, Huger, and Magruder pressing down on the right by the way of the Charles City road, overtook the enemy late in the evening posted on Frazier's [Frayser's] Farm, when a bloody struggle ensued, in which Generals Hill and Longstreet were the principal participants—the battle continuing long after dark with frightful fury; and, although the enemy had selected his ground and massed heavy bodies of men, yet again he had to yield before the conquering armies of the South.

BATTLE OF MALVERN HILL.

On Tuesday morning, July 1st, our men, after crossing the bridge, found the out-post of the enemy in strong positions and numbers, which made our movements necessarily slow. About one hundred prisoners and fifty wagons were captured during the morning. The first notice we had of the contiguity of the enemy in force was announced by an exploding shell in the midst of the 1st Texas, which killed and wounded some fifteen men. And it was followed by another, which caused about the same injury. The right wing was also in motion, and pressing upon the enemy, who, after the slaughter of the night before, were making haste from the bloody field.

We were now in the neighborhood of Malvern Hill, and discovering the situation of affairs, we were moved to the left, and soon were thrown forward to support a battery, which had been sent up to drive the enemy's guns and feel his position. But we were soon ordered to the timber in the rear. Here two men in Co. I and one in Co. D, 4th Texas, were wounded.

At 4 P. M., the infantry in great force moved up and engaged with great vigor, and until 10 o'clock at night the earth, air and water were in commotion. From sixteen batteries by land, and their gun-boats by water, they beclouded the day and lit the night with a lurid glare. Add to this the light and noise of our own artillery which had been brought forward, and like an opposing volcano with a hundred craters, it gleamed and flashed streams and sheets of burning fire—while long lines of human forms cast their shadows upon the darkness in the background, and each joined, with his fire-lock in hand, to contribute to the terror of the awful scene. One could easily imagine, while witnessing this bursting storm of human passion, that he was within one step of the council chamber of his Satanic Majesty, and that he had assembled all the furies from the far-off region of his empire, and let them loose upon this devoted spot in the Old Dominion. For both in sight and sound it was awfully terrible. For the outline of human forms, as seen by the light of burning powder through the smoky air, looked like ghosts in human shape, while the heavens were vocal with unearthly sounds from the passage of masses of iron and globes of lead. Death now held carnival over whole fields of living men. And his was the victory on both sides. McClellan was making his last exertions to save his army. And by this powerful effort, he succeeded in checking the triumphant march of our arms, until he had placed his broken and routed army beyond our reach—under the fire of his gun-boats—which, however, during the night, had been more destructive to his own men than ours. But this he never could have done, had not General Huger failed to check him by not taking possession of the ground before he arrived. The whole plan had been admirably executed from the time General Hood left Richmond, on the 12th inst., to reinforce Gen'l Jackson, at Staunton, down to the last day's conflict, except in this one instance. And we are sanguine in the belief, that had he [Huger] done his part as well as others, the whole Yankee army would have been captured. But they have escaped, and the whole of this bloody chapter will have to be repeated on some other field.

McClellan having made his escape and reached the "base" of his future operations, he produced one of the most remarkable documents known in the history of this great revolution. For having been defeated in half a dozen battles, and forced to the necessity of applying the torch to hundreds of thousands of dollars in stores, the most valuable to his army, he speaks of it as change "contemplated," and as having been "accomplished with success," and, no doubt, he has made thousands of his admirers believe it.—And after his army, for a week, had been running as for dear life, and making good their flight over the distance of about thirty-five miles, having frequently, both by day and by night, to turn and fight, while thousands of his men were being slaughtered, and thousands more were captured, without gaining anything except another chance to run, he said to his soldiers, "your conduct ranks you among the celebrated armies of history." I think he had more truthfully expressed it, by saying, "you rank all the armies, both of ancient and modern times, for you can out *run* any soldiers in the known world; which you have proved on various occasions, from the days of Bull Run, til now."

PURSUIT TO WESTOVER, AND RETURN TO RICHMOND.

Wednesday morning, July 2d.—When the sun cleared away the darkness of the night, it was discovered that the Yankees had also cleared out. We withdrew from the field, and prepared our rations for further pursuit. At the same time, strong parties were scouring the fields and woods beyond, to find their position, or the trails by which they had made their exit. And on Friday, while we were marching down to the neighborhood of Westover—McClellan's new "base," he was at work with the following Fourth of July speech:

Headquarters, Army of the Potomac,
Camp near Harrison's Landing, July 4th, 1862.

"Soldiers of the Army of the Potomac:—Your achievements for the past ten days, have illustrated the valor and endurance of the American soldier. Attacked by superior force, and without hopes of reinforcement, you have succeeded in changing your base of operations by a flank movement, always regarded as the most hazardous of military operations. You have saved all your guns except a few lost in battle, taking in turn, guns and colors from the enemy.

Upon your march, you have been assailed day after day with desperate fury, by men of the same race and nation, skilfully managed and led. Under every disadvantage of number, and necessity of position also, you have, in every conflict, beaten back your foe with enormous slaughter.

Your conduct ranks you among the celebrated armies of history. None will now question that each of you may always, with pride, say, "I belonged to the Army of the Potomac." You have reached this new base, complete in organization, and unimpaired in spirit. The enemy may, at any time, attack you, we are prepared to meet them. I have personally established your lines, let them come, and we will convert their repulse into a final defeat.

Your Government is strengthening you with the resources of a great people. On this, our National birth-day, we declare to our foes, who are rebels against the best interest of mankind, that this army shall enter the Capitol of the so-called Confederacy—that our National Constitution shall prevail, and that the Union, which no longer can insure internal peace and external security to each State, must, and shall be preserved, cost what it may, in time, treasure and blood."

George B. McClellan.
Major-General, Commanding.

McClellan says "you have saved all your guns, except a few lost in battle." When General Lee counts his guns, we find that McClellan has a different idea as to what the word "few" means, to that which

Southern people have. And of those which he says they "took in turn," our men know nothing. But we give you the address of

GENERAL LEE TO HIS SOLDIERS.

Headquarters in the Field,
July 7th, 1862.

General Orders,
No. 75.

"The General Commanding, profoundly grateful to the only Giver of all victory for the signal success with which He has blessed our arms, tenders his warmest thanks and congratulations to the army, by whom such splendid results have been achieved.

On Thursday, June 26th, the powerful and thoroughly equipped army of the enemy was entrenched in works of vast extent and most formidable in character, within sight of our Capitol.

To-day the remains of that confident and threatening host lie upon the banks of James river, thirty miles from Richmond, seeking to recover under the protection of his gunboats, from the effects of a series of disastrous defeats.

The battle beginning on the afternoon of the 26th June, above Mechanicsville, continued until the night of July 1st, with only such intervals as were necessary to pursue and overtake the flying foe. His strong entrenchments and obstinate resistance were overcome, and our army swept resistlessly down the north side of the Chickahominy, until it reached the rear of the enemy, and broke his communication with the York, capturing or causing the destruction of many valuable stores, and by the decisive battle of Friday, forcing the enemy from his line of powerful fortifications on the south-side of the Chickahominy, and driving him to a precipitate retreat. The victorious army pursued as rapidly as the obstructions placed by the enemy in their rear would permit—three times overtaking his flying columns, and as often driving him with slaughter from the field, leaving his numerous dead and wounded in our hands in every conflict.

The immediate fruits of our success are the relief of Richmond from a state of siege, the rout of the great army that so long menaced its safety, many thousand prisoners, including officers of high rank, the capture or destruction of stores to the value of millions, and the acquisition of thousands of arms and fifty-one pieces of superior artillery.

The service rendered to the country, in this short, but eventful period, can scarcely be estimated, and the General Commanding cannot adequately express his admiration of the courage, endurance and soldierly conduct of the officers and men engaged.

These brilliant results have cost us many brave men, but while we mourn the loss of our gallant dead, let us not forget that they died nobly in defence of their country's freedom and have linked their memory with an event that will live forever in the hearts of a grateful people.

Soldiers! your country will thank you for the heroic conduct you have displayed—conduct worthy of men engaged in a cause so just and sacred, and deserving a nation's gratitude and praise.

By command of General Lee.

[Signed]

R. H. CHILTON,
A. A. General.

This address contrasts well with that of the infidel Yankee leader of Northern fanatics, whose crusade upon the South is as unholy and unjust as that of Northern Europe, which sacked the cities and deluged the Southern States in blood. They claimed that their cause was holy, and upon their banners was emblazoned the cross—which is the star of hope to a sin cursed earth. And in their march they filled the earth with weeping. And so our enemies boast a superior religious morality, and demand a holier Bible and purer religion than was taught by Prophets and Apostles. And in their social compacts and moral creed, reject the institution of Abraham, and the teachings of the Son of God himself. Then the bombastic rant of self-conceit in McClellan's Fourth of July address, is in perfect harmony with the large pretensions, high profession and extravagant pomposity of the people whose great leader and representative he is. But instead of that majestic air and omnipotent pomp with which McClellan addresses his army, General Lee begins, "Profoundly grateful to the only Giver of all victory," &c. How beautiful! how befitting a great General! bending before the Throne and acknowledging the supremacy of his God, while McClellan declares in his own name, "This army shall enter their Capitol," &c.

From the 5th to the 8th, the command was on picket duty; and in the afternoon of Tuesday evening we received orders to march, and took up the line towards Richmond, and on the tenth, pitched our tents on the same ground from which we had moved on the morning of May 31st, to march to the battle of Seven Pines.—Thus we completed a tour of five hundred miles, passing through several bloody engagements, and at the end of forty days, were right where we had started. But the chapter of incidents which occurred during the time, will long be remembered by the Brigade—who, way-worn and battle-begrimed, are heartily glad of another opportunity to rest. All through the camp they are seen stretched upon the ground under the shade of their "flies" and the surrounding trees, while some are gone into the City to look after wounded friends.[65]

SAD REFLECTIONS.

After the engagement at Gaines' Farm, we came with the wounded to the City, to do all in our power for their comfort. And on learning the command had returned, we visited the camp, and will long remember the greetings we met from both officers and men.—But how sad were the hearts of those we met, could easily be discovered in the cloud which immediately chased from the face the smile of pleasure that lit the countenance at our meeting. Many, both officers and men, were absent from camp. Some of them were in the hospitals, while others were left to sleep on the battle-field in the soldier's grave—they will no more attend the roll-call of their companions, command the men on parade, nor march to the music of the fife and drum—nor shall we any more meet them in the private walks of life even when this cruel war is over. They will not return with us when we take up our line of march for our homes in the far west. No, they will not go—they have already got their discharge, sealed in blood upon the altar of their country, but they have not gone to the flowery Prairies of Texas. And though friends may often look for them, and listen for their foot-fall upon the threshold, it will not be heard—sad thought.—But when we return, we will tell his father that he fell with his battle harness on—sword in hand, and his face to the foe, and died with "forward" on his lips. We will tell his sister that even in death his face was lit up with a living lustre, which had burned there since the day that Butler's order of New Orleans was first read on dress parade—when he swore his strong right arm should avenge a sister's wrongs. Yes, we will tell his mother where he fell, and where we buried him. We will tell her that we wrapped his blanket around him, covered him with his martial cloak, and buried him in a soldier's grave. And to that loved one whose image he wore, we will return *this ring,* and tell her he was a *gallant* boy.

THE HOSPITALS.

By visiting the hospitals throughout the city, which are from three to four miles to the extremes, we can see what we suffered during six day's battles. There had been no arrangements to quarter the men of different States separately, except in a few instances. And the inconvenience and consequent suffering, no one can describe. If you had two friends wounded in the same fight, you would be fortunate, if in the city, you found them within two miles of each other. And as it was our duty to look after the welfare of the whole regiment, over two hundred and fifty of whom had been wounded, no one can properly imagine the trouble and labor it required to look them up, enquire into their wants and relieve their necessities.[66] And how often and warmly we felt to reproach the authorities of our State for thus neglecting the wants of men who had left their homes to do and die for her honor and her liberty, the reader will be left to imagine. What a shame upon our State pride. And when we remember how well they had done their part, and how high they had written the name of the Lone Star State above the honors of every other at Gaines' Farm, we felt that Texas was unworthy of such sons. For they, as will be seen by official report, stormed and took the strongest position in that living wall of fire and bayonets, which the enemy had thrown round the Confederate Capitol. They broke his ranks, and led the way to victory, crowding the road to death, as if it had been the high-way to festivity and mirth. And now when wounded and unable to care for themselves, they are found crowded together in unhealthy rooms, on miserable beds, and are without adequate attendants and nourishing food. They suffered much on account of the inadequate arrangements, and also from the inefficiency of Surgeons, and the neglect of hospital officers and nurses—some of whom, in the dignity of their official position, felt at liberty, not only to be cross to the sufferers, but to insult friends who were looking after the wounded, unless they complied with all the formalities and technicalities of "red tape" diplomacy, and that too, during "*official hours.*"

Having tryed to have our wounded removed from Chimborazo & failed I reported the whole matter to Gen. Hood. He told me he would meet me in the City in evening & have the matter arranged. He did so and Dr. [*Francis*] *Sorell promised if I would present a list of those to be removed he would order the transfer. I did so. But he refused again "Said he could not see that it would be for the benefit of the Service." I then asked him to be kind enough to furnish me with some clothing for the men who had been shot down on the 27th. & never changed, but this he did not do. & I went to the Y.M.C.A. And there succeeded in procuring 2 doz. Shirts & as many drawers. The balance I had to get as best I could and went & distributed them myself. I also gave them money from 5 to 10 as they needed—such as were without. This I could see they appreciated from their heart. And altho' in many instances I did not expect it ever to be repayed yet it did my own heart good to have an opportunity to relieve the pressing wants of the brave fellows who had fallen in defense of My country. And especially did I take the greater pride in doing so when I remembered how well they had Sustained the pride of the Lone Star State. They were now looked upon by thousands as the flower of the Southern Army who had Surrounded our Capitol, a living wall of fire & steel, sent the enemy in broken confusion back in the direction he had come . . . Chimborazo that charnal house of living sufferers . . . is situated at the extreme eastern portion of the City—too remote for many of them* [*the Ladies of Richmond*] *to visit even if circumstances had made it otherwise agreeable; which in all candor & honesty I must say in behalf of the ladies & in vindication of the wrongs of more than ten thousand of sick & suffering men was not the case. The place was so foul and the wards so filthy. The bed so lousy & the clothes so dirty, and the clothes of many of the men so nasty & many others so naked, that it was unreasonable to expect the ladies to minister their kind attentions there. And when I attempted to remove our men to other hospitals the Surgeons seemed offended. And why I could* [*not*] *tell; unless thereby the other hospitals would see the manner in which patients were treated under their care. There some of the Surgeons did their duty & some of their wards were under the circumstances well kept. But this was not the case with all—no not one half. And that the reader may have an idea of the place I will describe it. A plat of ground layed out from east to west & from north to south in regular blocks & streets, the blocks each has a ward built upon it about 100ft. long & 30ft. wide. The streets from north to south is about 25ft. wide between each ward & the streets from E to W are about 50ft. There are about 100 of these wards on 5 or 6 acres of ground. Each ward will contain about 75 beds, now multiply 100 by 75 & you have 7,500 men thus crowded together & then take into the account the privys under the hill, all along the N. & S sides so that when the wind blows from either direction, which during the summer is not verry infrequent, and then imagine the chambers carried a little below the brow of the hill & emptied. Together with the stench of several thousand wounds you can imagine how sweet* [*the*] *place where Lt. Wood, John Roundsavall, Johnny Young, J. T. Park, D. M. McColister, G. B. Scott, S. T. Owen, George Daugherty died, after having offered their best efforts & their lives upon the altar of their country*[*'s*] *liberty. Burning Shame will follow the men in authority at Chimborazo while the present generation lives. For the men who suffered will not forget. . . . In view of the neglect & mistreatment of our men I did all that I could to remedy the evils by visiting the hospitals daily—which caused me to walk from 8 to 12 ms per day & inquiring into their wants—as all who have survived their wounds will bear witness—and as far as possible afford the best means I could to render them comfortable—And having become so familiar with the whole sanitary program in & about the City I feel positive in the opinion that official dignity with surgeons & stewards & laziness of avocation with cooks & messes have resulted in the death of hundreds of as good soldiers as ever answered the roll call in the army & as good men as lives in the South. To give the reader an idea I will further state that it was not uncommon to see wounds that had not been dressed for from three to five days at a time. And then when the bandages were removed it was not unfrequent to find the wound filled with living creatures. This will show to some extent the kind attention of both Surgeon & nurse. Many of the men told me that they had a little cup of sut black coffee, tong*[*ue*] *& sour bread & beef or bacon as the case might be & that frequently cooked the day before, as their only diet for days together & this will give you a view of the loving kindness of Stewards & cooks. Mr. Brundridge of N. Ala. who waited on a wounded son there had a better opportunity to observe the conduct of the nurses & he told me it was not uncommon when a patient asked for anything—a cup of water for instance—to hear the nurse curse him. Or if he were a Negro & the man wanted a piece of meat or bread he had to be hired to bring & sometimes paid in advance. Noe* [*Noah*]

Bible of Co. E, poor fellow—wounded in both arms both legs & in the head told me in inquiry, that he had used the money furnished him as well as he could. Sometimes he could hire someone to go & buy a little milk & vegetables, who paid a high price for them & then he had to pay the cook at least a quarter of a dollar each time to cook them for [him], and of course his money did not last long. I wrote a note to Gen. Hood stating the facts and feeling discouraged from frequent failures I concluded it best as many of them were improving & some dead that the best plan would be to do what I could for them where they were & try to be prepared against the future.[67]

THE LADIES OF RICHMOND.

We would do injustice to those at whose hands we received a thousand kindnesses, were we to close this part of our narrative without a word of praise for the Ladies of Richmond. Thereby we should do violence to our own feelings, and be guilty of ingratitude, for kindness gratuitously bestowed. For the kind relief, smiling with a thousand sympathies, which they not only sent but brought and delivered with their own hands, will never be forgotten by our suffering men. Early in the morning, and often through the rain, they were seen gathering round the hospitals, each one ladened with just such things as woman knows how to prepare, and none so well as a soldier with ghastly wounds and exhausted frame, hundreds of miles away from home and friends, knows how to appreciate. And through all the day long, they were seen hovering round these scenes of suffering, like convoys of ministering Angels on errands of love. And they would not only come and bring such things as make the sick man glad, but would see that his sheets and clothes were changed, and, with their own hands, make up his bed, smoothe his pillow, and often comb his hair, and bathe his feverish hands and face—then with their soups, meats, cakes and teas, appease his hunger, and revive his drooping spirits with well flavored wines and cordials, and then talk with him in words of sweetness, of his mother and home. This they continued until the shadows of evening admonished them that the days work was done, and on leaving, many were the sacred admonitions and cheerful encouragements given to look to the great Physician who has a balm for the soul and the body too.

The attention of Mrs. Webb, Mrs. Davis and Mrs. Stevenson *who waited daily around the beds,* will long be remembered by the friends of Captains Porter, Ryan and Owen, and Lieutenants Lambert and Reich.[68] Their names will be often repeated by others also who have recovered and gone to their distant homes, where they will tell of the acts of benevolence bestowed by the hands of strangers, and that they wanted for nothing, that the sympathies of these and other ladies could imagine, would afford comfort to either body or mind.

Beyond the river too, we saw them gathering round the hospitals of Manchester, to do offices of mercy for suffering strangers on their couches of straw, and with liberal hands they supplied their wants as if they had been their brothers. They knew they had fallen while defending their homes and their honor from the brutal invasion of men, who, in their official orders, neither respected the altars of religion, nor the honors of woman, and this was quite enough.

The one general expression of the suffering is heard every where they have gone—"God bless them. I'll never forget them." They have treated me as kindly as a sister, a mother. Thus it is that Texas has been bound to Virginia & Virginia to Texas. Texas Soldiers have fallen on Virginia's soil. And Virginia's ladies have dressed & healed their wounds. And may [God] grant that the bonds made under our mutual affections may never be broken. But grow stronger ever after the sunshine of peace shall gladden & bless the land.[69]

The brigade remained in camp until the 8th of August, during which time, the number of recruits returning from the hospitals, increased it to within a fraction of the number on duty at the battle of June 27th.[70]

During our stay at this place, the subject of making some permanent hospital arrangements for our sick and wounded had become so apparent that the officers determined to take action in the matter. The sufferings of our men were so great, in consequence of being scattered in almost every ward throughout the city, so that no systematic relief could be rendered by their friends, that they determined to erect a ward for the benefit of the 4th, provided I would superintend the building and furnishing of the same. And although this did not belong to the duties of my office, and would give me a great amount of labor and annoyance, in consequence of the unwillingness of the department to furnish the material necessary, and the great scarcity of such things as were needed, making it almost impossible to purchase, yet with the hope of having a place where our sick and wounded could be gathered and cared for after they had behaved so well in the defence of our country, I felt willing to do any thing in my power for their comfort. And in fifteen days after receiving the orders for its construction, it was ready with forty-six beds, and we began to receive the sufferers into it.[71]

Each Sabbath while thus engaged in the city, we went to the camp to preach for the 4th and 1st, who were sufficiently near each other to assemble at the same place—either in the morning or evening, and at other hours of the day had service either with the 5th, or in the sick camp near by. Never had the men attended so well nor listened with so much interest. The terrors through which they had passed, had made their impressions deep, and we trust, lasting upon their minds. And from many private interviews, we learned that numbers of them had resolved to become soldiers of the cross, as well as soldiers of their country. The Testaments and tracts—as many as we could procure, were received and read with unusual interest. And to Rev. William Brown, D. D., and lady, we feel greatly indebted for aid in procuring religious matter for the soldiers to read.

And we cannot pass the Young Men's Christian Association, without the highest word of praise known to our language. From them we received the first word—which spoke out in action—of encouragement when trying to relieve the temporal wants of our men. They gave me clothes for them, when they had none, they gave me something for them to eat when they were sick and hungry. And we hope they will not be forgotten by our men in time to come, and that their thoughts will speak in actions too. They well deserve the name they bear.

The campaign thus far, had been a stirring one in all its details, from the Potomac, until the six day's battles around Richmond was ended. But the end is not yet. For by the time it was over, long lines of troops begun their march towards

CEDAR MOUNTAIN.

After the successful movement of the "Stonewall" to the rear of McClellan, General Jackson led his brave army back in the direction of the Valley. But instead of crossing the mountain, he moved up to the above named place, and opened another campaign, which proved to be as brilliant as either of the preceeding ones.—On the 8th of August he began an engagement with the commander who dates his orders from, "Headquarters in the saddle—" "always looking at the backs of his enemy, never studying the base of operations, nor the line of retreat." But it would appear after the "Stonewall" had become a mountain avalanche, that he performed the task well for one never having "studied." For after losing two thousand five hundred men, if he did not turn his back upon the "rebels," he must have had a hard way and road to travel. For by the 30th of August he is found near Bull Run, and running again. Our loss amounted to about six or seven hundred. But not having "studied" the science of retreating, [Gen. John] Pope halted to take another view on the Rappahannock, in a

BATTLE AT FREEMAN'S FORD.

After resting and recruiting up until the 11th of August, our Division received orders to move. But the place of our destination was, as it ever had been, a mystery. We were to go north, but to what point, and how far, no one knew.[72] Jackson and Longstreet had gone, and we were to join one or the other, but which, we did not know. At 1 o'clock, P. M., we took up the line, and marched thirteen miles, and on the next day, ten miles, and camped near Hanover Junction. The next day we moved to Anderson Station. Here we remained several days, and then passing near Orange Court House, we joined General Longstreet. The weather was oppressively warm, and several in the Division were smitten with sun-stroke, but as warmer times were just ahead, we moved forward to the Rappahannock. Arriving at Freeman's Ford on the 23d [22d], we were ordered up to relieve General [Isaac R.] Trimble in the front. But on arriving, we found that the enemy had crossed in force in the immediate front of General Trimble. The preliminaries of the battle, as old soldiers could readily see, had already begun.—The artillery had been at work for some time, and now the sharpshooters were marking their objects, and ever and anon, you could see some prominent Yankee go down to bite the dust. Soon the skirmishers engage, and in a few moments, the fire flashes along the main line. On arriving, the Texas Brigade took position on General Trimble's right, and Colonel Law's Brigade on his left.—With line of battle thus formed, the "Forward" was given; the line of the enemy was instantly broken, and driven headlong into the river. And pouring a dreadful fire into their crowds of confused and broken lines, as they were huddling together to cross, many were shot in the back, and others drowned by the crushing crowd which pressed for the other shore. It was the work of but a few miuntes, yet about three hundred of their killed and wounded were left upon the ground and in the river. Here Major M. D. Whaley, of the 5th, fell mortally wounded. His thigh was shattered by a shell, and had to be amputated. He died on the next day. We lost only ten men in the fight—all of the 5th Texas. (See the list in the appendix.)

It rained that evening and night, so that the wagons could not cross the stream. Green corn was the only chance for food; and from the same field we drew rations from one side, and the Yankees from the other.[73] At night, on the 23d, the wagons came up; and while the men were cooking their beef and bread, they received orders to march immediately. Supper was in every imaginable shape and condition, except one—ready to eat. Some had just drawn [their rations], others were washing their frying-pans; some had their beef on the fire; others had only got their flour in the pan, and had their hands well bedaubed with the dough—in short, they had supper in such a shape that they could neither eat nor carry it along. And whether they said any bad words at such a disappointment, it is not my business to tell, nor yours to guess. Some objected and others complained, but it was no use; for the order had come for the wagons to go to the rear and the men to the front. They were near Waterloo, but it was not the Waterloo of history. And although we had suffered no defeat in arms, the boys wet, hungry, and with a long night's march ahead, did suffer a dreadful defeat in their supper. And when they found they had to go, they charged it to the account of profit and loss, and moved off. The next day they had another chance to mix up their dough, but they were not disappointed this time. On the evening of the 26th, they quit camp, marched all night, rested an hour in the morning, marched until noon and rested two hours—having crossed the Rappahannock—continued to rout through Salem until 10 P. M., and halted within four miles of Thoroughfare Gap.[74]

PASSAGE OF THOROUGHFARE GAP.

The next morning (28th) it was found that the enemy had taken possession of the gap, and was ready to dispute the passage. Jackson had passed without molestation, they being unaware of his movements. But the news had gone out, and they were unwilling that another army of equal force should pass a gap where five hundred men could hold five thousand with but little exposure or danger. We had every prospect of a hard time at this place—a narrow defile, only sufficiently wide to admit a line of men in double files, with high mountains and long slopes on either hand, all occupied by the enemy, who were drawn up in line of battle to receive us. But disputed or undisputed, we were not to be checked long at this point. For Jackson had gone ahead, and every one knows that he cannot live long in the same country with the "blue jackets," without a fight; and for us to remain here and fool away our time with a few dirty Yankees, would leave him liable to be cut to pieces, or captured by the enemy in full force, who were near at hand. Gen. D.[avid] R. Jones was ordered forward; and on reaching the gap, immediately opened upon them, and pressing virgorously, drove them before him from the slopes and gap, and led his men to the other side. The whole line quickly following, passed through and bivouacked on the field beyond on the night of the 28th. All were aware that hot times were just ahead; for the booming of Old Stonewall's cannon was distinctly heard. We killed and captured about one hundred during the evening—but few casualties on our side.

ADVANCE TO MANASSAS.

When the morning of the 29th had scarcely dawned, the Texas Brigade was thrown to the front;[75] and a party of select riflemen of this brigade, under Lieut. Col. [John C.] Upton, of the 5th Texas, constituted the advance guard.[76] Moving forward, they came up with the rear guard of the enemy before sunrise. Pressing them vigorously, this gallant officer and his splendid marksmen drove in the rear of the enemy so rapidly, as to be frequently under the necessity of halting for the troops to come up. They did not move as if they were afraid to come in contact with the enemy. But following closely at their heels, they had frequent opportunities to try their marksmanship at the retreating guard. They also captured more prisoners during the morning than there were men in their own party. Early in the day they came up with the main body of the enemy on the plains of Manassas. They had driven them back about eight miles, and were now near the ground where Jackson's cannon was heard on yesterday evening. Forming upon line of battle as established by him, they rested and waited for orders.—Jackson had renewed the attack, and was now engaging them to our left; and from the thunder of artillery, and the roar of musketry, which came up from that direction, no one had to be told that the work of human slaughter was going on. Gen. Hood posted one of his brigades (Col. Law commanding) on the left of the Warrenton and Alexandria Pike, and the other (Texas) on the right. The line of battle, as established by Gen. Jackson, running nearly north and south, and facing to the east, crossed the Pike about one mile from Groveton—or three miles west of the Stone Bridge, across Bull Run, as it is better known in history—it being the one over which the enemy passed when attempting to flank our army last year. This line as now formed, was in sight of that classic ground. And the tide of battle is soon to roll its dreadful wave over the same field—to rage and break over the same hills—making the earth tremble under the charge of rushing squadrons, filling the air with its hideous roar, and the heavens with clouds of dust and mountains of smoke.

THE PRESENT AND PAST.

Thousands of living warriors stand trembling with eager anxiety upon the same ground, waiting for the word, to tread where fallen heroes sleep, and wrench from the hand of our enemy another palm for our country's glory. The position of the two armies is nearly the same as it was twelve months ago, only reversed; and it is now to be tested, whether or not we can whip them on either side of the field.

All the recollections of the past crowd upon the mind. Many of the heroes of July 21st are here. The 'Old Third Brigade,' now under the command of Col. Law, floats its colors proudly up, remembering the hard-earned honors of the past, and are resolving that their flag shall have "Manassas" inscribed upon it a second time. The 4th Alabama, which then stood like a giant in his strength, has again nerved itself for the combat. The names of Colonel Jones, Captain Lindsay, and Lieut. Turner among their first officers, and Landmand, Arnold, Kees, Bradford, Preston, Bailey, Briggs, Pitts, and many others, who stood with them in the ranks, bled upon this very ground. The living now re-resolve to do their country honor, and avenge the death of their fallen friends. For their very blood crieth unto them from the ground, and they hear their voices amid the roar of firearms, calling upon them by all the sacred fidelity of bye-gone days, to defend their graves from the polluted tread of sacriligious hordes, and their country from dishonor and oppression.

This field presents one of the liveliest scenes in the grand drama of war which the world has ever beheld. We might here stand and gaze upon it in mute silence, as it stretches away towards the sunrise, until every hill and vale had told its story—each a history of itself—of the 21st of July, 1861. But living scenes of real life are more interesting. The roar of cannon, which now disturbs the ear, and the long black lines of moving armies, are more attractive. The chivalrous knights of antiquity, and the marshals of Napoleon, of half a century ago, may pass in review before the mind in times of peace, when the fife and drum are not heard upon the soil of the South, and when the thunder of artillery ceases to be heard over the grave at Mount Vernon. This is no place to tell what Cromwell did; nor describe the fields where the Caesars fought. Neither does Yorktown, nor New Orleans have claims upon our time now—no time nor attention for the history of the past. To-day, we *make* history for the world to read. To-day and to-morrow we will write more than one of its pages in human blood. On yesterday, the roar of battle and the purple stream begun.

SECOND DAY'S BATTLE.

To-day a broader and bloodier scene is opening up before us.—For now (4 o'clock P. M.) the enemy moves forward in tremendous force, both in number and effort, upon the lines of Jackson (on our left) from one end to the other; but he holds his ground, and piles them in scores as they come. A courier from Longstreet arrives with orders to Gen. Hood to lead his Division forward. But before they had time to come to order, the enemy having advanced under cover of the woods, opened fire. The order was instantly given, and the whole line moved down on both sides of the road, into the open field. Their step is steady, and glistening steel flashes along the line. The artillery has been planted upon the hills; and as the infantry moved down, the artillery filled the heavens with shot and shell. Finally, the "make ready" is heard, and instantly a sheet of fire flashes along the line. The advancing line of the enemy falters, halts—another volley, and they give way, fall back, and take up another position to the rear; but only to be driven again and again, as our advancing lines draw near the ground upon which they assayed to stand. Thus, on and on they are driven, until night puts an end to our progress, and gives shelter to a vanquished army. But it was not until 9 o'clock at night the warriors were called off from the chase, and ordered to rest upon their arms.

After thus pressing and driving them a mile and a half, our officers supposing the enemy would withdraw to some little distance, to make arrangements for the morning, aimed to take advantage of all they had gained by quietly moving up and taking position upon the abandoned ground. But they were mistaken; for they had gone but a short distance, when they found themselves in the midst of the enemy. It was so dark that one flag could not be distinguished from another; nor the Yankee troops from Southern soldiers; and our men had to resort to the bayonet and butts of their guns to drive them back from the ground. [Lieut. Col. Work was twice struck with a clubbed gun and once brought to the ground, but a timely thrust with the bayonet by faithful men left the assailants bleeding on the ground; and notwithstanding the severe shocks received the Colonel remained calm and still kept the field.][77] And owing to some little confusion among our own regiments, they had to call out their names and numbers to prevent being fired into by each other. The enemy heard it, and took advantage of the information gained. One of their brigades, by our movement in the dark, had been cut off. But as they came up, they sung out, "5th Texas, don't shoot;" and so passed. At the same time, to divert our attention, they dashed a squadron of cavalry upon us, or else the trick might have been detected in time to have captured or shot them down upon the spot; for the 5th Texas was at hand, and the deception would not have lasted long enough for their purpose. But the cavalry paid well for their visit. Many of them slept upon the ground by their newly made acquaintances, and their slumber was so deep that the rising sun did not wake them up. —The order, "Right about," was quietly given, and our men fell back about two hundred yards. Pickets were then posted within about sixty paces of the enemy. One of our men went forward to look out the position and strength of the enemy. But he had not gone far when he received a shot, and crawled back to the line.

Colonel Law's command captured one piece of artillery during its brilliant march on the other side of the Pike. The Colonel had not only smelt powder on that field a year ago, but the battle scar which he then received, was to be avenged in the second fight.—General Hood was in charge, not only of his own Division, but received and sent forward three or four other Brigades.

It was now discovered that this Division was far in advance of Jackson's Corps; and at midnight, orders were sent round to fall back to the line from which the charge had begun. Here the weary warriors rested, and wait and wish for the coming morning.

THE SECOND GREAT VICTORY AT MANASSAS.

The morning of August 30th finally dawned. And the deeds of this day, will be read long after these warriors have ceased to hear the roar of battle. And as the reader would love to witness the struggle from morning til night, and watch the advance of our conquering arms to the farthest end of the field, we will take our stand on the heights where our line of battle was first formed; and to the left of Colonel Law's Brigade, which brings us near to Jackson's right; but a little to the rear of where he is now engaging the enemy. This position places us in the centre, Jackson's army on the left, and Longstreet on the right. It is true, that the position to which I have invited you, is one on which there are many Yankees posted, but you need not be afraid of them, for Jackson passing on Thursday, and Hood on Friday, located them there, and now they are as peaceful as you would have them be, except the stink of those left by Jackson. But as this is a common failing with the Yankees, to the smell of Southern people, you must put up with it for one day. And, as you are not accustomed to the music of shot and shell, nor the melody of grape and canister, it may make you a little nervous. But I will advise you of the fact, that you should not dodge, when you hear them pass, for in trying to get your head out of the way of one, you may put it right in the way of another. And while you are thus putting the head out of danger, you may get shot in the foot, and if you turn around to avoid a scar in the face, you may get shot in the back. Having taken our position, and facing to the east, we have the battle field of Manassas before us. The Warrenton and Alexandria Pike, passes two or three hundred yards to our right.—The field upon which the battle was fought last year, lies to the right of the Pike, which crosses the Run on the Stone Bridge, about three miles off, but which we cannot see, in consequence of a skirt of timber a little beyond Young's Branch; and the position from which we fell back last night. To the right, and about a mile distant from the bridge, may be seen the position occupied by General Johnston, as he watched the movements of the enemy, and sent forward troops to Beauregard. The artillery has taken position upon all the surrounding heights.

Picket firing and artillery dueling, begins at an early hour in the morning, on different portions of the field. The enemy have followed up, and occupied the ground which we abandoned for want of support—and looking beyond Groveton, you can see the "red breeches Zouaves," and old United States Regulars, crossing Young's Branch, and taking position in the rear of Groveton.—Towards noon the enemy are seen in great force, the artillery they post on every hill, and form their infantry in the valleys and gorges below. The preliminaries having been arranged, heavy lines of skirmishers are thrown forward. The field begins to present to the eye a little world of commotion. Bayonets bristle, the long lines, and heavy masses are moving yonder and yonder, on both sides of the road. The hopes of Southern Liberty are in line of battle, and officers are standing in little groups, while aides and couriers are dashing from one position to another, receiving and conveying orders to the different commands. Clouds of smoke are rising from the hill-tops, and growing and blackening, as the number of guns is increased, and more vigorously served by the cannonniers. Conspicuous, and a little to our right and rear, is Riley's splendid batteries, throwing shot and shell into their midst. Yonder to our left, the skirmishers are hastily drawn in, and a sheet of fire blazes along the line on the Peach Grove Farm. It is 4 o'clock, P. M. A desperate effort is being made by the enemy to turn Jackson's right. But, having his position in the railroad cut, his men are but little exposed. And with good aim, they thin the ranks of the advancing line. At last, they reach the top of the hill, and are piled in scores upon the ground. Their lines waver and fall back, yet it is but to rally and renew the charge.—Another and another line moves up to their support; but they only meet the same deadly fire more murderous than before.—There is a rail fence between them, and their lines are not more than seventy paces from each other. That fence was literally shot to pieces, and many of the rails cut in two, and shot into splinters by rifle balls. Their lines were again driven back—and not to be rallied. But, giving way in great confusion, were pursued by brave men, who checked the speed of many a Yankee, as he made haste from the range of Jackson's riflemen. Listen, and you may hear the shout of victory from Jackson's little band of heroes, in pursuit of the flying foe. The surge of that mighty cheer, rises above the storm of battle.

But gazing so intently upon this part of the line we have lost sight of the field. Look yonder on the Pike, they have driven in the skirmishers, and the battle begins under Longstreet's command.

HOOD'S DIVISION IS MOVING,

and, having crossed that open field, the Texas Brigade is entering the skirt of timber to the right. They are gone for but a few minutes, until the roar of a thousand muskets is heard, and the great iron balls break, and rend the forest like a storm. The bodies of the trees are scathed and severed, and the giant arms of the oak are broken like the reed. Soon the Texas Brigade is struggling like a giant, with the flower of the enemy's army; but in a few minutes the work is done, the ground is covered with the dead, and the hills with the flying foe. They charged gallantly on, with their usual daring and enthusiasm, driving them in great confusion, for a mile and a half. These were the Zouaves and Regulars, to which your attention has been called; and in testimony of the manner in which our boys disposed of them, we quote a few lines from [Edward A.] Pollard's [*The First Year of the War* (Richmond, 1862)] history of the battle: "Hood's Brigade formed Longstreet's left, and, of course, charged next the Pike. In its track, it met Sickle's 'Excelsior Brigade,' and almost annihilated it. The ground was piled with the slain." They had been selected and pitted against the Texans, as we have since been informed by prisoners captured. They had been feeling for our position for a day or two; and the collision of the evening before, had revealed to them the part of the field we were on. But, coming in sight of them, our men were not frightened at their red breeches, nor the appearance of their red skull-caps, with cow-tail looking tassels, but they seemed to be fired afresh for the combat. And I guess it will be some time before those Zouaves will hunt up the Texas boys again, to "skeer" them with their scarlet trowsers.[78] This is the second time we have met and whipped them; but, if they are not satisfied, let them look us up again. At the far edge of this timber, they lay thick over the ground, and then scattered up and down Young's Branch, and far over the field beyond. The line of their flight was marked by the carcasses, which fell from their ranks as they were making a brave charge in the wrong direction. Hundreds of them, after our own men were buried, were hilled up like a potato-patch on the field. But many of their stinking carcasses lay for weeks polluting the air, and their bones now bleaching in the sun, on the very soil which their polluted feet had desecrated. So the number was small that was left to gloat over a victory, won from the soldiers of Texas. And they, instead of rejoicing in the glories of a victory, have to mourn the shame of a disgraceful defeat.

THE FOURTH CAPTURES A BATTERY.

Soon after the enemy had been driven from their first position, a courier arrives to inform General Hood, that General Longstreet wished to see him immediately. Ordering his command to "press the enemy back to the branch, and there halt under shelter of the hill" from the battery, he rode back to receive the orders of the Commanding General. Although the officers and men of our brigade are usually strict in their obedience to orders, they did trespass, to some extent, on this occasion. And General Hood might have known better than give such orders, at such a time—for having been with the brigade as long as he has, he might have known, that with such a temptation before them, they could not obey it. They, however, did obey the first part of the order, "drive them back to the branch," to the letter, but the "halt" part of the order, they could not obey. For, with the red breeches "skedaddling" over the field, and that fine battery in full view, they marched right on, and in one bold dash, cleared the guns, and swept every thing from the field before them. It was here that Major [W. P.] Townsend fell wounded, while gallantly cheering his men to the charge. And, as if in defiance of the cannon, moved right up to its front, discharging his six shooter at the men that worked the guns, and fell within a few steps of its mouth.

When General Hood returned, they were not to be found where he had ordered them to halt, but passing up the hill, he found that they had run over the battery, and were in the valley beyond pouring their deadly fire into the backs of those splendid troops, which McClellan had eulogized so highly below Richmond, on the Fourth of July. Here they were moving in glorious confusion—Zouaves, Regulars and Artillerists, all together. When the General came up, instead of having them arrested for disobedience of orders, and sent to the guard house, he said, "boys you don't know how proud I am of you. You have behaved gallantly; you have done nobly. For you have fought like heroes. Men who fight in this way, can never be whipped."

The brigade was now far in advance of the other portions of the army—the 4th [5th] Texas leading the van. They had looked neither to the right nor to the left, to see if others were doing their duty, and coming up to their support, but with the red breeches before them, they had been pressing forward to the "mark." After driving them sufficiently on to gain a position of shelter from the fire of the enemy, [they fell back and were resting a moment in order to make another charge so soon as they could reform their lines,][79] the General, riding in front of the 18th Georgia,[80] halted the command, that it might have time to rest, and moving on to the right near the Chinn House, took position upon an eminence, where he could watch and direct the movements of the line over that portion of the field. Some five or six brigades were there received, and posted by him, under the fire of the enemy's guns. Too much cannot be said, in honor of the gallant manner in which he had behaved and handled, not only his own Brigade and Division, but those also which were sent to him for disposition, while the fight was going on. He won for himself a name that will go down in history. For not only did he command his own men, viz; the 1st, 4th, and 5th Texas, 18th Georgia and Hampton Legion, and rush them like a whirlwind, over the field—directing the destiny of the "Lone Star" to a higher position upon the roll of honor, but had immediate command of nearly all the troops on this portion of the ground.

While our Brigade was resting at the point where General Hood had halted it, General [N. G.] Evans rode up on his grey charger, and rallied himself for a moment, waving his hat and eulogizing the men. The boys, some of them, were foolish enough to think that he was lost from his command, but if he was, it was not long before he found them again, and led them on to the fight in his usual way.

As soon as the men had time to rest, and our advancing lines came up in supporting distance, our Brigade was again led forward. And others who had not participated in the fight, were brought forward and thrown upon the field, until the whole concentrated army of the enemy found itself flying in a second Bull Run defeat across the same stream which they had crossed a year before in grand confusion, and hastening might and main towards Washington as for dear life. Or, in more modern language, they were "skedaddling at Bull Run speed,"[81] to effect a "splendid change of base."(?)[82]

Gen. Longstreet was in the rear, sending forward the men as fast as they arrived, and watching the behavior of his corps as they strove successfully with superior forces. And I will take occasion here to remark that it seems that our commanding officers have at last learned to be prudent, and not unnecessarily expose themselves, and thereby their army and their country, to dangerous perils, by taking their position too near the enemy's fire. True, the highest in command, under certain circumstances, should lead the charge, and go with the men even to the cannon's very mouth. But this is not often. Our men do not need their chief officers to set them an example of bravery and daring. They only need to be told when and where to go.

At the battle of Gaines' Farm, Gen. Hood commanded the 4th Texas in person. This was a trying hour. He had already sent forward the other regiments of his command into the fight. This regiment had been held in reserve. The time had come and the place found in which it was most needed. He knew the men and they knew him; and each knew the confidence which the other had, in an hour of trial, and with a mutual confidence thus sustained, there was no fear of failure. The battle had been raging all the afternoon, and our advantages were but small, if indeed, they could be called advantages at all. Our lines had been held in check. Brigade after brigade had been led rapidly forward, and as rapidly repulsed; and some of them driven from the field. The fate of the day, which was almost at a close, now depended upon one single bold dash, that would break and penetrate the enemy's front, and throw his lines in confusion. We could afford to hazard the destiny of one of our best officers in the dreadful attempt. It was *made* and *done*. The shout of victory was first heard in the 4th Texas, under Hood's command. And we may here say, that no one doubted the bravery of Colonel Marshall, who fell just as the charge begun. Nor did they question the gallantry of their daring Major, Bradfute Warwick, who fell mortally wounded, soon after they had stormed and taken the first breast-works. But every one knows, that the presence of an officer high in command, nerves the men to almost super-human exertions in an hour like this.

And it was again necessary on the plains of Manassas that some one should stand forth upon the field, whose proud spirit and noble bearing would inspire each officer and man with the perfect assurance of victory. And for this high, though dangerous position, the General commanding again selects General Hood, who performed the duty assigned with great satisfaction, and filled the most sanguine expectations of all upon the field.

But in thus presenting the noble part which this officer acted on the Plains of Manassas, we would not detract from one of the gallant officers who were in command, nor from a single soldier the praise due to his valor. For the whole army, with the fewest exceptions, did their duty on this day. For the very thought of the presence of the spirits of fallen brothers, who bled on this field a year ago, and over whose graves we now tread, was sufficient to make each man a giant in the fight. And each one will be held in rememberance by a grateful country for the part which he so nobly acted. And even the scars received will not, like the mark on Cain, point them out as monsters to the world, but make them respected wherever they may go.

Thus the day ended, and so did the second battle of Manassas, after three days bloody conflict, and with as much honor to our arms as on last year.[83] And August 30th, 1862, will be written by the historian with as much pride to our country as July 21st, 1861.

Jackson's victory on the north side of the Pike was quite as complete as our own, and our victorious army slept beyond the battlefield, near the Sudley Ford road.

The brave and gallant Upton, Lieut. Colonel of the 5th, was left dead upon the field. He did his duty on both days of the fight.—His loss is deeply felt. Lieut. Colonel Ruff and Major Griffis, of the 18th Georgia, were wounded. Col. Robertson, of the 5th Texas, was also severely wounded, while leading his regiment far out upon the field.

Col. Wofford, of the 18th Georgia, Lieut. Col. [R. A.] Work, 1st Texas, and Lieut. Col. Garey, of the Hampton Legion, being in command of their respective regiments, deserve the highest praise for their coolness and bravery. Lieut. Col. Carter, in command of the 4th Texas, had an opportunity to show his value as an officer upon the field; and to his gallantry may be attributed, in a great degree, the brilliant dash made upon the battery of six guns, five of which were captured by his regiment. And we would again call to mind the conduct of Major Townsend, whose bravery amounted almost to recklessness at the time the charge was made upon these guns; and being wounded, the regiment lost his services during the remainder of the day. Capt. Hunter, while leading his company forward upon the same battery, received a serious wound, which, although dangerous, was not mortal. But those who were not wounded deserve equal praise with those who were more unfortunate. Among whom were Captains Winkler, Cunningham, Bassett, Martin, Darden, Brandon, Barziza, (who received a slight wound in the arm,) and also Lieut. McLaurin and Dugan, who were in command of their respective companies. I would love to give the names of all the subordinate officers and privates who fought so gallantly. But the limits of the present work will not allow me that pleasure. But as the conduct of our whole brigade, as well as that of Col. Law's Brigade, is better described by Gen. Hood, under whose eye they fought, I content myself by giving it in his own language; and this short sentence says all that good officers and brave men could ask. After speaking of the trophies which they won upon the field, he adds, "As to their gallantry and unflinching courage, they stand unsurpassed in the history of the world."

The trophies won are justly distributed among the regiments as follows: Hampton Legion, three stands of colors; 18th Georgia, two; 5th Texas, four; and the 4th Texas, two, and five pieces of artillery. This battery, commanded by Capt. Curran, had volunteered under a call on that morning to support the Zouaves and Regulars, in their attack on the Texas Brigade. The commander of which remarked to one of our men, while he lay mortally wounded, "I promised to drive you back or die by my guns, and I have kept my word." And so he had, for when the men returned from the charge, he lay dead under one of his guns. This officer had a heart and a courage worthy of a better cause. Colonel Law's Brigade captured one gun and three stands of colors, making in all six guns and fourteen stands of colors, captured by Hood's Division.

But it becomes my painful duty, after recording the history of these regiments, and the glory of our arms upon this day, also to open to the reader the

CHAPTER OF OUR MISFORTUNE.

Yes, we must be sad in the midst of joy. For after we have scattered and driven the enemy in broken masses over the hills and beyond the stream, we must look back over ground which was marked by blood and fire at every step. Many of our officers, who were never absent from their post, and men that were never known to flinch from the fight, are not to be seen. The roll is called, and the "marks" run up, and it is found that one-half of our men are gone. They are left upon the field, scattered from this spot to the place where the fight begun—a distance of more than two miles. Some are dead and others are bleeding. And to form an idea of this horrible day, you have but to imagine a field over which the sword has flashed, and fifty thousand bayonets have bristled the hills from morning till night, and as many rifles poured their volleys of lead, while a perfect storm of iron hail rained all over the ground. Its extent from north to south is about three miles, by two in width. This done, and you have the field over which death rode in his chariots of fire, and held his conquering reign August 28th, 29th and 30th, 1862.

Our entire loss is supposed to amount to about six thousand, in killed and wounded; but the loss of the enemy is astonishingly greater—thirty thousand at least in killed, wounded and prisoners. Of this we have the means of positively knowing; for we were left in entire possession of the field, and, consequently, of the killed and wounded on both sides.

On the next day, after the killed and wounded had been cared for, the march was continued to the Sudley Ford, and from thence to the Leesburg Pike, three miles from Germantown. Here Gen. A. P. Hill, on Monday, completed the work of a battle which I may say begun at a distance of fifty miles from this place, and lasted for twenty days—for from August 9th to Sept. 1st, the work went on. Here we remained until next evening—the object being to cut off the enemy's trains and harrass his rear; but their good speed enabled them to save the greater portion. Yet the whole line was strewed with abandoned guns, caissons, wagons, ambulances, commissary and quartermaster's stores, ordinance of every kind, and small arms of every pattern—knapsacks, cartridge-boxes, canteens, haversacks, blankets, overcoats, camp-kettles, tin cups, and frying pans at almost every step in their splendid race from Groveton to the Stone Bridge, and for miles beyond.

MARYLAND CAMPAIGN.

After reaching Drainsville, we found we had accomplished about all we could expect in that direction. But there was another field for operation, and a part of the army was already wending its way in that direction. So we were faced about, and passing through and beyond Leesburg about four miles, we came to White's Ford and crossed the Potomac into Maryland.

Sept. 6th.—Passing through Buckeystown, we arrived at the Monoccacy river, at the crossing of the Baltimore & Ohio Railroad. Here also is the junction of the Frederick road. The command was halted here for two days; for we were now in supporting distance of Jackson, who had gone above for the purpose of falling upon Harper's Ferry. And to prevent McClellan from reinforcing the enemy at that place, and also from moving upon Jackson's rear, we had been sent forward to occupy this line. While here, the boys amused themselves in blowing up the splendid Railroad bridge across the river, which must have cost thousands of dollars. From thence we moved through Frederick city, Boonsboro, and on to the vicinity of Hagerstown.

ENGAGEMENT AT BOONSBORO GAP.

On the morning of the 14th, we moved back to Boonsboro Gap, or South Mountain, a distance of thirteen miles. Arriving between 3 and 4 P. M., we found that General D. H. Hill had already begun the engagement, with a heavy body of the enemy, who were aiming to reinforce [Colonel Dixon S.] Miles at the Ferry. General Hood took up his position on the left of the Pike, but was soon ordered to move to the right, as the troops on that part of the field were giving way to superior numbers. On his march to the right, he met General [Thomas F.] Drayton coming out, saying the enemy had succeeded in passing to his rear. At this information, Hood immediately inclined his command still farther to the right, over a rugged country, and hastily put his men in position to receive them. [The contest soon became general and severe. The overpowering numbers, who had forced the brave Drayton to quit his ground, were checked. And the well-directed fire of Hood's men soon taught them that they were advancing over dangerous ground; for at every turn they found their numbers lessened, and their position growing more critical. Several attempts were made to charge our lines; but they were only able to utter a few huzzas and move up but a few paces, when another volley would check and cause them to waver and stagger like drunken men. Finally the expected "forward" was heard, and then came the full grown shout of success, which always tells what the Texans are doing, when they struggle for victory in the presence of mighty foes.][84] Soon he ordered the two Brigades forward with fixed bayonets.[85] The order was promptly obeyed, and our lines restored upon the ground, which had been lost. Night coming on, prevented further pursuit. We lost but very few; yet had foiled the enemy in his effort with seventy-five thousand men, to relieve Miles at Harper's Ferry.

SHARPSBURG.

Soon after night, orders were received to withdraw from this position. [Col. Wofford was in command of the Texans, and Colonel Law of the 3d Brigade.][86] All our forces were to fall back in the direction of Sharpsburg, or Antietam river; and we were again to act as the rear guard of the army. But there was little or no annoyance on the march. Arriving on the heights beyond the Antietam river, near the Town of Sharpsburg, about noon on the 15th, we took position on the right of the road leading to Boonsboro. But, as it was found that the enemy was threatening an immediate attack on the other flank, we were ordered to move to the extreme left, and take position on the Hagerstown road, near St. Mumma Church.—Here we remained, under the shot and shell of the enemy, until near sunset, on the evening of the 16th, at which time the enemy made a vigorous attack upon our left. They had crossed in great force higher up the Antietam, at Smoketown. Hood's Division, of two small Brigades, were all the troops in this portion of the field. Yet he succeeded in checking, and then in driving them back for some distance, when night put an end to the contest.—During the night, General Jackson's troops having arrived, they were thrown to our left, and at almost a right angle with our line, and with a space of some little distance between our left, and his right; his line facing west, and ours north.

[GEN. HOOD ARRESTED.

On our way from the Monoccacy river to Hagerstown many of our men gave way under the hard marches which they had to perform, destitute as many of them were of shoes and blankets, and frequently without rations. This caused our ambulance train to be filled with the sick. Our train at this time was larger than usual, for Gen. Hood's command having captured a large number at Manassas, Gen. Longstreet allowed him to retain as many of them as he wanted. General Evans, being Hood's senior, was in command, and having through negligence or some other cause failed to supply his own brigade with the requisite number, ordered General Hood to turn over those which Gen. Longstreet had allowed him to reserve, to his (Evans') brigade. But General Hood positively refused, upon which Evans ordered him under arrest, and to follow in the rear of the command. I need not say that this produced a sensation in the camp. And on Hood's application for trial he was ordered with his staff to return to Winchester to await a court-martial. This of course did not make Hood's division the less indignant. The next morning, while making arrangements to leave, he received orders from Gen. Lee to remain, for it was no time to be sending officers to the rear, nor had any one the authority to do so without his approval. To show the feelings of his men for him under the circumstances, at night he was treated with a grand serenade by the band, and on the way back from Hagerstown the men of Col. Law's brigade as well as our own, made every demonstration which the discipline of the army would allow, of their appreciation of him, both in view of that act, which was in defence of his own sick men, and also of him as an officer. And as they drew near to Boonsboro Gap, where the roar of the enemy's cannon was already heard, and an occasional shot or shell was howling in the air, Captain [E. D.] Cunningham approached Gen. Lee and asked that Gen. Hood be immediately released and placed in command, for the men were not willing to go into an engagement without him, and many had positively declared that they would stack arms on Gen. E. before he should lead them. But Gen. Lee knew too well the value of such an officer as Hood to suffer him remain under arrest for a trifling offence, and consequently sent an order to have him restored.[87] As he rode to the front he was cheered long and loud by each regiment of the division.

True, when he refused to obey the orders of a senior, there was no alternative left Gen. Evans but to order him under arrest. But the men felt that Evans had no right to our ambulances, and consequently should not have issued the first order. And Gen. Hood felt that the men who had captured them and to whom they had been given ought to ride in them when sick; consequently he subjected himself to arrest and humiliation before he would see the men who had followed him over so many battle fields thrown out upon the road side when they were unable to follow him on foot to the next battle ground, and our own ambulances given to others.

Our boys were frequently heard to say, if Evans wants ambulances, why did he not get them before leaving Richmond! And having neglected it, then let him capture them as we did, and we will never ask him for them.][88]

The officers and men of this Division, having been without food for three days, except half rations of beef and green corn, General [Alexander R.] Lawton, with two Brigades, was ordered to relieve us, that we might have a chance to cook. On the morning of the 17th, the firing commenced at 3 o'clock, along the line of General Lawton. At 6 A. M., General Hood received notice from him, that he would need all the aid he could render, in order to hold the position. In a few minutes, another courier arrived, and informed him that General Lawton was wounded, and he must come forward immediately and take the command. His men were ready for the word, and were instantly moved out upon the field, where they met [Lawton's scattered army retiring before][89] the advancing lines of an immense force, consisting of not less than two entire Corps of their army; and according to their own statements, were soon reinforced by several Brigades.

"Here," says General Hood, "I witnessed the most terrible clash of arms, by far, that has occurred during the war." A little world of artillery was turned loose upon us—and the line of their shot and shell screaming, blazing and bursting as they flew, made a perfect net work in their passage through the air. "And here," says he, "the two little giant Brigades of my command, wrestled with the mighty force, and although they lost hundreds of their officers and men, they drove them from their position, and forced them to abandon their guns on our left." [Lawton's men had done all that brave men could do. But so greatly outnumbered, they were swept back by the overpowering tide, but not until two-thirds of their comrades had fallen; and when Hood arrived they rallied like men to join in the charge.

The Texas Brigade was moved several hundred yards to the left, and reaching a cornfield it was halted to await the approach of the enemy, who had opened a brisk artillery fire upon our position, which they had ascertained by the firing of a few shots from a little battery of our own, situated a little to our left. But as soon as the enemy commenced throwing a few shell at them they basely fled the field and left us to our fate.

Captain Turner, in command of the 5th, was on the heights, and was ordered to dislodge the enemy from a wooded hill they had gained, and from which they were doing us considerable damage. True to this trust as on former occasions, he led the "bloody" 5th right up in their face, and in a few minutes routed the enemy and cleared the hill. He held his position until 9 o'clock at night, when the brigade was relieved by Gen. Lawton, who arrived at an important moment, as the cartridges were nearly all expended.

The Hampton Legion and 18th Georgia had advanced far to the left to prevent the enemy from flanking our position, and becoming closely engaged with superior numbers, the 1st Texas was ordered up at a double quick, and in the report of Col. [LeRoy A.] Stafford he says they moved in a rapid and gallant manner, pressing the enemy until he fell back to his guns, which now poured a dreadful fire into both flanks and centre of their well dressed line, which was two hundred yards in advance of our line of battle.

The position of the 4th was on the extreme left. "They had been," says Col. Wofford, "taken by Gen. Hood from their position (between the 5th and 1st Texas) and stationed on the Pike road to cover our flank by holding the enemy in check." Many efforts were made to drive them from the ground; but they had been placed there with orders to stay, and they did stay until they were ordered away. But many of them had to bleed for their bravery on that day. But it fell to the lot of the 1st to suffer most. The 4th lost most at Gaines' Farm, the 5th were the greatest sufferers at Manassas, and now the 1st has to mourn the loss of three-fourths of the number led into battle; and besides their men, they lost their flag, which they had carried through every battle of the campaign.][90]

Thus the battle raged furiously until 9 o'clock. The enemy had been driven some four or five hundred yards by this little band of gallant men. But, fighting at right angles, with our general line of battle, it afforded the enemy an opportunity to pour a heavy fire into the right and rear of Colonel Law's Brigade, which made it necessary for the Division to move to the left and rear, into the woods, to close up the unoccupied space, between our left and Jackson's right, at the angle of the two lines, near the St. Mumma Church. And especially was this move necessary, as Jackson had moved the troops from his right flank, without our knowledge, thereby leaving our left entirely exposed. Moving back near the Church, they formed and held their position bravely until 10:30 A. M., when General [Lafayette] McLaws arrived with his command, which, being formed, was immediately thrown forward upon the field, and becoming engaged, Hood's Division was withdrawn to the rear, to replenish their cartridge boxes. At noon they returned, and were ordered to form in rear of the Church, and hold their ground, which they did, until about 4 P. M., when the Division moved to the right, near the centre, and there remained until the night of the 18th. [We mourn the loss of the gallant Major Dale of the 1st Texas, who fell in the thickest of the fight.][91] During the day, we waited their advance, but they did not move. Two or three guns were fired, as a challenge to the contest, but still they did not come.—They had received a shock, so severe, and lost so many officers and men, that they were not willing to hazard another attempt.—And they felt so proud that they had not been run entirely off the field as usual, they were perfectly willing to make the child's bargain with us—"I'll let you alone, if you'll let me alone." They knew from their facility at lying, that they could manufacture a splendid victory out of the fight, and not fire another gun, notwithstanding we had waited all day, and challenged them to renew the fight. And, sure enough, they have so published it to the world. But it is like those splendid victories won by McClellan, around Richmond—and by Pope, at Manassas.

HOOD SENDS FOR AID.

On the morning of the 17th, Major Blanton was despatched to General D. H. Hill, to ask for troops to assist in holding the left of our position, but he returned a negative reply—"He had no troops to spare." Again and again, General Hood sent for aid, while his little devoted band of heroes were struggling with the many thousands of the enemy, who were pouring in, in a constant flood. In hopes of aid, they held their ground, and even drove them back over the field, long after every prospect to the eye of the observer of their final success had fled. They were frequently cheered with the indefinite promise, "You will be reinforced soon, hold on a little longer." They had never been beaten upon the field, and knew not how to give up the ground. They were out-numbered, twenty to one. But there they stood, amid the storm of death, until they became the astonishment and admiration of their enemies. And in their report of the fight, they pay this Division, the following well earned tribute of praise:

FROM THE NEW YORK "HERALD," SEPT. 20th.

"General [James] Ricketts at once assumed command. But our victorious movement had lost its impulse. Our right had advanced and swept across the field so far, that its front, originally, almost in a line with the front of the centre and left, formed almost a right angle with them. While our lines rather faltered, the rebels made a sudden and impulsive onset, and drove our gallant fellows back over a part of the hard won field. What we had won, however, was not to be relinquished without a desperate struggle. And here, up the hills and down through woods and standing corn, over the plowed land and the clover, the line of fire swept to and fro, as one side or the other gained a temporary advantage. * * It is beyond all wonder, how men, such as these rebel troops are—can fight as they do. That those ragged and filthy wretches, sick, hungry, and, in all ways miserable, should prove such heroes in the fight, is past explanation. Men never fought better. There was one regiment that stood up before the fire of two or three of our long range batteries, and two regiments of infantry. And though the air was vocal with the whistle of bullets and the scream of shells, there they stood, and delivered their fire in perfect order."

As to the regiments here referred to, it will detract nothing from the honor of our troops, to tell the reader that this was our whole Brigade. Numbering in all, when this fight begun, only eight hundred and fifty-four men. Not the number of one full regiment. They had passed through so many battles, that regiments looked like companies, and brigades looked like regiments. Yet, small as they were, they did the work of strong, full commands.[92]

[In view of some statements about the Texas Brigade retiring from the field, I insert the following, which will explain itself:

Fredericksburg, Va., January 20th, 1863.

To the Editor of the [*Richmond*] *Whig*:

I read, a few days since, in one of the Richmond periodicals, a notice of the charge made by the 24th North Carolina Regiment at Sharpsburg, in which it is stated that "Hood's Division was driven back in confusion." Allow me space to make a correction.

At that time Hood's Division consisted of but two Brigades—Hood's Brigade, consisting of the 1st, 4th and 5th Texas, 18th Georgia and Hampton's Legion, and Law's Brigade, (formerly Gen. Whiting's) consisting of the 2nd and 11th Mississippi, 6th North Carolina and the far famed 4th Alabama. These two Brigades aggregating 3000 men, including teamsters and attachees, went into the fight with but

40 rounds of cartridges to the man. After breaking through and thoroughly routing two successive columns of the enemy, their ammunition was exhausted. Unwilling to abandon the advantage so bravely won, scouting squads gathered from the field the cartridges of the dead both friend and foe—and with this supply endeavored to hold their ground until relieved by fresh troops. But their coming was so tardy, that the last of Hood's ammunition having been expended, he was compelled to withdraw his Division, which was done *in the most perfect order*. During the continuance of this fight many of his division fired more than 70 rounds, and the general average was 60 rounds per man.

No! Mr. Editor—Hood's Division has never yet been beaten on *any* field, and whenever they *do* retire—if ever they should—no other body of men in this or any other army of equal numbers need make any attempt to repair the loss.

A VIRGINIAN.][93]

The great misfortune on that day was, that our higher officers did not discover in time, that it was on this part of the field, that the enemy had staked the fortunes of the day. Of this, they could not be convinced, though frequently advised by General Hood and Staff, that they were moving in sight, and in tremendous force. And in connection with this matter, General Hood remarked, that he was "thoroughly of the opinion, that the victory of that day, would have been as thorough, quick and complete, as on the Plains of Manassas, on the 30th of August, if General McLaws had reached the field with his men, even as late as 9 o'clock."—The reasons for his tardiness, we hope, will be satisfactory, when he renders his report. But, if he moved carelessly up, stopping at the river and losing two hours, as we are told he did, waiting for his men to strip and roll up their clothes, to prevent getting them wet, and then halting for some time, for them to make their *toilette* on the other side, not only the loud condemnation of a country, which had, in part, entrusted him with its destiny, should fall upon him, but the strong arm of the law should take hold, and by one way or another, remove him from a position, in which he is able to jeopardize her future weal. This is not the first time that a single man has thwarted the plans of a great army, and made its victory only half complete.

EVACUATION OF MARYLAND.

On the evening of the 18th, we received orders to recross the Potomac. Our march to and across the river was undisturbed.—This, of itself, will show to the world the nature of McClellan's victory. And if he had beaten and driven us, as he publishes, why did he allow us to pass quietly away, after holding the field a whole day and night? Why did he not follow our army as we did his, near Richmond, forcing him to turn and fight, to save his routed men?

We had accomplished our object, as far as we were able, and, of course, were ready to return. Harper's Ferry had fallen, and its rich prizes were ours. They, it is true, expected us to move against Washington, Philadelphia and Baltimore; and whether we would capture one or all of them, they could not tell. But we had started out for Harper's Ferry, and as much else as circumstances would allow us to accomplish. And having won it, we saw that the magnitude of further invasion was greater than our preparations, and we returned to await another "on to Richmond." Our loss will not exceed seven thousand men, in killed, wounded and missing, while McClellan's friends set down his killed and wounded at fourteen thousand seven hundred and ninety-six, up to the 18th. And, by adding about two thousand for the number that were slaughtered and drowned, in attempting to follow us across the river, and thirteen thousand killed and captured by Jackson on the 14th and 15th instants, you can see whether our Maryland campaign was a failure or not. The sum total of their loss in men, is twenty-nine thousand seven hundred and ninety-six; and in property we captured seventy-three pieces of artillery, fourteen thousand muskets, great quantities of ammunition of every kind, and finest quality, with quartermaster's and medicine stores to the amount of thousands of dollars, and two hundred wagons, with fine teams, all in harness made by Yankee labor, with which to haul the other property away. And so ends the brilliant campaign of twelve days across the Potomac.

It is due to the memory of those who fell, either killed or wounded, that their names be written and preserved for the pen of the historian, who will write them with other fallen sons of the South, and that Texas may see that her brave men were at their post when her honor and her liberty called for a sacrifice of blood. We have given them a place. (See appendix)

HOSPITAL ARRANGEMENTS.

Having been left at Richmond to build and furnish a Hospital Ward for the sick and wounded of our regiment, it was not my pleasure to participate in the trials and marches of this brilliant campaign. It was expected that the wounded especially would be sent to me there; but ascertaining that orders had been issued after the battle of Manassas Plains, by the Surgeon General, that the wounded should be stopped at Warrenton, Gordonsville and Charlottesville, we immediately set out for those places; but on visiting the two last named places, and finding but few, and they well cared for, we continued on to Warrenton, where we found quite a number of each of the Texas Regiments. They had been quartered by Dr. Fennell, immediately after the battle and were as pleasantly situated as circumstances would permit.[94] For the number of wounded was so great, that their wants extended beyond the capacity of the town. After being with them five days, and doing for them as much as we could, the Doctor and myself left to take

A STROLL OVER THE RENOWNED FIELD

on which we had won two great victories, and had so many of our men killed and wounded. A train of ambulances was going down to gather up a few of the wounded, who had been left at private houses, and so we had the pleasure of a ride to the field. When we reached the place where the line of battle had been formed, we left the ambulance and begun our walk, following the line over which our Brigade had fought on both days of the battle. There were a thousand objects of interest yet to be seen. We could easily see where the two armies had met, and track them by the marks of shot upon the trees, and the graves upon the ground.—There were yet many bodies of the fallen enemy unburied, and the hands and feet and heads of others were exposed. The air was foul upon the field, and for a great distance around. You could mark the spots where the batteries had stood, by dead horses and the graves of men. From the discharge of the guns the grass had been fired and burned over the ground. On that portion where our gallant boys had met the Zouaves, the dead lay thick, and especially on that portion where the 5th Texas fought. And passing on to an eminence in the field, my attention was arrested by two boards standing at the head of one grave. And on approaching it, I read on one Niles Fossett, and on the other James Thomas. Brave boys—they belonged to the same company, were from the same town, had marched hundreds of miles, and fought through several battles together, fallen side by side before the same gun, died upon the same spot, and now sleep in the same grave. We passed on and around, and at last came back to the Peach Grove Farm, where Jackson had left the enemy in swaths upon the ground. But the declining sun admonished us to be going, or else we could not reach the house of Mrs. Hunton—that good woman under whose care Major Townsend and Captain Hunter were being healed. On the next day we returned to Warrenton, and there learned that a part (four) of the ambulances that had gone down with us had been captured. And we also learned, that while we were leisurely walking over the field, and interesting ourselves with all the broken relics of that blood-stained ground, that the "sinners" were on both sides, and, at one time, within a few hundred yards of us. It was too late then to become frightened; but I must confess that it did even at that time make me feel a little wild, and, especially so, when I remembered that I had no arms of defence, that was much better than a goose-quill tooth-pick.

Soon after reaching the village, I heard that General Longstreet had had another engagement; and I felt certain that if he had, our Brigade had borne their part, and so I immediately determined to go on in that direction, and look after the condition of the wounded. During the evening I made every effort to procure conveyance, but was unsuccessful. The next morning a man promised to take me on; and about 10 A. M., I left for Winchester. But we had gone but a short distance, when the Yankee news from ahead became so thick and strong, that he, after telling me how much he thought of me, told me he would go my way no farther, and set me afoot. That evening I made eighteen miles and the next day, Sunday as it was, I made twenty-five miles, which brought me to Winchester a little before sunset. I had narrowly escaped the enemy's stealing party a second time. For by the time I reached the town, they had possession of Paris in my rear—a little village at the gap in the Blue Ridge, which I had passed in the day. They made a dash at our cavalry that were stationed there, and frightened them off, and captured their baggage. But it would have made but little difference if they had captured the men too, for they were no account, or they would not have been surprised in this manner.

When I got within half a mile of Winchester, I met about fifteen of our men returning, wounded, from Maryland. This was the first direct word received of their fight, and I believe both parties were glad to see each other. I directed them to camp, some where near, as they were looking for a place where they could have their wounds dressed, get something to eat, and have a place to lie down. Stopping at a private house until morning, I went to the surgeon of the post, and he had the door of the basement of the M. E. Church, South, opened for me. Going to work, I had it arranged as soon as possible, and here received our men of all the Texas Regiments as they came. It was not long before the news reached the other hospitals and sick camps in the neighborhood.—And at the end of the 6th day, we had a hundred and ninety-four of our Brigade. True, about twenty of this number were not of the Texas Regiments, but they were of the 18th Georgia, who were in our Brigade, and having been so pleasant in the camp, and behaved so gallantly in the fight, and, in fact, sometimes calling themselves the 3d Texas, they felt like our own boys, and we took them in. And if there had been room, I should have taken the wounded of the Hampton Legion, another gallant regiment from the Palmetto State, who are also in our Brigade. For they have ever behaved like true sons of the South, when fighting was to be done. Brave as Spartans and true as steel, they are winning honors for South Carolina.

I need not say how glad the men were, with the prospect of attention. It was with great difficulty that we were able to procure the necessary appliances. For there were so many coming in to be accommodated.

VISIT TO THE CAMP.

On the 26th inst., learning that the army had moved back to within six miles of the town, I went out and had the pleasure of seeing those of my old regiment, that were left, after marching several hundred miles, and passing through the fire of six days, in battle. The men looked worn and tired. Their clothes were ragged, and many of their feet were bare; and in their coats, pants and hats could be seen many marks of the bullet. They had many times performed long marches, and fought hard battles, without rations. The weather was warm and dry, and the dust had settled thick over their clothes. But they were cheerful and lively, and as resolved to fight to the bitter end as when wading the swamps of Louisiana, to get to Virginia. After such an arduous campaign, I expected to see them worn down and somewhat discouraged; but in this I was agreeably disappointed. They had marched long and fought hard—they had buried many comrades on different fields; but that same unconquerable spirit, gleaming through every feature of the face, and speaking in every act they performed, stood forth as defiant as when the first blast of the bugle was heard.—They had believed that "a people could never be conquered who were determined to be free," and they believe so yet.

REVIEW.

October 7th and 8th, I was again in the camp, and Gen'ls Longstreet and Hood were reviewing the troops. On the 8th, as I sat looking on, while one regiment after another passed in review, (eighteen in all,) I saw one flag, in which were many holes, made by the bullets of the enemy. I watched it until it had gone some distance past. For it was a matter of great interest to me, to see an object upon which the history of the recent battles was so plainly and truthfully written. From the manly step of the Ensign, one could easily see that he was proud of his colors. It was a "Lone Star" flag, and belonged to the 5th, and, after the parade, I learned that it had been pierced forty-seven times, and seven ensigns had fallen under it. By the time I turned from looking after it, another was passing me. I knew it. It was an old acquaintance. Many times had I seen it on dress-parade, but never with such mingled feelings of pride and sorrow. It called to mind all the hardships and sufferings, fire and blood through which we had passed. It was made and presented by Miss Loola [Louise] Wigfall to Col. Hood, for the 4th, with the motto

"Fear not, for I am with thee. Say to the North give up, and to the South, keep not back,"

which was graven on the spear-head. [And for this act of respect, Miss Loo was made the adopted daughter of the regiment.][95] Nine Ensigns had fallen under it on the field. It had gone through eight battles, which in all had occupied eleven days, and brought off the battle scars of sixty-five balls and shot, besides the marks of three shells. It was the only flag to be seen, that had gone through so many battles, and had so many marks of honor. It was understood that this was the last time it would appear upon parade. For it is an object of too much pride to the Regiment, and honor to the State of Texas, to be kept in the camp. On to-morrow, it is to be committed to the care of Captain [Stephen H.] Darden, to be sent home to report our conduct in the hour of our country's struggles, and be deposited among the archives of the State. And knowing that hundreds would desire to see it, I had a drawing made, and here present it to our friends and relatives at home, that they may see the battle-flag, around which the 4th rallied in so many struggles for our country's liberty—and beneath which so many of our brave men have fallen. It is with great pride that we can send it home without a single stain; and to it the men of the 4th can point for the record of their deeds as long as Texas exists an independent and sovereign State. Beneath the flag I have written the name of our first Ensign, who carried it through the fire of Eltham's Landing, Seven Pines, Gaines' Farm, Freeman's Ford, and fell wounded on the second day on the Plains of Manassas, but is fast recovering, and will soon take his place again under the new flag.

And that the reader may the better understand our appreciation of it, we here spread before him the letter of Lieut. Colonel B. F. Carter, which accompanied the flag when it was sent home to the Governor of Texas.

HEADQUARTERS 4th TEXAS REGIMENT,
NEAR WINCHESTER, VA., OCT. 7th, 1862.

To his Excellency, F. R. Lubbock,
Governor of Texas.

SIR: I have the honor to present to you, by the hand of Captain S. H. Darden, the battle-flag of the 4th Texas Regiment, borne by them in the battles of Eltham's Landing, Seven Pines, Gaines' Farm, Malvern Hill, Freeman's Ford, Manassas Plains, Boonsboro Gap and Sharpsburg. From its torn and tattered condition, it can no longer be used; and it is returned to you, that it may be preserved among the archives of the State, as a testimonial of the gallantry of her sons, who have fought beneath its folds. I need not dwell upon the services of my Regiment. Its deeds in battle will go into the history of our country, and speak for themselves. And this silent witness bears eloquent evidence, that the men who followed it in action, were where shot fell thick, and death was in the air.

You will readily believe, Governor, that we part from the old flag with painful feelings. More than five hundred of our comrades in arms have fallen beneath its folds. And it is to us an emblem of constancy under multiplied hardships, gallant and dauntless courage in the storm of battle, and devotion unto death to our cause. Let it be preserved sacredly, that the remnant of our little band may, in future days, gaze upon its battle-stained colors, recall to mind the sufferings they have endured in their country's cause, and their children incited to renewed vigilance, in the preservation of those liberties for which we are contending.

Our General has presented us with another "battle-flag," and we hope to be able to acquit ourselves as well with that, as we have done with the old one.

Respectfully your serv't,
B. F. CARTER.
Lieut. Col. Commanding.

[HEADQUARTERS 4th TEXAS REGIMENT
CAMP NEAR FREDERICKSBURG, November 26, 1862.

Miss Louise Wigfall—

In February last our regiment had the honor of receiving from your hands a battle flag, and of adopting you as the Daughter of the Regiment.

In the few eventful months that have elapsed since then, our regiment has passed through hardships not often paralleled in history; and the torn and tattered old flag bears few traces of its original beauty. How well the 4th Texas has redeemed the promises made by our then Colonel, (now Major-General Hood,) on the reception of the flag, let history tell, but in a communication of this character a recital of some of its deeds may be pardoned.

Upon its folds are now inscribed the ever-memorable names of Eltham's Landing, Seven Pines, Gaines' Farm, Malvern Hill, Freeman's Ford, Manassas Plains, Boonsboro Gap and Sharpsburg. In the last named battle its colors were so torn and the staff so shattered by hostile shot, as to render its further use as a regimental standard impossible, and it has accordingly been transmitted to the Governor of the State of Texas, with a request that it be sacredly preserved among the archives of the State, where the name of its fair donor will be linked with the ever-living memory of the gallant dead who fell in its defence. I speak from the record in saying that in the three greatest battles of the present campaign in Virginia, that flag was seen floating in the very front ranks of the Southern army; that it was the first carried through the entrenched lines of the enemy at Gaines' Farm; that it waved over the first battery captured from the foe on the classic plains of Manassas, and that on the bloody heights of Sharpsburg, where the feeble remnant of the Texas Brigade struggled in the face of death for hours against overwhelming numbers, it longest maintained its position, and was the last to leave the field, supported and defended by the feeble arms but stout hearts of but sixty members of its regiment. Is it too much for me to assert that not one of that sixty would ever have left the field without it? Endeared to us as the gift of a daughter of our State, it has been baptized in the blood of our fallen comrades, and is hallowed by memories that will linger with life. When we have passed away it will stand a silent witness to heroic deeds, and cast an imperishable lustre over the humble names of those who died beneath its folds.

Daughter of the Regiment! have the soldiers of the "Fourth Texas" acquitted themselves as become Texans, and as men worthy of their flag? In their names I am commissioned again to thank you for its gift, and to assure you that in future days the few surviving members of our little band will ever hold in grateful remembrance its fair donor, and will approach with reverence to gaze upon its folds, consecrated to us by so many recollections that can never perish.

I have the honor to be, very respectfully,

Your obedient servant,

B. F. CARTER,

Lieutenant-Colonel Commanding.][96]

Our regiment numbered about one thousand men when we first entered the service, and last spring we were recruited by about five hundred more; and we now number one hundred and seventy-six for duty—who were on parade this evening. But it will not be understood that the balance have all been killed, or have died; but many of them are scattered over Richmond, in the hospitals, and along the road, to this place.

The First, carried its old flag through every battle, until at Sharpsburg, when the Ensign was shot down, unobserved in the corn field, as the regiment was changing its position to prevent being flanked, and it fell into the hands of the enemy, who, we learn from some of our men that were made prisoners, rejoiced over it exceedingly—mounting it upon a music wagon, and running up the Stars and Stripes over it, drove it through the camp, to the tune of "Yankee Doodle," and then to McClellan's headquarters, when they delivered themselves of several "Spread Eagle" speeches on the subject of capturing a Texas flag. Well, let them make the most of it, for it is the first Texas flag they have got, and I guess many of them will bite the dust before they get another.

The regiments are small, but recruiting from the hospitals in the rear every day, and I suppose they are quite as full now, as when they fought at Sharpsburg.

The loss sustained by this Division, (of two Brigades,) since leaving Richmond, October 11th, is two hundred and fifty-three killed on the field, sixteen hundred and twenty-one wounded, and one hundred missing—making in all, one thousand nine hundred and seventy-four.

In closing this part of the campaign, I present you with the General's address.

HEADQUARTERS—DIVISION,
NEAR WINCHESTER, Sept. 28th, 1862.

GENERAL ORDERS,
No.—

The Brigadier-General, Commanding, takes much pleasure in tendering his thanks and congratulations to the officers and men under his command, for their arduous services and gallant conduct during the recent campaign. After having distinguished yourselves at the battle of Gaines' Farm, June 27th; your long and continued and tiresome march since leaving Richmond—dashing courage at the battle of Manassas Plains, August 30th, your truly veteran conduct at the battle of Sharpsburg, Md., September 17th, has won for you the merited praise and gratitude of the army and our country.

In less than three months, you have marched several hundred miles under trying circumstances, participated in several battles, and made yourselves the acknowledged heroes of three of the hardest fought battles that have occurred in the present war.

In none of these, have you elicited so much praise from our Commanding Generals, or so justly entitled yourselves to the proud distinction, of being the best soldiers in the army, as at the battle of Sharpsburg. Called upon to retake ground, lost to our arms, you not only did so, but promptly drove the enemy twenty times your number, from his guns, and, if supported, would have led on to one of the most signal victories known to the history of any people. Your failure to do so, was attributable to others. And it, was here, by your conduct in rallying and presenting front to the advancing columns of the enemy, that you earned higher praise than in any of the brilliant charges you have made. No achievement so marks the true soldier, as coolness under such circumstances as surrounded you on that memorable day. And it is with peculiar pride, the Brigadier-General Commanding, acknowledges, that, such of his command as had not fallen in that terrible clash of arms, were in ranks again, ready and willing to meet the foe.

By order of J. B. HOOD

Brigadier-General, Commanding

McCLELLAN ATTEMPTS ANOTHER "ON TO RICHMOND."

McClellan, after the battle of Sharpsburg, was ordered to follow our army across the Potomac. He made an attempt, but the shock he received at the river, was so great, that he turned aside from the direct road, to look out an easier way than following in our rear. He, however, kept up appearances, as if he intended to drive us in full chase through Winchester, or capture Lee and his "rebels" before they could get out of the Valley. After making all his arrangements, and taking possession of all the Gaps in the mountains, to prevent our troops from interrupting his newly conceived plans, he made a dash for Gordonsville, but on arriving at Warrenton, to his astonishment, the "rebels" were all at Culpeper Court House, ready to receive him. Lee's eye was upon him. We had left Winchester on Wednesday morning, October 29th, and camped that night near Front Royal. The next morning we waded one branch of the Shenandoah, and passed through the Village at an early hour. After a hard days march, we camped on the mountain, near Gaines' Cross Roads. Friday morning the wagons and artillery separated from the troops, and took the road by New Washington Turnpike—the troops marching by the nearer dirt road, and both parties camped that night near Culpeper Court House. On the next morning, we passed through the Town, and camped one mile below. We had good roads for the march, but the weather was very cold.

Colonel Robertson, of the 5th Texas, after the promotion of General Hood, received the appointment of Brigadier-General.—He gave F. L. Price, Adjutant of the 4th Texas, the appointment of Assistant Adjutant General. Captain Littlefield, of the 5th, was appointed Quartermaster. Dr. Scott, of the 1st, Aide-de-camp.

On the 3d of November, the camp was moved to the battle field of Cedar Run, six miles from the Town. Here we had but little to do, but to watch the enemy, and guess what would be his next strategy.[97]

On the 18th, the Hampton Legion was detached from our Brigade, Lieutenant-Colonel Garey, being promoted to the Colonelcy. This is a noble regiment, and we regret the removal.

McCLELLAN'S REMOVAL.

When Lincoln and his friends learned that Lee had headed McClellan off from the great Mecca of their hopes, whither in their pilgrimage, they had been journeying as earnestly and as *circuitously* as Moses for the Promised Land—for so many long days and wearisome nights—while their clothes were waxing old, and being burnt, and much of their meat and bread was being captured by Jackson in the wilderness; and thousands of their carcasses were falling on the way—whose bones could not be carried along in their journeyings to the land they were going to possess, they determined to be revenged on some body, and as they could not manage Lee, they determined to decapitate McClellan.

And so it was when the great Napoleon, (who never has won a battle yet,) was doing his best—feeling the strength of our army, and contemplating a "change of base," and in company and conversation with General [Ambrose E.] Burnside at the lone hour of midnight on the 7th of Nov., an unwelcome courier arrived from Washington, and informed him that he should be captain no longer, and that he should not lead this great army over to the promised possession.—For he had acted "unadvisedly" with the men in his march—not that he had led them by the wrong way, but that he had let the captain of the hosts on the other side, get possession of the fords, so that he could not "make the crossing." At these sad tidings, Mac was sorely troubled, and wept much—and Burnside wept—and there was great lamentation and weeping throughout the camp. And Lincoln killed him, and he gave up the ghost, and went to Jersey, and his grave has not been seen until this day, for nobody has buried him.

BATTLE OF FREDERICKSBURG.

As soon as Burnside was placed in supreme command, he began to devise a strategy by which he could capture the Confederate City. After making all his arrangements, he opened a tremendous fire upon our lines, with the hope of getting away from his position, by hiding behind the smoke of his artillery. He made a bold and rapid move for Hanover Junction. And, on arriving at Fredericksburg, he hastily demanded the surrender of the City. But imagine his surprise when General Lee, who he thought still at Culpeper, answered his demand —"I do not wish to occupy the Town myself, and *you shall not,*" to which Burnside agreed, for it was a "military necessity."

We had left our camp on the 19th, and crossed the Rapidan on the Railroad bridge late in the evening; on the next day, we marched sixteen miles; and on the 21st, camped near Spottsylvania Court House. On Saturday morning, we moved up to the Fredericksburg Railroad, and camped within four miles of the old City. The rain fell almost incessantly, and the roads were very muddy over the entire march.

As it was evident that the enemy intended attempting a crossing as soon as he could make the necessary preparations, General Lee and his officers examined the ground, and made ready for his reception. On the night of the 10th of December, they began to throw their Pontoons across the river, at the City—and to defend them, they opened fire with artillery, at daylight on Thursday morning, which they kept up all day, at the rate of sixty shot per minute. Thus protected, they finally succeeded, with two Brigades [bridges], after many attempts and much loss. About a mile and a half below, another bridge was thrown over, and by noon on the 11th, was completed. The position was such, that we could offer but little resistance. On the 12th, under cover of the darkness, and a dense fog, a large force passed the river, and took position on the south-side, under protection of their guns on the other shore. But notwithstanding the terrible fire of a hundred guns, which raked every street and lane of the city, [Gen. William] Barksdale's Mississippi Brigade held the Town. They had resisted the bridge-builders with energy, and now kept them at bay in the streets. From the enemy's guns, the houses were shattered and set on fire in many places. This incessant fire of artillery was kept up upon the doomed City, from dawn till dark. When night closed down upon the scene, and hushed the roar of cannon, the burning houses of helpless women and children, who were driven out to wander through the dark, and over the frozen ground, without shelter or fires; destitute of food, and some of them of clothes—lit the landscape, and still revealed the barbarity of the cruel and heartless invader. Harmless old men, women and children, were slaughtered in the streets, and even in their own houses. But Heaven is preparing a righteous retribution for them in the very streets which they have so wickedly baptized with innocent blood. And we are persuaded that the slaughter with which they are soon to be visited in Fredericksburg, is but the introduction to the miseries with which their foul souls will soon be familiar.

Our gallant men had fallen back to the edge of the town; and those noble Mississippians were relieved by Gen. [Thomas R.] Cobb's Brigade, supported by [John R.] Cooke's command. Their position was behind a stone wall, and in ditches, while the enemy occupied the houses, in the out-skirts of the town.

Of the 18th Georgia, we have good news on this occasion—for after they had maintained their position a long time, relief was sent up, that they might have a little rest; but their reply was—"This is as good a place as we want," and refused to go, but continued at their work, as if they intended to finish the "job" before they quit.

Here it was that General Cobb was killed, and General Cooke was wounded.

Saturday morning, Dec. 13th.—On the right wing, while it was yet dark from the heavy fog, the enemy commenced feeling Jackson's position, and advancing in heavy force. About 9 o'clock, A. M., the fog was lifted, and their position and numbers were in view. In a few minutes the battle was joined. The strength of the artillery on both sides was now displayed. More than two hundred guns were belching forth their sulphuric flames, filling the fields and the heavens with hideous sights and unearthly sounds. The positions of our guns were well selected, commanding all the regions below, and sweeping the enemy down by hundreds as they moved on to the attack, or changed positions in the fight. Toward evening the infantry, sixty thousand strong, moved up to drive our men from their position. Then ensued a struggle of terror, full of grandeur. The long-drawn roar of musketry, with fitful gleams of fire, uniting with the bellowing surges of artillery, stunned the ear and made the earth vibrate beneath the feet. Every species of projectile known to modern warfare was hurled back and forth, from guns of every pattern and calibre. At the onset they forced A. P. Hill back upon the second line, but by its aid, under command of General [Jubal A.] Early, they were soon driven back under their guns, and it was not until after dark that the fighting ceased. They had been repulsed at every point, and were gradually falling back. Before the day-light had gone, we could discover their confusion. But we had no idea as to the extent of the demoralization and slaughter they had suffered. Over the ground where A. P. Hill met them, hundreds were left, dead and dying. Hundreds more were slaughtered on the left wing, while the artillery had slain them all over the field. But we did not suppose they would so easily abandon the highway to the "Rebel Capitol." We had not brought one-fourth of our men into the fight. Many on each wing had not fired a gun, while the centre, except Hood's right wing, had all the while been but playing the spectator, to the scenes below. General Stuart did valuable service throughout the whole fight. [Major Pelham won for himself a name that will never perish, by the manner in which he used his guns and handled his battery.][98]

On Sunday morning, Gen'l Lee expected them to renew the attack in full force, and with great violence. But instead of an attack, a flag of truce was sent in, for permission to bury the dead and care for the wounded. The petition was granted; and after occupying the day in carrying the wounded to the other side of the river, there were still hundreds not removed.

On Monday, the great Yankee army *en route* for Richmond, was drawn out and marshaled over the lands below. As many as sixty thousand were in full view from one point. They displayed all their stars and stripes with all the pomp and circumstance of Yankee glory; but instead of renewing the fight, as was expected, they waited until dark, and then begun "a change of base." At daylight next morning "Burnside *non est*" was the general rumor.—He and his army had adopted the old maxim—

"He who fights and runs away,
May live to fight another day."

THE RESULT: Our loss is about three thousand, in killed and wounded and missing. General [Maxey] Gregg was mortally wounded.—The Yankees lost about eighteen thousand, killed and wounded, and one thousand six hundred and twenty-six prisoners. Several General officers fell. [In consequence of the terrible defeat of their grand army, the War Department at Washington sent out a Court of Inquiry to ascertain the cause of the great disaster. Many were the reasons assigned; but of all that were given they fail at last to find the only reason why they did not gain a victory, (which was simply because we *whipped* them) assigning some that were truly childish—we give the following as a sample:][99] Burnside, among other reasons assigned for this defeat, while before the Court of Inquiry, states that Lincoln had told him that "he did not want the Army of the Potomac destroyed." This being the case, we agree with him and his officers in council of war, that the only way to prevent its total destruction, was to move them out of harm's way as soon as possible, and place them on the other side of the river, and then cut the bridges; which he informs the court he "did with success."

What a terrible retribution for their slaughtering those innocent ones in the city, and destroying the furniture, clothing, &c., in all the houses, and then setting fire to the buildings to consume what they had left. Their dead were left in every street, and scores were found in the shattered houses.

This is the fourth defeat, of the grand army of the Union, in its "on to Richmond." And this last repulse, must prove, if possible, more disastrous than the preceeding. For the defeat of their whole army, which must have numbered one hundred and forty thousand strong, which Burnside in his telegram to Washington says, had crossed the river, by about fifteen thousand of our own, will have a powerful effect on the minds of their soldiers, as well as the public mind of the Northern people. And as to the influence it will have abroad, I have but little care; for it is not to the nations that we should look for help, but to Him who made the nations, and "giveth the kingdom to whomsoever he will."

The "New York World" says, that their "army will now go into winter quarters, *because it can go no where else.*" But if it should attempt to go any where else, we suppose General Lee will be there, waiting for them when they arrive.

A few more such defeats will give us peace. For a peace-party is already forming in the North.[100] This is the reaction. The ebbing of a tide, which has flown beyond all bounds, assisted by every prejudice, and driven and lashed by the storm of envy and fanaticism. And a peace-party, originated by blood and suffering, cannot be checked. It may be next spring before they will give us another chance; but, whenever they do, it will end this unholy war.

BY WHAT NAME SHALL WE CALL THEM?

Abolitionist, Unionist, Federals or Yankees. We should speak the same language, with as much concert as we should act together in strife. All of the above names, have by different ones, and by the same ones, at different times, been applied to our enemy.—Words and names are the signs of ideas, and the vehicles of thought. We then should adopt the vehicle which would most certainly convey our meaning. Names are also significant. And while we would represent and convey our thoughts in words, those words should be properly selected, that our whole meaning—nothing more nor less—may be understood. Each of the above names are significant, and have a different meaning, and it is impossible that they can, with propriety, be indiscriminately applied. Then to determine which is the more, or rather the only applicable one, let us notice the meaning of each.

Abolitionist: says Webster, is one who is desirous of abolishing any thing, especially slavery. This word then will apply, provided the abolition of slavery is their only object and aim. But all will say that this is not their sole avowed intention—but to subjugate and despoil—make the South their inferior, and the bearer of their burdens, &c.

Unionist: one who desires concord agreement in mind, will, affections and interest. This, we readily see, will not apply to them. For there can be no union where there is discord—that they desire the South to remain in union of government with them is evident, but they seek a union which is a moral impossibility. And the name does not convey to the mind, their true character.

Federalist: says Webster, is an appellation in America, given to the friends of the Constitution of the United States, and to the political party which favored the Administration of President Washington.

I have but to inquire if they have been the friends of the Constitution? or have they not declared that sacred instrument to be "*a covenant with death, and a league with hell?*" Have they favored that line of policy pursued by the great champion of liberty—who so successfully led the armies of the first rebellion against oppression and tyranny, to victory, and finally to a peace as broad and as deep as the rivers? I know when you have learned the meaning of the name, you blush to know that you have ever soiled the native dignity of the name by which your ancestors were known, by applying it to a nation of thieves and murderers.

The next and last, is the only one that will apply. YANKEE: The popular name for the citizens of New England. This is what Webster says it means—and this is what we want—a name for the people of New England. And, as their history is well known to the civilized world, the whole world will understand us, and we will understand ourselves when we call them YANKEES. It is the only name or word in the English, or any other language, living or dead, that can be applied with full scope and force. It extends to all their ten thousand schemes of deception and fraud, and comprehends their every act of lying and stealing, from the days of Washington till the present hour, in all their political, legislative, executive, commercial, civil, moral, literary, sacred, profane, theological and diabolical history.

The word, has ever been used in contemptuous ridicule of their conduct towards each other, and their dealings with the rest of the world. And there is no other word in all the range of human learning, which will convey to the mind of every man, both in Europe and America, in Africa and the Islands of the Sea, so many, and correct traits of character, as the word YANKEE, when applied to the Yankee. And thus applied, it means meddlesome, impudent, insolent, pompous, boastful, unkind, ungrateful, unjust, knavish, false, deceitful, cowardly, swindling, thieving, robbing, brutal and murderous.

With this name, we involuntarily associate the story of the Clock Peddler who stole the land-lady's counterpane off of her own bed, and then sold it to her—shoe-soles made of birch-bark, wooden hams, patent medicines, chalk milk and wooden nutmegs. It carries us back to days of yore, and enables us to look at the different phases of society, from the time they burnt old women for witches to the days of the inauguration of the "woman's-rights conventions." Exhibiting the style of dress worn by Puritans in beautiful contrast with the fast age that puts their women in breeches.

[To answer the ends of their greed for gain, they have not failed to use all means in their power, however dishonest, and when detected, they have ever been ready to seek a difficulty to hide their shame. But when they have been insulted and kicked for their pusilanimity, they will even then make friends for the hope of a dime.][101]

This Yankee country has given birth to Socialism, Mormonism, Millerism, Spiritualism and Abolitionism, with every other Devilism which has cursed the naton of Unionism. And, as there is one word that will express all these and a hundred more *isms*, I prefer to use that word, and thereby say all that can be said on this subject—the term is YANKEEISM. And we will call them *Yankees*; General Beauregard and the newspapers to the contrary, notwithstanding.

BIOGRAPHIC SKETCHES OF GEN'L HOOD AND STAFF.

As these sketches will be of interest to our friends at home, I take pleasure in transcribing them from my journal for publication.

Brigadier General John B. Hood was born in Owensville, Bath county, Ky., June 29th, 1831, and was brought up at Mt. Sterling, Montgomery county. He entered upon his collegiate course at West Point, in 1849, and graduated in 1853. He was then assigned to duty in the 4th Infantry in California, where he served twenty-two months. And when the two new regiments, raised by Jefferson Davis, then Secretary of War, were called out, he was transferred July, '55, to the one (2d cavalry) in which Gen. Albert Sidney Johnston, who fell at Shiloh, was in command, and Gen'l R. E. Lee, the Lieut. Colonel. This regiment furnished many valuable officers to the South. Gen'ls Earl Van Dorn, E. K. [irby] Smith, [Charles W.] Fields, Evans and [William J.] Hardee were from its ranks.

In the winter of 1855-'6, Gen. Hood entered upon the frontier service of Western Texas, where, in July following, he had a spirited engagement, and was wounded by the Indians on Devil's river.

A short time before the beginning of the present war, he was ordered to report for duty at West Point as Instructor of Cavalry. But anticipating the present difficulties, he was allowed at his own request, to return to duty in Texas—his object being, in view of all the prospects of impending dissolution, to be in that portion of the country which he most loved, and so greatly admired. He could see no hope of reconciliation or adjustment, but every indication of a fierce and bloody war; consequently, he had determined to cast his destiny with the South. On the 16th of April, 1861, he resigned his commission under the United States Government, and tendered his services to the Confederacy. His name was entered upon the roll with the rank of First Lieutenant, and ordered to report to General Lee, in Virginia, who ordered him to report to General [John B.] Magruder, on the Peninsula. He was at once placed in command of all the cavalry of the Peninsula, with the rank of Captain of Regular Cavalry. Having several successful engagements with the enemy, he was soon promoted to the rank of Major. On Sept. 30th, he was ordered to Richmond, and receiving the rank of Colonel of Infantry, was placed in command of the 4th Regiment Texas Volunteers, then in camp near the city. Very few of the men had ever seen him, and doubts were entertained whether a Colonel could be appointed, that would give satisfaction. For an attempt had been made to organize the regiment under Colonel Allen, of Texas; but in consequence of a protest of some of the Captains, the appointment was withdrawn. This produced a feeling with others, and it was thought that they would not be satisfied with any one that might be appointed. But in a few days this feeling was gone, and every one seemed to be perfectly satisfied. His commanding appearance, manly deportment, quick perception, courteous manners and decision of character, readily impressed the officers and men, that he was the man to govern them in the camp, and command them on the field. And his thorough acquaintance with every department of the service, satisfied every one of his competency for the position. For they found him able and ready to give all the necessary instruction, not only in drilling them for the field, but also in the forms and technicalities of the clothing, commissary, ordinance and transportation departments—for the want of which information, regiments entering the service frequently go hungry, and commissaries and quartermasters make many fruitless trips.

The General is about six feet two inches high, with full broad chest, light hair and beard, blue eyes, and is gifted by nature with a voice that can be heard in the storm of battle.

On the 8th and 9th of November, the 4th and 5th Texas Regiments left Richmond, and arrived at Dumfries on the 12th instant, where we were with the 1st to be crganized into a Brigade, under Colonel

Wigfall, who, to this end, had received the appointment of Brigadier General. But, as he was the Senator elect from the State of Texas, after the meeting of Congress, he resigned. And on the 3d of March, 1862, Colonel Hood was appointed to take his place. Thus we see, within the short space of ten months and seventeen days, he was promoted from the rank of Lieutenant to that of a Brigadier General. And having been personally associated with him during his term of service with the Texas troops, I take pleasure in saying that his rapid promotion, has not filled him with that official vanity and self-importance which so often kills the pleasure, and cuts the acquaintance of former friends.—For while with him, there is no effort to make you feel the dignity of his official position; but you enjoy the pleasure of a social companion, familiar and kind. But as a companion, his friendship cannot be cultivated to an extent that will allow a pretext to the neglect of duty, by either officers or men. He is a disciplinarian; and the discharge of duty is the way to his society and friendship.—And, notwithstanding his rigid adherence to discipline, I am persuaded that he is as much admired and esteemed by the men under his command, as any General in the army. And to this one thing, I would in a great measure, attribute his promotion in rank, and our success in battle. Its importance is admitted by all. For it is this that makes the army of well drilled soldiers so much more efficient than the raw militia. Our success depends upon it; and the sooner our people, our army and our Congress are willing to see it properly enforced, the sooner shall we see our enemy beaten, our liberty won, and our country free.

An army half disciplined, cannot be efficient. For while they are in camp, they are scattered all over the country. While on the march, they are strung from one end of the road to the other.—And the result is, when we have to go into the fight, which is to decide the fate of an empire, one-half of the army is not there, and a few must meet the foe, and do the work of all. And when the fight is over, the straggler comes in for a portion of the honor, and will claim an equal share of the blessing of liberty, which has been won by the toil and blood of others.

But absence from the labors of the camp and from the dangers of battle, are not all the evils growing out of this loose method of soldiering. If you will but go round through this city, (Winchester, Va.,) and adjacent country, or any where else, that our army has either camped or moved, you will find abundant argument for a more thorough adherence to army regulations than we have yet had. Men straggling every where, and doing almost every thing—begging, taking, destroying, stealing and robbing almost every one they pass, of nearly every thing they have, until our country *groans to be delivered from its friends.* And what difference whether a man is robbed of his bread by a friend or a foe? Will he not perish, and his children starve, whether it is taken by the one or the other? Does any one doubt whether or not such things are done by our own men? I ask you to go to the people and ask them. We know it is so. For we have seen it with our own eyes more than a hundred times. And now, in all candor, we ask, are these things so to continue? Are we to leave desolate in our rear, and gaunt hunger to feed upon the lives of helpless women and innocent children? If so, would a home under Austrian oppression not be preferable?

But how are all these evils to be remedied? How are the men to be prevented straggling from the camp and along the march?—From robbing the country as they move, and brought up to the fight, so that all will fare alike in the burdens of the campaign and in the battles for our country? The answer is simple, and in a single word—DISCIPLINE.

All that is now necessary to make the name of Hood immortal, and fill the earth with the fame of the soldiers of Texas, is to bring forward a sufficient number of men to fill up the gallant regiments—now the honor of the Army of the Potomac—under his command, and add to their number some eight or ten new regiments of those now in Mississippi and Arkansas, and give him the rank of Major General. All of which we hope will shortly be done. Then our movements will not depend upon the inefficient and tardy movements of other officers and troops. But, thus constituting an independent Army Division of Texas, we will not have to watch and wait and fall back from ground hardly won, to keep from being flanked by the enemy from other portions of the field, after we have beaten and driven our foe in the fight. No one can look back over the history of past engagements without being struck with the brilliant dash and successful charges made by our men; and seeing how rapidly they press to the front, none will fail to admit the importance of their being supported by men of their own metal, and under the same commander, so that they can support themselves in the contest, and hold the ground they have conquered.—The records of Gaines' Farm, Plains of Manassas, and Sharpsburg, give sufficient comment upon its importance. For on each one of these fields they had to halt, and sometimes fall back from ground which had cost the lives of many of our men to conquer, to prevent being flanked by troops that should have been engaged, and driven from the field by other portions of our army; and, instead of our falling back, the whole of the enemy's line would have been hurled back in one grand rout, and driven in confusion before our conquering march. Other troops are brave enough, but they fight too slow. We want more of our own men. Men who, when the fight begins, will not stand and "listen the battle shout from far," but will rush forward at the word, and carry the field by storm. These are the men, and this the *modus operandi* for success. For when the enemy's lines are once driven from their advanced position, they should not be allowed to "face about," and form on new ground; but pressed and shot in the back, until they have effected a splendid "change of base."

Some of our men, both in and out of the army, are trying to make the impression, that our men are used by the Government, as a kind of portable breast-work for Virginia; and that they are required to occupy positions of danger, to screen the other portions of the army. But this is wrong. For we have seen as much of the treatment of the Government and of the officers of the army towards our men, as any body else, and we have been able to discover no such discrimination. But on the contrary, we have had our share of favors in almost every thing. And in many instances, we have been favored more than others. It may be possible, that the President will not give up our command, to be controlled and disposed of as some desire, but there are not many of our men that have complained even on that point. And if any are disposed to think that we have had to march further, and fight harder than other troops, I ask them to get the history of Jackson's campaign, and compare it with ours. They have marched further and fought oftener than we have. See also the history of Col. Law's Brigade, who have been with us in all our fights, and marches, too; and were in the battle at Manassas, before we left Texas. That we have had to perform long marches, and do hard fighting, I do not deny. This was what we came for, and the men were willing to do it. But that we have had to occupy *all* the most dangerous places on the battle-field is incorrect; and this idea should not be allowed to obtain, for it has no foundation in fact. True, in two or three instances, when the fortunes of the day hung trembling upon the command of a single Regiment or Brigade, we have been called to the rescue. And of all the positions on the field, our men would if left to their own choice, have stood upon the very ground where they fought. For they were willing that none should occupy more dangerous ground, do more, nor win greater laurels for their State than themselves. They had come to fight, and were willing to stand where the storm broke in its fury. And none have made a brighter record.

It is also stated, that an attempt is being made to remove our Regiments beyond the Mississippi, to rest and recruit—put upon the invalid list! We have no doubt, but that the motive which prompted our friends, is the love which they have for the men of our State. But that it is not from a broad philanthropy, which embraces the whole Confederacy, nor with a proper view to the final success of our arms, will be apparent to all. And especially will this appear, when they read the letter of the Commander-in-Chief of the Army to Gen. Wigfall, and there see the importance and confidence he places in them in view of success. As this letter will give pleasure and pride to every Texan, both at home and in other portions of our army, I hear spread it before the reader. It was written four days after the battle of Sharpsburg, where our men covered themselves with glory on the field.

HEADQUARTERS ARMY OF VIRGINIA,
NEAR MARTINSBURG, Sept. 21, 1862.

GEN. LEWIS T. WIGFALL—

GENERAL: I have not yet heard from you, with regard to the new Texas Regiments, which you promised to endeavor to raise for the army. I need them much. I rely upon those we have in all tight places, and fear I have to call upon them too often. They have fought grandly and nobly, and we must have more of them. Please make every possible exertion to get them in, and send them on to me. You must help us in this matter. With a few more such Regiments as Hood now has, as an example of daring and bravery, I could feel much more confident of the campaign.

Very respectfully, yours,
R. E. LEE, General.

I now ask, if, in view of the importance which we sustain to the final success of our cause, in which our all—life, liberty, and sacred honor, both for ourselves and our children is embarked, there is a single Texan that will say for us to return, or refuse to send us the men to fill up our thinned ranks? We think not. And we hope our friends will not, by persisting in their opposition in this matter, strike the honors which we have won for the "Lone Star" flag from our hands. Such efforts do harm. They tend to make the men dissatisfied, and feel that they are badly treated—worse than others—which is not so. And what would be the effect produced upon our army, if the request to remove our Regiments home, were granted? Arkansas would soon file her claim, and then Louisiana, and Mississippi, and so on, until the last man would be sent out of Virginia, to his own State. And there is no one so blind that he has failed to see the just indignation which the whole country pours upon the Governor [Joe Brown] of Georgia, for the factious opposition which he has raised against the Government. And all are proud to see the people and soldiers of that State condemning his course in unmeasured terms. He wants to be noticed.

We hope that the Legislature of North Carolina will be made to feel the withering contempt that now rests upon Gov. Brown, for the course it has recently taken.

This course persisted in, and it will not require the foresight of a prophet to tell the future destiny of our young Republic, in honor to whose arms the lips of the nations of Europe now glow with anxious praise. And McClellan would no longer be under the necessity of transforming a grand "skedaddle" into a "strategic movement," nor a dreadful defeat into a "change of base." But the iron yoke of despotism would be riveted upon our necks, and the heel of Yankee oppression grind our children in the dust. We call upon our countrymen, one and all, to lay aside all their sectional prejudices and selfishness, and let the whole people, burning with the living fire of patriotism, view the grandeur of our cause, and still rally around our country's battle-flag, and help us roll the tide of victory onward, and by the grace of God we will come off conquerers in the end. Let Texas send us the men, and with Hood to lead them, we feel safe in saying, they will make a bright record in our country's history, while they hasten the end of our toil and suffering. Texas need not fear; for if an attempt is made to invade the State, troops will be sent to her relief. For the Western Army must in a great measure be subsisted from the Prairies of Texas.

Since penning the above lines, I am proud to learn that Hood has been made a Major General, and the President has ordered the desired number of Texans; and a messenger has gone to bring them forward. We will hail their coming with pleasure, and promise them for a leader, one of the best officers in the Confederacy, who has never been incapacitated for a single moment from commanding his men by intemperance; nor been absent from the post of duty twenty-four hours, from the time he took command of the 4th, (Oct. 1st, 1861,) up to the present time, (Dec. 25th, 1862.)

W. H. SELLERS, A. A. G.,

Was born in Tennessee, and emigrated to Texas in '35; was a member of the celebrated Mier Expedition, captured Dec., '42, and held a prisoner in Mexico and Perote twenty-one months.

In the spring of '46, he entering the service in the Mexican war, was made 1st Lieutenant in Capt. Tom Green's Company of Col. [Jack] Hay's Regiment of Rangers, and was present at the battle of Monterey, September, '46.

In 1861, he entered the service of the Confederacy, with the rank of 1st Lieutenant of Co. A, 5th Texas Regiment; and when the Regiment was organized, received the appointment of Adjutant, which office he filled until March, '62, when he was appointed Assistant Adjutant General on General Hood's Staff, with the rank of Captain. In this position he has given the most entire satisfaction. And of his coolness and gallantry on the field, he has had no superior, rendering the most efficient service in every battle, especially at Gaines' Farm, Manassas and Sharpsburg, having his horse shot at Manassas, and twice at Sharpsburg. But he has passed unhurt through every fight.

CAPTAIN JAMES HAMILTON, A. D. C.,

Is a native of South Carolina, and in his twenty-second year. He entered West Point in 1858, and continued until his State seceded, when he resigned; and returning, tendered his services to his country, and was placed upon the Staff of General [Richard] Taylor. With him, he continued, acting gallantly and with credit to himself through the engagements around Richmond—after which, at his own request, he was transferred to the Staff of General Hood. At Sharpsburg, his horse was shot under him. And although his coolness and gallantry enabled him to go when and wherever sent—not shunning to pass through the midst and fury of the battle—eliciting the praise of the Generals upon different occasions; yet he has passed all unscared and unhurt, with the honor of having been under fire on fourteen different occasions—some of them, the bloodiest of the campaign.

Notwithstanding his youthful appearance and delicate constitution, with rather effeminate features; he has a brave heart and lion-like courage—that predict for him a future as brilliant, as his record is clear and honorable.

MAJOR B. H. BLANTON, A. I. G.,

Is a Kentuckian, and from Frankfort. He took position on the Staff on the 1st of May, and was in every battle with the Brigade up to the 1st of October. At Gaines' Farm his horse was killed, and at Sharpsburg he met with the same misfortune. His unflinching courage and gallantry, won for him the high respect and praise of the command. He received an appointment as Major in the Quartermaster's Department in Kentucky, and started for that army, but on arriving in Richmond, was allowed to return; and is yet with our command. And as he is a favorite with all, his return will be greeted with pleasure by both officers and men.

LIEUTENANT D. H. SUBLETT, ORDNANCE OFFICER,

Is from Waco, Texas. He entered the service a Lieutenant in Co. E, 4th Regiment, from his Town—and served in that capacity until the 16th of March, 1862, when he was received as a Volunteer-Aid to General Hood. And on the 1st of May he was made Ordnance Officer of the Brigade. In all these positions, he discharged his duty with satisfaction and credit.

COLONEL JOHN MARSHALL,*[102]

Commanding the 4th Texas, was born in Charlotte County, Virginia, in the year 18___ . He was at one time Editor of the Vicksburg "Sentinel," and afterwards took charge of the "Mississippian" at Jackson. And at the earnest solicitation of the leading members of the Democratic party of the State of Texas, he disposed of his interest in the "Mississippian," and removed from Jackson, Mississippi, to the City of Austin, Texas, where he conducted the "State Gazette," which was the leading organ of the Democratic party; and having made a reputation as a party leader and an able writer, was elected Chairman, of the Democratic State Convention at Austin, in 1858, over Governor [Elisha] Pease, by a considerable majority. (And as a testimonial of the manner in which the party appreciated him as a leader, they presented him a fine gold headed cane.) He continued to hold this position until he left Texas to join the army in Virginia.

Colonel Marshall was a literary man, of liberal views and fine attainments—an excellent writer and a close logical reasoner, of quick perception and excellent forecast, in so much that he did not wait the full development of events, in order to comprehend the end and aim of politicians, before the results of their policy were seen and understood by the masses. His friends knew well the value of his services, and his enemies felt the weight of his opposition.

When the 4th Regiment Texas Volunteers was organized, he received the appointment of Lieutenant-Colonel, and although the appointment was not altogether satisfactory, the Regiment soon learned to appreciate his value. For, possessing high business qualifications, and being a warm personal friend of the President, they found that through him they would be able to procure all the necessaries and comforts for the campaign, that would be enjoyed by the most favored.

He was ever watchful for the well-being of the Regiment, and fared and shared with them, both by day and night. Many officers, when there is no prospect of an immediate approach of the enemy, leave their post in camp, and spend a week or two at a time in the city or town nearest at hand. But Colonel M preferred the post of duty to the place of pleasure. He was promoted to the Colonelcy on the 3d of March, 1862.

We had no braver man in our army than he was. But he, it seems, was not long allowed an opportunity, to show his devotion to his country, and his gallantry on the field, until the missile of death sought and found the shining mark. Colonel Marshall fell, pierced by a minnie ball, on the field of Gaines' Farm, on the 27th of June. He had been in the battle of Eltham's Landing and Seven Pines, and was just wheeling with his Regiment to make one of the most brilliant charges known in history, when he fell from his horse.

And we have reliable information, that, had he survived this bloody scene, he would have received the promotion of Brigadier-General.

His death will be felt and regretted, not only by the army, but the State of Texas will mourn his fall.

LIEUTENANT COLONEL BRADFUTE WARWICK.

Was the son of Corban Warwick, of Richmond, Virginia; born November 24th, 1839, and entered upon the study of medicine—having been thoroughly prepared, at the University of Virginia in his 17th year.

This profession, however, was not his first choice; for with an ardent temperament and ambitious aspiration, he preferred a life of more hazardous enterprize. But his parents not consenting, and much preferring the life of a civilian for him, he reluctantly yielded his own ambition to their wishes. And as a second choice, begun the study of medicine—with their approbation—as it opened up before his young and aspiring mind, the widest field of benevolence and usefulness. That he did not enter upon this arduous field of labor with a view to its lucrative rewards, is quite evident, from the fact that the great wealth of his family, made it unnecessary that he should subject himself to the trials and labors, the fatigue and exposures to which this calling would necessarily lead. His estate would have furnished him all the comforts and luxuries of life. But not willing to live in the enjoyment of the world's blessings, without being a blessing to others, he placed his eye upon an exalted mark, and soon his foot-print is seen in the path that leads to a high circle of usefulness.

After attending a course of lectures at the Medical College in Richmond, he entered the Medical College of New York, where he graduated at the close of the first year, and not only received a diploma, but quite a complimentary one. And being only nineteen, he felt unwilling to assume the responsibilities of a profession, in which he would be charged with the life of others, at so early an age—yet unwilling to spend his time in idleness, and also desiring to leave no branch of his profession unattained, even in its highest degree, he went to Paris and prosecuted his studies until the following summer. When the exercises of the College suspended, he concluded to spend a few months in a tour through Europe, visiting the battle-field of Solferino, Venice, and many other places—returning to Paris, he made a pedestrian tour of the Desert.

On resuming his studies, his health began to fail, and he was advised to travel. This was welcome counsel to him, and he immediately determined on a trip to the East, where every city and village, every town and hamlet, every mountain and valley, river, spring, and almost every rock is the subject of history—either ancient or modern, sacred or profane. Italy, Greece and Turkey, afforded a wide field of pleasure and literary investigation to his well cultivated mind. But his trip through Asia and Africa were of greater interest, for, although not more classic than the former, yet there was more adventure than in other countries. He often wrote back to his friends, the most graphic accounts of the ancient relics and living generation through which he passed. And it was his lot to be in Palestine on the eve of the great massacre of the Christians by the Druises.

On his return from Jericho, his party of seventeen men encountered a band of Arabs, seventy in number, which they put to flight after a severe conflict, in which they killed several of the marauders, and lost one of their own men. On their arrival at Jerusalem, they were received with the wildest enthusiasm by the inhabitants. For the savages had been roaming the country and robbing travellers for years, and this was the first time they had been overcome for a long period.

Having visited almost all the places of interest in the country where Prophets and Apostles had dwelt and traveled, and where the Saviour of the world had lived and taught, he returned via Constantinople to Europe. On his arrival in Italy, he found it in commotion. Italy, long bound and trodden under foot, was struggling to be free. And ere he was aware, all his desires for military life, which he had yielded at the request of his parents, were revived, and he was fired anew with the prospect of entering upon the profession of arms. But as he had declined a course which he felt would give uneasiness and pain to those whom the scriptures taught him to obey, and thereby failed to receive a course of training at West Point, qualifying himself for the science of war, and having qualified himself to heal, and not to inflict wounds, he could not feel willing to offer himself in any other capacity than that of a Surgeon in the army. But presenting himself to Garibaldi, which was in the following language, viz: "I wish the appointment of Surgeon, because I think by it, I can do more good, but place me any where, if you do not, I will get me a rifle and fight on my own hook. For to fight or physic in this war, I am determined"—he was unable to conceal that fire, which, no doubt, he had long since believed to be extinct. And we will here remark that his parents had but little idea when they objected to his military course, that he would fall on the bloody field, and in the terrible charge which should disconcert the foe, and contribute so largely to the relief of Richmond, his native city, from a state of siege.

The great Dictator [Garibaldi] received him cordially, and gave him a place on the Medical Staff as he desired. But he did not remain long on this duty. It was too near the place for which his ambition was struggling when he abandoned the idea of a military career. At the end of two months, he resigned his commission and took his place in the ranks as a common soldier. But the eye of his leader was upon him, and having a knowledge of men as well as of nations, he gave him a commission; and serving in his new capacity—to the great satisfaction of the Commander, he was called out on the battle-field and promoted to the rank of Captain, for his bravery and daring during the engagement.

It was at Palermo, that he identified his fortunes with this military chieftan, and he continued with him, until he arrived in triumph at Capua. During this time, Lieutenant-Colonel W. participated in eleven regular engagements, besides many skirmishes; and also rendered much valuable service in other important matters connected with the success of the campaign. At one time he was sent over into Calabria as a spy, and by the successful manner in which he performed this duty, won for himself the Cross of the Legion of Honor. At another time, he was sent to London, recruiting for the Dictator's army, of which the "Southern Literary Messenger" speaks in the following language:

"What an example Doctor Bradfute Warwick has set the young men of wealth throughout the South! Scorning the delights of Parisian life, and burning with love of the sacred cause of liberty, he joined the army of Garibaldi. Not content with this, he repaired to London, and by his personal exertions succeeded in enlisting three hundred recruits, many of them, like himself, young gentlemen of family and fortune. Deeds like this must not be permitted to go unpraised. We trust our young Virginian may share fully the undying fame which shall attach to the deliverers of Italy. It will be a proud day for him when the shout of liberated millions shall proclaim, "Italia is free!" a day worth ten thousand years of the stagnant, idle, useless, semi-idiotic existence which the great mass of men born to wealth pursue."

It has been our pleasure to read in the Richmond "Dispatch," a short sketch of him, after his return from this brilliant tour in the East which so beautifully and correctly presents the bearing and deeds of this gallant young officer, that we give it in full.

AN OFFICER OF GARIBALDI.

"We had yesterday the pleasure of meeting with Doctor Bradfute Warwick, who, as our readers are aware, has been serving with Garibaldi throughout his late campaign. We have rarely been more pleased with a rencountre. Doctor W. is an exceedingly intelligent young man, and gave us a most interesting account of his adventures. They are narrated with great modesty, and without the least appearance of bravado or presumption. Doctor Warwick is but twenty-one, and yet he has already been in eleven pitched battles and innumerable skirmishes. He joined Garibaldi at Palermo, fought in all his battles and left him only when he resigned at Capua. Doctor W. is a Captain in the Sardinian service, Victor Emanuel having adopted the soldiers of Garibaldi. He literally fought his way up, from a common soldier to a Captain, in six months! That speaks far more than Captain Warwick's modesty allows him to say."

On his return from Calabria, he received information of the troubles in his native land. He immediately resigned, and set out for America. On reaching Paris, he ascertained that the "Vanderbilt" was ready to sail for the United States. He made all his arrangements, and registered his name with the passengers on board, and set-sail on his homeward-bound voyage on the following morning. His eye and heart were fixed on home; and his mind was occupied, and his thoughts absorbed, with the new and undeveloped events about to transpire on a theatre to which he was more nearly allied. He had entered the army in the Old World to assist in the common cause of Liberty. But *Home* and Liberty are now blended in the same scene. When he started out on his trans-atlantic journey, he left a nation smiling with peace, and rejoicing in prosperity and wealth, but what was to be the condition of affairs, and the state of public feeling on his return, was left to conjecture. And as the vessel was bound for a northern port, he knew not the destiny that awaited him on his arrival. And thus through the whole period which elapsed from the time he embarked, until he reached the American Continent, he was the subject of alternate hopes and fears. But on his arrival, the storm cloud, which, in its course, was to sweep over—first brightning, and then blasting his brilliant career, had not sufficiently culminated, nor broken over his path, to prevent him pursuing his way unmolested.

On reaching home, although passionately fond of his family, he remained but a short time. The sound of the bugle was moving the heart of a great nation, like the wind moves the waves of the mighty deep. But as Virginia had not formally placed herself in the ranks with her Southern sisters, he could not enter the service under the folds of "*Sic Semper Tyrannis.*" Consequently he hastened to join the Southern army. For the cause for which they had begun to martial their hosts was that of freedom, and having already offered himself upon that altar, he hastened to the place where the camp fires were burning, and whether Virginia ever became a member of the Southern Confederacy or not, he determined to identify himself with the Southern cause, and become a member of the Southern army. He reached Charleston, only in time to see Fort Sumter surrender to Beauregard, which he regretted, as he wished to participate in every contest for liberty.

When the Ordinance of Secession was passed, and Virginia became a Southern State, he returned, and with the rank of Captain, was placed on the Staff of General [Henry A.] Wise, in Western Virginia—who was often heard to speak of his young Aide in the warmest terms; and when the Texas troops were organized near Richmond, he was honored with the appointment of Major to the 4th Regiment, in consequence of his military reputation and daring spirit.

When Hood took rank as Brigadier-General, Major Warwick was made Lieutenant-Colonel, and as there had been no opportunity of testing the coolness and bravery of their young Virginia officer, many of the men had their fears as to his efficiency on the field. But at the battle of Eltham's Landing he satisfied them that he would not only stand his ground, but was ready to advance and meet the foe. He here won great credit for himself, even among western soldiers. From this time, he won upon the feelings and confidence of those who had objected to him, because he was a Virginian—not because they did not like Virginians, but because of their own State pride—they felt that we should have had Texans for our officers, which feeling, I believe, is common with soldiers of every State.

At the battle of Gaines' Farm, June 27th, Colonel Marshall fell soon after the Regiment entered the field in front of the enemy's guns. Lieutenant-Colonel W. was then in command, and none behaved more gallantly than he did on that day. As we were advancing, preparatory to that memorable charge which broke the right arm of the enemy's power, he picked up a battle-flag which had been left by some of our troops on the field, and carried it in his hand, and waving it over their heads, cheered them on to glory and to victory. But he was not long to enjoy this triumph in the full bright beams, with which it will radiate the brow of his command in future time. He had passed the second line of the enemy's defences with his men, and was about to plant his flag upon a battery which they had captured, when a minnie ball pierced his right breast, and he fell mortally wounded.

Thus ends the brilliant career of one of our most gallant officers, and one of Virginia's bravest sons. A man of military talent, and high literary and social attainments—capable of adorning in the high circle which nature had indicated, and, for which, no pains had been spared in fitting him to move.

The 4th Texas, will, while recounting the incidents of this eventful campaign, ever speak of him in terms of unmeasured praise, and think of his deeds with the greatest pride. While his family will treasure his honors as an inheritance bequeathed, and acknowledge him worthy their ancient name.

And knowing the state of his mind, both before and after he fell, we have reasons to hope that he lives beyond the land of misfortune in the regions of peace. For about two hours before he received that mortal wound, we asked him how he felt in view of the anticipated struggle, he said, "If we have an engagement today, I expect to go down." Then how do you feel in view of such a result? He replied, "I never prayed so fervently, nor so constantly during any day of my life, as I have on this day."

After a few sentences more, the command moved forward, and on leaving him, we added, "Put your trust in the Son of God, and whether you go down, or come through safely, it shall be well with you." He replied, "I will," and led on to the field.

On the 6th of July, he was relieved by death of all his sufferings.

His funeral was attended by Rev. Dr. [Charles] Minnigerode [St. Paul's Episcopal].

BRIGADIER-GENERAL J. B. ROBERTSON,

Was born in Woodford County, Kentucky, and at the age of twelve, was left an orphan, and without means. He was bound out for the period of his minority, but by his industry and economy, purchased his liberty at eighteen, and begun the study of medicine as soon as he had made sufficient literary advancement to enable him to do so. He had gone to school regularly, only three months prior to his 18th year.

About the time he completed his course, he left Kentucky with a company of volunteers, to join the Texans in 1835, in their struggle for independence. The battle of San Jacinto was fought while they were *en-route* from New Orleans to Velasco. They joined in the pursuit of the enemy to the Rio Grande, and he was promoted to the rank of Captain, which he held until the Army of the Republic was furloughed in June, 1837. He then resumed his profession of medicine in Washington County; but owing to the unsettled condition of affairs with Mexico, and the hostilities of the Indians, he was again called to the field, and put in command of a regiment and during the years 1839 and 1840, the savages were made to fear and feel the force of his command. He was an active participant in all the stirring events which transpired from the independence of Texas, both with the Mexicans and Indians, until annexation with the United States.

In 1848, he was elected to the State Legislature, and was one of its ablest and most efficient members. In 1850, he was elected to the State Senate; and at that early day, advocated the necessity of preparing for a contest with the Yankees, which he then saw was coming. He was one of the members of the Convention that passed the Ordinance of Secession, and was one of the first to raise a company and hasten to the contest. He was promoted to the Lieutenant-Colonelcy of the 5th Texas Regiment, on arriving at Richmond. And on the 2d of June, when Colonel Archer received the appointment of Brigadier-General, he took the rank of Colonel.—And as to the gallantry of his conduct at Gaines' Farm, Freeman's Ford, Manassas and Boonsboro Gap, the preceeding pages have already testified. Physical exhaustion after the last named battle, was so great, that he had to be hauled off the field; and was thereby prevented from participating in the engagement at Sharpsburg.

But the recommendation of General Hood, and the appointment of this brave officer to the rank of Brigadier-General, November 1st, 1862, speaks more in his praise, than I am able, otherwise, to do. He is now in command of the Texas Brigade, in the Army of the Potomac.

[LIEUT. COL. P. A. WORK.

This gallant officer is a native of Kentucky; was born February, 1832, in Breckinridge county. His literary attainments are good, and at the age of 21 was admitted to the bar, where he soon took a favorable stand for one so young.

In 1854 he entered the service of his country in a campaign of about six months on the Western frontier as Orderly Sergeant in Captain Walker's company. By his constant and prompt attention to his duties he won the good feelings and confidence of the command.

He took an active part in the last Presidential canvass in the United States, advocating the claims of J. C. Breckinridge for that position. He was elected to represent Tyler county in the State Convention, and his name stands recorded against the old tyranny and for Southern independence. Returning home he raised a company and repaired to Montgomery to tender his services to the young Republic. His Company was accepted, and in May, 1861, in company with four other Companies they reached Richmond. At the expiration of twelve months he was elected Lieutenant-Colonel of the 1st Texas Regiment, of which he has been in command since the battle of Gaines' Farm; and from his gallantry in the field and constancy with his command, he well deserves to have rank as he has command; for although Colonel Rainey is a gallant officer, he has been unable since his wound at Gaines' Farm to be on the field. Colonel Work has been present in every battle, and with his men in every march of the campaign.

MAJOR MATT DALE.

Major Matt Dale, of the 1st Texas regiment, who fell while gallantly charging the strong lines of the enemy at Sharpsburg, was born in or near Nashville, Tennessee, and at the time of his death was about thirty years of age. His father dying when he was very young, he was bound out by his elder brother to a printing establishment in the city of Nashville. Being a young man of strictly moral and sober habits, and possessed of considerable native intellect, by a zealous prosecution of his studies and a close application to business, he very soon acquired a thorough knowledge of the art of printing. He continued this business in Nashville until he was about twenty-one years of age, at which time he removed to Texas and located in Palestine, Anderson county. By strict economy he had managed to save a small sum of money, with which, upon his arrival in Palestine, he purchased an interest in the "Trinity Advocate," a newspaper published in that town, and became one of its editors. Being an able editor as well as a good practical printer, he succeeded in making the "Advocate" a very useful and influential paper. He soon made many warm personal and political friends, and in 1857 was elected by the voters of Anderson county to represent them in the State Legislature. He made a good member of that body, and was distinguished for his sound practical views upon all subjects of legislation. He was no orator, but wielded more influence in a legislative body than more ostentatious and less substantial members. After his return from the Legislature he continued the publication of his paper until the commencement of the struggle for Southern independence, for which he afterwards fell a martyr. He was a zealous State Rights Democrat, and was an able advocate through the columns of his paper of that political doctrine, and of the right of secession. Upon the secession of the Southern States he was amongst the first to respond to the call of his country, and did so by aiding in the organization of a company of volunteers in Palestine, of which he was elected Second Lieutenant, and Jno. R. Woodward, Captain. He left his home on the 23d day of June, 1861, and upon his arrival in New Orleans on the 10th of July, was mustered into the service for the war. He continued to serve as Second Lieutenant of his Company, which was a part of the 1st Texas Regiment, until the 20th day of May, 1862. In the meantime he participated in the battle of Eltham's Landing, where he acted with great coolness and bravery.

On the 20th day of May, 1862, it became necessary to reorganize the 1st Texas Regiment, and Lieutenant Matt Dale, of Company G, the subject of this sketch, was elected Major by a vote nearly unanimous. He was no office seeker, but his gallant conduct and general affability won him a host of friends, who forced positions upon him.

He took an active part in the various battles around Richmond, the second battle of Manassas, and various engagements of minor importance, in all of which he acquitted himself in an honorable manner, and fortunately without injury to his person.

At Sharpsburg he again went into the charge. Here it was that he fell. The 1st Texas, with other regiments composing the Texas Brigade, made a desperate charge, and forced overwhelming numbers of the enemy to retire in confusion before them. The enemy poured a perfect hurricane of grape and canister from their batteries, while their infantry, which had been heavily reinforced, rained missiles of death from their small arms into our advancing columns. Our men were mowed down like grass, and our ranks being so terribly thinned, it was thought prudent to order a halt. Major Dale had been first in the charge, and seemed lost to all sense of danger. When the halt was ordered, and what few of the men that were left had laid down for protection from the perfect hail-storm of bullets that were making the air hideous with their noise, there stood Major Dale, seemingly as cool and collected as if nothing was going on. While he was thus standing the fatal bullet penetrated his body in a vital part, and he fell, and in a few moments breathed his last. No braver or better man fell on the field of Sharpsburg. We can ill afford to spare such a man and such an officer—but he is gone, "like the summer dried fountain, when his need was sorest." He was a kind, generous and magnanimous friend, a noble and devoted patriot, a faithful and wise statesman, and a heroic and gallant soldier. One had but to know him well to know the number of his virtues. He leaves several brothers and many warm and devoted friends to mourn and avenge his loss.

LIEUT. COL. H. H. BLACK.

Harvey H. Black was a native of Kentucky, which State, although divided in its poltical sentiment and martial power, yet it has been as fruitful in gallant and noble spirits as any State in the South. It is saying much, but in the estimation of the writer, and, indeed, of all who knew him, no purer or more noble spirit ever grew up on Kentucky soil.

At the age of eighteen he, together with two brothers, emigrated to Texas, where he settled in Hopkins county, and confined himself chiefly to stock raising. Though engaged in an occupation so strictly private, he soon became known through all North-Eastern Texas as an energetic, intelligent and liberal minded citizen.

At the first intimation of the mighty disruption which was about to rend the American Union, he joined heart and hand with the secession party of this State, and immediately after secession he engaged actively in raising one of the first three companies raised on Texas soil to defend the South. The company was organized and mustered into service on the 27th day of April, 1861, and was called the "Marion Rifles," and known as company A, 1st Texas Regiment. Black was one of the leaders in getting up this company of patriots, which numbered 115 men. As he did not profess to be a military man, he expressed his willingness to go into the ranks, but his exertions in raising the company entitled him to some position, so he was unanimously elected 3d Lieutenant. These men, too impatient to await the slow process of reporting to the Governor of the State for duty, determined at once to go to Virginia, and if necessary, pay their own way. On the 28th of April, 1861, they left Texas, and on the 4th of May reached New Orleans. Here they were informed that the Confederate Government would not receive troops from west of the Mississippi, consequently the company was detained about three weeks.

While detained here the post of Captain became vacant, and Black was at once elected to fill the vacancy. He immediately obtained orders to move to Virginia. After a tedious journey he arrived in Richmond on the 28th of May. Here by the exertions of Hon. L. T. Wigfall these companies were made the nucleus of the 1st Texas Regiment.

By the 1st of August the regiment was fully organized, and was immediately ordered to Manassas, though not in time to participate in the first battle. Capt. Black, however, did not waste his time, but indefatigably studied the duties of his position, and soon became in all respects a good officer.

In the Spring Captain Black received the promotion to Lieutenant-Colonel. While in winter quarters near Dumfries his restless spirit would not permit him to remain idle in camp. With squads of volunteers from the regiment he performed several daring feats.

One night in January, at the head of fifteen or twenty volunteers, he procured two boats and set out across the Potomac to visit the Yankees, and change the spirit of their dreams. They moved silently unobserved close to the Maryland shore, when they perceived a company of the enemy's pickets, and poured into them a volley that killed and wounded several, and sent the balance panic stricken to wake up their whole army, and caused the long roll to run through all their camps. Black and his comrades finished their observations, and quietly rowed back unharmed by the muskets and cannon that were fired after them.

On another occasion, when Capt. Black and his company was on picket duty on the river, one of our batteries opened on a schooner in the river and forced the crew to abandon her in the channel only about four hundred yards from the Maryland shore. Captain Black and Lieutenants Wincherly and Waterhouse and a portion of Company A immediately volunteered to board the schooner and fire her. This they did at mid-day and in the face of a furious infantry and artillery fire from the Yankees on shore. The schooner's colors and several other articles of value were brought off by the party. During the short two months of life that remained to him after his promotion, he ably filled his position. He was constantly present during the fatiguing marches to Yorktown and back to Eltham's Landing. On the morning of the 7th of May, when it became certain that the Texians would at last meet the foe face to face on the field, his eye flashed with joy and enthusiasm.

The determination not to follow but *to lead* his men into action marked his bearing. When the rifles of the 1st Texas thundered their first volley at the Californians (?), and when the enemy were broken as the waves dashed from the rock, I never saw more enthusiasm than the countenance of Colonel Black expressed. He galloped in front of the lines on his white horse and cheered his men, holding up at the same time his hand, which had been pierced by a minnie ball. General Hood in person now gave the order for us to "charge," and Black spurring in front of the colors, waved his hat, and exclaimed, "Follow me, 1st Texas!" Instantly, with a yell that doubtless struck terror to the heart of every Yankee, the regiment sprang after him as one man, and chased the foe almost to their gun-boats. After running two hundred yards the regiment halted a moment for breath, when Colonel Black dismounted from his horse and was standing by him, when the writer approached him and asked if his hand pained him. "Not much," said he; but the words had scarcely passed his lips, when a ball from some Yankee skulker pierced his side, when he sunk in my arms. He lived long enough to know that we had gained the victory; and almost his last words were, "Thank God, we've whipped them."

Thus, at the early age of twenty-eight, he fell on his first field and at the opening of what promised to be a most brilliant career. The decrees of God are wise and just; but a braver or more patriotic spirit, or one more beloved and regretted by his comrades, never died for his country than Lieutenant-Colonel H. H. Black.

COLONEL J. G. C. KEY, FOURTH TEXAS.

Colonel Key is one of our bravest men, and his conduct on the field bears sufficient testimony as to his gallantry as an officer.

In 1860 he organized and commanded a company on the western frontier, during the time of the Cortinas troubles, to assist in driving him and his Mexicans from our borders.

After the Ordinance of Secession he raised a company and repaired to San Antonio to aid General [Ben] McCulloch in taking that place, then in possession of the Yankees. And he was again in command of a company at Indianola, under Van Dorn, when the enemy were captured at that place. He was also among the first to pitch his tents on the San Marcos, with another company, for twelve months' service in the Confederate Army; and, on learning that no more twelve months' men would be received, he enrolled his command for the war, and was the first company, of twenty that were called for, that was mustered into the service; and, being the senior officer, he was placed by General Van Dorn in command of the first five companies and ordered to report them to the Secretary of War at Richmond, Virginia.

When the companies were organized into a regiment he took his position on the right of the 4th Texas; and, after the promotion of Colonel Hood, Captain Key was made Major; which position he held until after the battle of Gaines' Farm, when he, in consequence of the fall of the brave Marshall and the gallant Warwick, was appointed to the chief command in the regiment. After the fall of the above named officers he was severely wounded in the abdomen, but his duty would not allow him to leave his post, nor quit the field, until fainting from loss of blood he was compelled to retire. As soon as he was able to take the field again he reported for duty; but, after the fatigue and exhaustion of the battle at Boonsboro Gap, he was compelled to go to the rear, knowing at the same time that all was safe under the command of the gallant Lieutenant-Colonel Carter.

Colonel Key is a native of South Carolina, where he begun the profession of law, and was admitted to the bar in 1842, in his twenty-fifth year. In 1844 he removed to Louisiana, where he pursued his profession with success until 1854, when he removed to Texas and settled in Gonzales.

LIEUTENANT-COLONEL B. F. CARTER, FOURTH TEXAS,

Is from Maury county, Tennessee, and in his thirty-second year. He was graduated at Jackson College, Columbia, in 1850; and spent the years 1851-'52 in the Law School at the Cumberland University, Lebanon, when he procured a license and moved to the city of Austin in the fall, where he has since resided, and held various municipal offices, viz: Alderman, City Attorney, and Mayor two terms.

He was elected captain of the first company raised in Travis county, in April, 1861, at the call of Van Dorn. On returning home he raised a company for twelve months, which was changed as to term of service and were mustered in for the war, and went forward with the first detachment of the twenty companies that were ordered to Virginia. When upon the organization of the 4th Texas he was the second captain in rank, and took his place on the left flank. On the 11th of July he was promoted to the Lieutenant-Colonelcy. He commanded his company at Eltham's Landing and Seven Pines; but he was not present at Gaines' Farm, from the fact that he was left sick at Charlottesville as the command was leaving for McClellan's rear. His condition was such (typhoid fever) when we left him, that we did not believe he would ever rejoin his command; but by kind attention he recovered and reported for duty a short time before the beginning of the Maryland campaign, in which he proved himself a field officer of whom Texas deserves to be proud.

He commanded the 4th at Freeman's Ford, Manassas and Sharpsburg, and especially in the last two, his regiment found him to be everything that was necessary on those trying occasions. On both fields the struggle was long and bitter. Each one had witnessed the setting of the second sun before the enemy gave up the strife. And it is under circumstances like these that the best material is put to the severest test. But his gallantry and endurance was only equaled by the bravery and unalterable determination of the men under his command.

No man in the Texas Brigade is more esteemed as a soldier and an officer; and we are of opinion, if this war lasts long, that he will hold high rank among Confederate officers.

COLONEL R. M. POWELL,

Is now in command of the 5th Texas. He is a native of Montgomery county, Alabama, where he was admitted to the bar, and in 1849 emigrated to Texas; continued his profession until 1851, when he married, and settling a farm in Montgomery county he retired from the practice of law for the more quiet and pleasant pursuit of the farm.

In 1857 he was honored by the citizens of his county with a seat in the Legislature, as an advocate of State Sovereignty. His course in the Legislature was marked by that straight forward integrity which is so much dreaded by political tricksters. The single purpose and single aim to do the will of his people, and good for his country, were so marked that he had the confidence of the House.

In 1861 he was appointed A. D. C. by Governor Clark, and immediately organized a Camp of Instruction. But as he desired to enter the field he took command of a company, made up from Montgomery and Walker counties, and repaired to Richmond, where he arrived on the 9th of September, and was incorporated into the 5th Texas regiment.

After the death of Major Whaley he received the rank of Major; and when Lieutenant-Colonel Upton fell, in the second battle of Manassas, he became the Lieutenant-Colonel of his regiment. The position of Colonel becoming vacant by the promotion of Colonel Robertson, Colonel Powell was placed in command of the 5th Texas.

His brave spirit and gentlemanly bearing towards officers and men, has won for him the confidence and esteem of both.

We might also add, that early in 1861 he received notice from General Van Dorn that he needed help to capture the Yankee forces then at Indianola. In twelve hours after the notice was received his company was organized and he was on the way to the place designated.

When he left Texas for Virginia, his energy would not allow him to wait, and rely upon the slow and uncertain arrangements of the Government for transportation; but furnishing his own teams he moved immediately, and with much more comfort to his men than many others who passed over the same route.

His readiness for emergencies and self-reliance have characterized him through the campaign.

GALLANTRY OF PRIVATE STINSON.

When the Confederate Army was retreating from South Mountain to Sharpsburg, Private J. C. Stinson, of Company G, 1st Texas Regiment, a youth of only eighteen summers, being exhausted from a hard marching and loss of sleep, was forced to stop by the wayside to take a little repose; when he awoke he found that the entire army had passed, and he was hard pressed by the advance guard of the enemy. As the safest place, to avoid being captured, he left the road and took to the forest. He had not, however, proceeded far before he discovered a squad of Yankees, some half dozen or more, very near him. He perceived at a glance that it would be utterly impossible to make his escape by flight; so he determined to make fight; and as there was no time to be lost, he at once fired upon the foe, when the foremost one fell and the balance broke and fled, leaving our young hero master of the field. Young Stinson thereupon very boldly approached the lifeless body of the Yankee, and found that the victim of his unerring marksmanship was a Yankee captain. He found upon his person a splendid six-shooter, which he appropriated to his own use; and then made all possible speed to overtake our army. He was, however, so hard pressed by the enemy that he had to cross Antietam creek a good distance below where our army had crossed it; but finally succeeded in getting safely to his command, bearing with him the elegant six-shooter which he had captured.

AN EXAMPLE OF IMITATION.

A. C. Crombie, of Company G, 1st Texas Regiment, was Acting Assistant Surgeon at the battle of Sharpsburg, and had command of the Litter Corps of the regiment on that bloody day. He did not remain *a mile* to the rear, as is too often the case with Surgeons in charge of the Litter Corps, but went as far as the regiment, and made those under his control do the same. Colonel Wofford, of the 18th Georgia Regiment, then in command of the Texas Brigade, complimented him on the battle-field for his gallant and humane conduct on that trying occasion, and assured him that his conduct should not soon be forgotten, but would be remembered by him to his latest day, and that he would have his gallantry rewarded, if it ever lay in his power.

Dr. Crombie has continued to perform the duties of Assistant Surgeon in his regiment, drawing only the pay of a private; but it is to be hoped his meritorious conduct will be properly appreciated and rewarded yet. He served in the ranks from the time he entered the service in June, 1861, until detailed to his present position; and, while in ranks, no one made a better soldier. As to his efficiency and close attention to the suffering, I had an opportunity to witness while near Winchester, Virginia.][103]

DANIEL COLLINS AND THE BRASS BAND.

This part of our organization has to the mind of many, been of but little advantage in the camps, or service on the field. But to the mind of an observing man, it is evident they have done a great amount of good. For there is nothing better calculated to stir up all the soldier in the composition of the man, than the thrilling strains of martial music, as it rises and swells in harmonious euphony from a well trained band.

When the men are weary and exhausted, its soft notes on the night air, drive away the thoughts of fatiguing marches, and quietly lull the soldier to rest. And the bugle's blast at reveille reminds him, as he is aroused from slumber, that he is a soldier; and to his guardianship has been committed the weal of a great nation, as well as the peaceful enjoyment of his own little home.

This principle was well understood by the great Napoleon, who would have the mothers of France teach their children the science of war, ere they could handle the gun, or could scarcely climb over the doorstep. Each little man had his toy drum and corn stalk gun, and thus grew up from the cradle, a man and a soldier. Napoleon knew that music had a powerful charm upon the soul, and, consequently, by it, held the armies of France chained to his will, and led them through Russian snows and over Alpine mountains, whithersoever he pleased.

But, to make music for the braves, was not all the service rendered by the band. For being organized, they served as guard to the knapsacks and blankets, which the men could not carry into the fight, and also as nurses to the wounded as they were brought in from the battle to the Field Infirmary. And as it was our lot, on two occasions, to be present at these scenes of suffering, we take pleasure in saying, they labored with untiring zeal for days and nights together without sleep, and with but little food.

IMPROVED CONDITION OF THE HOSPITALS.

In the earlier part of the campaign, the sick and wounded suffered much for the want of efficient Surgeons, Nurses, Medicines and Hospital room and appliances generally. The reasons are obvious and many. We had been living at peace with ourselves and with all the nations so long, that we had but very few Surgeons who understood Military Surgery. Many of them had, though practicing Physic for years, never dressed a gun-shot wound. This was, although a great want of skill and fitness for army surgery, more their—and, consequently, our misfortune, than a fault on their part. There are now scores of young men, who had never begun the practice of medicine before the commencement of the war, much better *practical* surgeons, than any of the surgeons, in whose hands the knife was placed, except a comparatively small number. And while the young men have been thus qualifying themselves, the older ones have been making more than equal advancement.

In the next place, the nurses have acquired a skill and aptness in their duties, which, in a great measure, lessens the annoyance and pain of the sufferers.

The rules and regulations of the Hospitals have also been systematized and adapted to the comfort of the patients, as well as to the convenience of their friends, who come to look after, and do offices of kindness for them.

The room which has been provided, is now ample for any number that will ever, at any one time, have to be quartered for treatment.

The number and improvements in all the various appliances for the hospitals are almost, if not quite, as extensive as the quarters which have been fitted up.

The supply of medicines is yet limited, but the great accessions and improvements, in all the other branches of the healing department are so many and great, that they very much make amends for this *desideratum.*

And in addition to all the improvements mentioned, the regulations have been so amended as to provide a matron for each Ward. A woman is to be seen supervising the culinary department, the Laundry and Wardrobe, and keeping an eye to the cleanliness of the ward, and neatness of the patients. Nothing could have been suggested, that will add more to the comfort and cheer of these houses of suffering. It is a position of honor, and opens a wide field for usefulness, and deeds of love and mercy to the mothers of our country, which is hailed with as much satisfaction by the soldiers, as it will be a source of pride to the women of the South, as long as they live.

And the last, though not the least among the arrangements, which will add to the comfort of all concerned, that we will here mention, is the quartering of the soldiers of different States together. The importance of so doing is so obvious, both for the comfort of the sick man, and the convenience of his friends, that no one will fail to see and appreicate it.

And although the Surgeon General did take it upon himself, to attempt to give me a little lecture, for quarreling a little with some of the Surgeons at the Chimborazo Hospital, for the manner in which they treated some of our men; yet I will say that the present condition of the Hospitals does great credit to him, both as a Surgeon and a State officer.

[SURGEONS.

In the beginning of this war we were as completely wanting in the healing department as in any other. We had many good physicians, and many who were well qualified for civil surgery; but they had never been called upon to treat the . . . [type uninked] diseases as are developed in camp life; nor were they accustomed in their former practice to treat men in the open field and sometimes even without tents, where they were exposed to every change of weather, and many of them to an unaccustomed climate. Neither had they been in the habit of taking patients through a course of physic without medicine. All these disadvantages have been encountered; all these inconveniences have been met; and in all candor we are compelled to honor them for their patient endurance and incessant labors by day and by night. Many have been the unpleasant sentences indulged in by those who have not considered the trying position which they occupy.

The 4th will ever be indebted to Surgeon Jones for the efficient services he has rendered in the field, and many times under the direct fire of the enemy's guns. They will also remember the unceasing labor of Dr. Estis at Dumfries. The 5th will always love Surgeon Breckinridge for his kindness and constant attention both in camp and in battle. And there are a number of others who have endeared themselves to the men of all the Texas regiments—young men, who have ever heard the complaints of the men with sympathy, among whom are Drs. Leonard, Terrell, Bray, Hill, Sloan, Crumby, Roberts and Work.

Of the qualifications, efficiency, energy and kindness of the Medical Director of our division, Surgeon J. T. Darby, of South Carolina, too much cannot be said, for he is well suited to his position and does his duty well.][104]

And to Dr. Smith, the Post Surgeon at Winchester, the thanks of our men are due, and we take the liberty of tendering them through this medium, for the kindness that we received at his hands. For we have not seen an officer since our connection with the service who labored so incessantly, both day and night, to provide a place and means of comfort for the hundreds of sick and wounded, who were sent to the rear during our Maryland campaign.

Dr. Thomas and the Sisters of Charity, at the Infirmary St. Francis de Sales, have also favored us with all the benefits that kind treatment and attentive nursing could afford.

CONTRIBUTIONS.

In consequence of the immense demands upon the Quartermaster's Department, it has not been able to furnish the requisite amount of clothing, to keep the men from suffering during the winter.[105] And with a view to supplying the deficiency—as we are too far from home, and with many difficulties intervening, to look for help from our friends—the following card, prefaced by the Editor of that excellent paper, made its appearance in the "Whig," on the 5th of November:

"We call attention to the statement below, assured that the citizens of Richmond need no comments from us to induce a prompt response to the simple and touching appeal of the Texans—bravest among the brave. The 4th Texas, to which Mr. Davis is attached, distinguished itself greatly in the battle at Gaines' Farm, where Lieut. Col. Bradfute

Warwick fell, while leading it into action.—The 4th Texas has a special claim upon Richmond, which we doubt not will be fully recognized."

TEXANS BAREFOOTED

RICHMOND, November 4th.

To the Editor of the Whig:

I have just arrived from Fredericksburg; the prospects are good for a fight, but our men are not all shod. On yesterday evening an order was read on dress parade to the effect that, being barefooted would not excuse any man from duty. Those who were without shoes, were ordered to make moccasins of raw hide, and stand in their places; and we feel that Texans will come as near discharging their duty as any who will meet the next struggle; but I ask the good people of Richmond and surrounding country, if they will stand by and see them go into the fight without shoes. We are too far from home to look to our friends there for help.—We acknowledge the kindness shown us last winter, and many of the recipients have poured out their life's blood on the soil of Virginia.

We are from the far South, and the cold is severe to us. It will require at least one hundred pairs of shoes, and five hundred pairs of socks to complete one suit for our men. Those who are disposed to contribute, will please send forward their mite to the depot of the Young Men's Christian Association, or the depot of the 4th Texas Regiment, on 15th street, between Main and Cary, over Ratcliff's, and it will be forwarded immediately.

N. A. DAVIS,
Chaplain 4th Texas.[106]

In answer to this appeal, we have received from Miss Virginia Dibrell, (collected from various contributions,) $268.25; Miss Mattie M. Nicholas and Mrs. Garland Hanes, (proceeds of a concert at the Buckingham Female Institute,) $175.05; from the Ladies Soldiers' Aid Society, New Market, Nelson county, a box filled with clothing; Mrs. Wm. G. Paine, seventy-eight pairs socks; Mr. Wm. Bell, Chairman of the Purchasing Committee of the citizens of Richmond, one hundred pairs of shoes; Young Men's Christian Association, thirty rugs, one hundred and forty-six pairs of drawers, one hundred and nine shirts, ninety-four pairs of gloves, and four hundred and ten pairs socks, besides a number of smaller sums and packages, which have warmed both the feet and hearts of our men; who feel that it is unneccessary to attempt to express their gratitude for these unexpected favors. But, by way of acquitting the claims of the young ladies, the boys are willing to promise to take them home with them, and work for them as long as they live.

In return for the liberality extended to our men, the Brigade, after the battle of Fredericksburg, contributed near $6,000 to the sufferers of this unfortunate city—Hood's Minstrels giving about $400 of that amount.

[APOLOGY.

When I began to keep a journal of our campaign, it was my object to keep an account of the 4th alone, but added many incidents of the other Texas regiments. I made many efforts to get a more full account of the 1st and 5th, but did not succeed as I desired.

Before the work was issued from the press the idea had from some cause obtained credence that I was preparing a history of the Brigade. I regret that I have not yet been able to procure the data of those regiments so as to make it as complete as my own.

There have been some complaints for manifesting a partiality for my own regiment, but I am persuaded that none will complain when they are in possession of all the facts. I promise finally to make the history all that the Brigade desires, so far as I am able, if they will be kind enough to furnish me the matter from which it can be written.

It is my purpose, when this cruel war is ended, unless providentially prevented, to publish my journal in a neatly bound book, with a neat lithograph of all the field officers and captains of all three of the Texas regiments now in Virginia, with a short biographic sketch of each; and to add many short paragraphs of individual gallantry which I cannot publish now. I therefore earnestly request all who feel an interest in this work to aid me in a matter in which they and their children will ever feel the greatest pride.

I should not have put the work to press so early and in such an imperfect form, but from the fact that the press at Richmond had not given Texas the credit due her gallant sons, consequently I determined to publish it in a form that it might be conveniently circulated and assist in making up the final account, and let the world know who had done their duty in this struggle. This being my object, I was not prepared to expect complaints from Texans, although the account of one regiment is more complete than another, and although the deeds of some individuals are recorded, while others are not published.

A HISTORY OF CHANGES IN THE FIFTH TEXAS REGIMENT,

From Its Organization, October 4th, 1861, Richmond, Va.

No. from right to left.	Order of Rank.	October 4th, 1861.	October 10th, 1861.	November 1st, 1861.	June 3d, 1862.	July 17th, 1862.	July 25th, 1862.	August 22d, 1862.	August 30th, 1862.	November 1st, 1862.	Number.	Company.	Captains at Organization.	
1	1	A	A	B	C	D	D	F	G	H	1	A	Captain	W. B. Botts.
2	6	F	F	G	H	K	I	A	B	C	2	B	"	J. C. Upton.
3	4	D	D	E	F	G	H	K	I	A	3	C	"	D. M. Whaley.
4	9	I	K	I	A	B	C	E	D	F	4	D	"	R. M. Powell.
5	3	C	C	D	E	F	G	H	K	I	5	E	"	J. D. Rogers.
6	8	H	H	K	I	A	B	C	E	D	6	F	"	K. Bryan.
7	5	E	E	F	G	H	K	I	A	B	7	G	"	J. C. Rogers.
8	10	K	I	A	B	C	E	D	F	G	8	H	"	J. S. Cleveland.
9	7	G	G	H	K	I	A	B	C	E	9	I	"	J. B. Robertson.
10	2	B	B	C	D	E	F	G	H	K	10	K	"	Ike N. M. Turner.

FIELD OFFICERS AT ORGANIZATION OF THE FIFTH TEXAS REGIMENT.

Colonel, J. J. Archer; Lieutenant-Colonel, ________ Schaller; Major, P.[aul] J. Quattlebaum.

Captain J. B. Robertson, of Co. I, appointed Lieutenant-Colonel, *vice* Lieutenant-Colonel ________ Schaller, removed, October 10, 1861.

Captain W. B. Botts, of Co. A, appointed Major, *vice* Major P. J. Quattlebaum, resigned, November 1st, 1861.

Captain J. C. Upton, of Co. B, promoted Major, *vice* Major Botts, promoted Lieutenant-Colonel, *vice* Lieutenant-Colonel Robertson promoted Colonel, *vice* Colonel J. J. Archer promoted Brigadier General, June 3, 1862.

Captain D. M. Whaley, Co. C, promoted Major, *vice* Major Upton promoted Lieutenant-Colonel, *vice* Lieutenant-Colonel Botts resigned, July 17, 1862.

Captain J. D. Rogers, Co. E, resigned July 25, 1862.

Captain R. M. Powell, Co. D, promoted Major, *vice* Major Whaley killed at Freeman's Ford, August 22, 1862.

Captain K. Bryan, Co. F, promoted Major, *vice* Major Powell promoted Lieutenant-Colonel, *vice* Lieutenant-Colonel Upton killed at Manassas No. 2, August 30, 1862.

Captain J. C. Rogers, Co. G, promoted Major, *vice* Major Bryan promoted Lieutenant-Colonel, *vice* Lieutenant-Colonel Powell promoted Colonel, *vice* Colonel Robertson promoted Brigadier-General, November 1, 1862.

NAMES OF THE PRESENT FIELD OFFICERS AND CAPTAINS OF COMPANIES, ACCORDING TO RANK, MARCH 1, 1863.

Colonel R. M. Powell;
Lieutenant Colonel K. Bryan;
Major J. C. Rogers
Adjutant, Lieut. John W. Kerr

1. Co. H, Capt. J. S. Cleveland;
2. Co. K, Capt. Ike N. M. Turner;
3. Co. I, Capt. T. T. Clay;
4. Co. A, Capt. D. C. Farmer;
5. Co. B, Capt. J. D. Roberdeau;
6. Co. C, Capt. J. J. McBride;
7. Co. E, Capt. T. A. Baber;
8. Co. D, Capt. W. T. Hill;
9. Co. F, Capt. W. D. Williams;
10. Co. G, Capt. John Smith.][107]

CONCLUSION.

For the present, we must take leave of the reader, with the promise of continuing our journal until the sunlight of peace returns. And then it is our purpose to present a history of the whole campaign. There may be, and doubtless, are many dark hours between this, and that long desired and much wished for time. But the same unyielding courage, and patience in suffering, which you have manifested hitherto, will bring it after a while. Too much cannot be said in praise of that noble, self-sacrificing devotion, which has been exhibited for the cause of Southern Liberty in your past history. And I am proud to say, that notwithstanding all the trials and hardships, privations and sufferings, you have been called to endure, that the same uncompromising, living patriotism burns as warmly in your bosoms to-day, as when you first left the quiet walks of civil life, and entered the army of your country. And, for which, your country will not only praise, but love you while you live, and your names after you are dead.

That there have been privations suffered by our army, which might have been avoided, we do not deny. And that the policy pursued by those in authority, in some instances, seemed unwise, we also admit. But it becomes us, as patriot soldiers, to regard these with a charitable eye. For while we have been exposed to the missiles of death from the enemy, and the diseases of the camp, we feel assured that our friends at home, and the authorities at Richmond, have been doing all the while, what they, at the time believed to be for the best. To believe otherwise, would be unkind and unjust. For it is as much to their interest as ours, that that policy be pursued, which will bring this cruel war to a speedy and honorable close. If, then, they have erred in some things, it does not become us to speak evil, or unjustly accuse them, for it is the misfortune of man to err.

It is the opinion of some, that "The danger is in such a contest as we are now waging, that we will be too favorably and generously disposed towards the Government, rather than prejudiced against it—that we will be blind to its faults, rather than eager and exacting in their exposure." We should not be blind, it is true. But that some are more eagerly exacting than is profitable, either to themselves or their country, is equally true. They are not blind, we know, when they can see so clearly as to discover a policy for the administration, and a plan of operation for the army, that would, while we were without the means of defence or aggression, have steered the Ship of State clear of breakers, and brought her into port, without a single defeat. They have never failed to charge the administration with every defeat we have suffered. They are ready whenever we meet a reverse, to show the causes, and blame the President. They make no allowances for the skill and superior numbers of the enemy—their great resources and superior arms and advantageous positions. But their conclusion is soon drawn—the authorities at Richmond, or some man with a commission from Jeff Davis in his pocket, was the cause of it. They are not only "eager," but "exacting;" and they are so eager in their exaction, that they do not wait to inquire the cause, but with their eyes open to the "faults" of the Government, they begin their unholy work of fault-finding. Oh, what a pity the President did not have his fault-finding seers in his Cabinet, so they could have prophesied before the battle was fought; whether Israel would prevail, or the Philistines succeed! But with their great wisdom, they could have always prophesied victory—and "a victory it must have been."

These wise men, tell you, soldiers, that you should not only be "eager" and exacting, but you should be "prejudiced" against the President and officers of State, whom you have called to these high positions, while you would go and fight the battles of your country. Why do they desire you to be prejudiced against them? What good can come of such "eager, exacting prejudice?" For my own part, I am unable to see any just cause for this gratuitous alarm, unless it be to attract attention to their important selves and have you claim a place in the cabinet for them. The President is the same man he was, when he was called to the chair in Montgomery. He is the same man, and with the same views and policy, as when you, in one united voice, a year ago, said he was the man which you desired to stand at the helm through this storm which had already broken upon the South in all its whirlwind fury. And he is still heading the ship in the same direction, as when you called upon him to take an oath that he would stand in the pilot-house for the next six years. His eye is still fixed upon the Polar Star of your liberties, and notwithstanding the false alarms of the frightened or fault-finding portions of the crew, they cannot divert his attention from its glorious light on the hills of American hope. The false lights that are kindling along the shore, have never caused him to veer from the course, and I am persuaded that the false cries of rocks and breakers ahead, by these "eager, exacting, prejudiced" ones, will not be able to move his nerves, or cause him to deviate from the light of that Star which has grown much brighter and nearer, than it was last February.

We know that it is unreasonable, to expect any one to fill the high position which he occupies, and be able to please every man. No form, nor period of any government, has ever been free from such "eager, exacting, prejudiced, fault-finders" as we already discover to exist in our young Republic. No, not even the Theocracy itself was free from such men, for Korah, Dathan and Abiram, thought Moses and Aaron took too much upon themselves. And so it is now. These men think the President takes too much upon himself. "He makes the members of his Cabinet act as chief clerks, &c., &c." The great difficulty seems to be, that the President examines too minutely, all the business of the different departments. But this is what you claimed at his hand, when you required him to take the oath of the office to which you elected him, and which he has filled as well as any other man in our nation could have done. And if he fails to scrutinize the whole national machinery with constant vigilance, then he should resign the solemn trust.

To speak evil of the authorities in our Government, seems to be the pleasing employment of the class of men referred to. They have not known, or if known, they have not learned to practice the sacred law of charity, which "hideth a multitude of faults." There is a God, and that "God doeth his will in the army of Heaven and his pleasure among the children of men." He has given us a Bible, and that Bible says, "Thou shalt not speak evil of the ruler of thy people," but they have never learned or practiced this command. And instead of practicing it themselves, they would have you prejudiced, and eagerly exacting in your demands. Oh what a shame!

When our army is successful, they say "the soldiers did it."—This is true. But did the soldiers win the victory without officers? And did the soldiers and officers in the army plan the campaign, and fight the battles without the knowledge and council of the President and his Cabinet? We are persuaded that the brave soldiers of our army would desire to claim no such thing. And while you are doing all you can to win our liberties, you are willing to do justice to all, from the highest to the lowest. And while you claim the honor due to your noble deeds, you are as willing to confer that honor due to both the officers of the army, and officers of State.

It seems to be the object of these men, if it be possible, to sow the seeds of discord in our country and our army, and thereby destroy the last hope of American freedom. For such would be the legitimate result of their conduct. But we are proud to know that the men whom they desire to disaffect, and persuade into the same unholy calling with themselves, have too much sense, and too much love of liberty and home at heart, to be influenced by those, who, instead of taking their muskets and helping you drive the invader from their own soil, are spending their days in ease, and their breath in slander.

We are proud to know that you cherish a soverign contempt for such men, and for the cause in which they are engaged. For you are aware that there were men in the days of your revolutionary sires, who did the same. And you know, too, that the contempt of the world rested upon them, and upon their children, ever afterwards.

And, in conclusion, we ask you to look back over the history of our national career, for the last twelve months. We have been defeated in several engagements, it is true, but it was in a branch of the service in which we never have had but little power. We have lost our little fleet, and some of our sea-ports. But how many victories crown your arms by land? And although some would have you believe that our administration has been characterized by imbecility, and the departments with inefficiency, we ask you now, to look at the army, which is the pride of our nation, and the admiration of the world. It is well trained and well armed, and stands in proud defiance of the mustering legions of the North. Less than twenty thousand of whom, but a few days ago, defeated the whole of the enemy's Grand Army at Fredericksburg, themselves being the confessors.

We admit the force, and quote the language of one of our great statesmen, viz: "Eternal vigilance, is the price of liberty," but we would also remind you of the fact, that confidence in each other, is the sheet anchor of our safety. For united we stand, divided we fall. And while we have enemies from abroad, and pressing upon our borders, let us not forget that we have enemies as subtle, malignant and dangerous at home. But with vigilance for our cause, and confidence in each other—in our officers of the army and of the State, we shall not fail to discover every attempt they shall make, and by the help of Almightly God, we will finally conquer our peace, and drive the aliens from our homes, and the secret enemies from our altars.

And although you long for the time, and signal to stack your arms and return to your distant homes, yet we know that it is your unchangeable determination to keep the camp fires burning around the borders of your bleeding country, until you have forced the hordes of Yankees from the land of wooden-nutmegs, [who have grown rich by plundering your commerce in unjust tariffs],[108] to acknowledge your independence—or else you will fill the soldiers grave. For you, by your recent campaign, have declared that you intend to die on the field, unless you shall be allowed the enjoyments of the liberties bequeathed by your ancestors. For an honorable death is preferable to an ignominious life. And you are also aware of the fact, that "while you are determined to be free, you never can be conquered."

May the living God preserve you from the pestilence that rides upon the winds, and shield your heads in the day of battle.

APPENDIX

In presenting a list of the killed and wounded, we have made it as correct as we possibly could. If we have made mistakes in spelling some of the names, we would be glad to have them corrected, in view of making it correct when the Journal is finally completed. And if we have not done each one justice in the Roll of the 4th, in the different engagements, we will take pleasure in making any corrections desired, provided the corrections are legally authorized by the company officers—otherwise we cannot take the liberty of altering it, as it was made by official order, and subjected to the examination of the officers who furnished it to me, as nearly correct as circumstances would enable them to make it. I am not responsible for the errors that may occur. For the tables were made out by others.

Many of you have made a bright record—one, of which you will be proud until the day of your death. And we hope we shall have the pleasure of concluding it with as much honor as it has been thus far sustained.

Killed and Wounded of the Hampton Legion, in the different Engagements of the Campaign, as furnished by B. J. Bouknight, Lieutenant, acting Adjutant.

	KILLED.	WOUNDED.
Williamsburg and Seven Pines,- - - - -	22	122
Gaines' Farm,- - - - - - - - - - - - - - - -	2	18
Manassas, - - - - - - - - - - - - - - - - - -	12	73
Sharpsburg, - - - - - - - - - - - - - - - - -	9	48
Total,	45	261

List of Killed and Wounded of the 18th Ga., in the different Engagements of the Campaign, furnished by order of Col. Wofford.

SEVEN PINES.

Co. H.—Wounded—A. J. Nallay, John Ward.

Co. K.—Wounded—G. M. Scott, J. H. Carroll. Total wounded, 4.

GAINES' FARM.

Co. A—J. E. Jackson, S. D. Price, Wm. Stansel.

Wounded—H. Gragg, S. M. Owens, J. M. Abney, A. G. Dempsy, G. W. Grisham, J. J. Mims, A. Nichols, F. M. Summers, J. W. Smith, W. J. Stanley, W. A. Steele, J. R. Thacker, W. J. Tanner.

Co. B.—Killed—J. B. Watkins.

Wounded—1st Serg't S. P. Doss, J. W. Allman, Elihu Allman, E. W. Chandler, S. A. Hill, J. D. Hill, A. J. Hendry, W. J. Lester, H. Miller, W. J. Morgan, L. J. Richardson, O. P. Richardson, W. B. Stowers, Jas. Veal, J. A. Winborn.

Co. C.—Killed—1st Lieut. McCulloch, J. T. Appleby, Willis Auglin, C. Harwell, J. J. Moore, H. W. McElhannan, J. H. Thurmond. Wounded—2d Lieut. Silman, 1st Sergeant H. W. Bell, 3d Serg't E. M. Eustace, T. C. Bowles, W. G. Harris, B. B. Morgan, J. M. Orr, W. M. Potter, R. T. Rogers, J. M. White.

Co. D.—Killed —W. A. Murray.

Wounded.—A. Bailey, G. W. Deriso, J. M. Dancer, W. R. Dancer, C. Faircloth, G. W. Rhodes.

Co. E.—Killed—J. M. Smith. Wounded.—A. W. Putnam, W. O. Harris, Wm. Howk, J. Nave, F. M. Sampson.

Co. F.—Killed—C. J. Hibberts, Wm. Jackson, L. C. Smith.

Wounded.—A. J. Earp, J. C. Reynolds, J. D. Foster, W. Byers, F. Durham, G. Freeman, T. D. Hackett, J. M. Lumpkin, L. J. Nichcols, A. J. Reed, A. J. Sarter.

Co. G.—Wounded—B. Cantrell, S. W. Dixon, W. Holl, J. M. Morris.

Co. H.—Killed—J. B. Vaughan. Total killed, 17; wounded, 65.

MALVERN HILL.

Co. A—Killed—T. J. Bennett, A. S. Tanner. Wounded.—J. M. Tanner, R. E. Turner.

Co. B.—Wounded—Corp'l R. F. McDonald, W. H. Shaw.

Co. G.—Wounded—W. Morris. Total killed, 2; wounded, 5.

SECOND MANASSAS.

Co. A.—Killed—J. D. Mullens, J. N. Tinsley, J. R. Whitener.

Wounded—Capt. J. B. O'Neal, T. P. Brown, A. Durham, J. P. Durham, L. A. Hicks, W. H. Jackson, C. Priest, B. R. Whitfield, D. B. Whitfield.

Co. B.—Killed—G. M. Polson, E. Watkins.

Wounded.—J. W. Allman, J. Guinn, R. Hollingsworth, J. King, E. McDonald, J. T. Smith, J. R. S. Sowel, Wm. St. John, T. T. Thrasher.

Co. C.—Killed—Capt. Jarrett, Wm. Clanton, J. C. McElhannan, J. H. Miller, J. H. Oliver, R. A. Williamson.

Wounded.—J. R. Howard, J. A. Espry, J. R. Mitchell, T. H. Niblack, W. T. Thurmond, W. O. Wilson, J. N. Williamson.

Co. D.—Wounded—Lieut. E. R. Laws, Lieut. Rhodes, Corp'l A. Brown, Corp'l C. R. Penick, J. E. Higenbothan, Corp'l J. W. Reed, W. J. Hurst, J. Hayse, J. A. Knight, W. J. Pierce, James Rhodes, Henry Sapp, A. J. Taylor.

Co. E.—Killed—2d Lieut. E. S. Brown, 3d Corp'l M. S. Collins, J. J. Jarrett, John Kelley, T. J. Smith, E. M. Smith.

Wounded.—3d Serg't F. A. Weems, 5th Serg't B. J. Baughan, 1st Corp'l B. F. Sanders, H. A. Baughan, Sam Edlemon, J. S. Guyton, W. M. Pannel, R. H. Russeau.

Co. F.—Killed—J. W. Calvert, E. Mosteller.

Wounded.—Capt. J. C. Roper, Lieut. J. F. Harden, Serg't Dolphin, Corp'l J. D. Foster, Corp'l J. R. Boyce, J. M. Conn, J. W. Conn, W. J. Guest.

Co. G.—Corp'l D. M. Stradley. Total killed, 20; wounded, 54.

SHARPSBURG

Killed.—Sergeant Major A. McMurry.

Co. A.—Killed—M. L. Davenport, Wm. Davenport.

Wounded.—F. A. Boring, J. S. Mason, M. S. Mason, T. H. Northcut, T. M. Peters, T. J. Pyron, F. J. Robertson, J. D. Scott, J. W. Wheeler.

Co. B.—Killed—H. B. Windborn.

Wounded.—S. P. Doss, T. D. Guinn, Wm. McKee.

Co. C.—Wounded—3d Lieut. Calahan, F. M. Bates, J. Roberts.

Co. D.—Wounded—2d Lieut. J. H. Macon, 3d Lieut. W. G. Gilbert, Serg't S. H. Woodall, M. A. Adams, R. C. Clifton, A. Jones, J. Mitchell.

Co. E.—Wounded—3d Lieut. O. W. Putnam, W. Arnold, J. B. Brooks, J. W. Caldwell, A. Holcomb, A. J. Sowry.

Co. F.—Killed—L. B. Arnold, S. Brooks.

Wounded.—Lieut. A. F. Wooley, Serg't A. J. Earp, Serg't J. C.

Reynolds, Corp'l J. D. Foster, Corp'l S. Cantrell, Jas. Brock, D. S. Brandon, Jasper Culwell, Thos. Dawson, J. M. Lumpkin.

Co. G.—Wounded—A. L. Myers, Serg't G. W. Whitten.

Co. H.—Wounded—2d Lieut. John Grant, Corp'l W. H. Windsor, J. R. Morrill. Total killed, 6; wounded, 43.

Grand total killed, 45; wounded, 171.

NOTE.—In consequence of the exceedingly high price of paper, press-work, &c., I have been under the necessity of omitting the Roll, as furnished at length by the 18th Ga., for the present; but it will appear in a future edition.

I should have omitted the Roll of the 4th Texas also, but for the means furnished by officers of that Regiment, which enabled me to publish it in this edition.

List of Casualties of the 1st Texas Regiment, in the different Engagements of the Campaign, Ordered and Signed by Lieutenant Colonel P. A. Work, Commanding.

ELTHAM'S LANDING.

STAFF.—Wounded—Lieutenant Colonel Black—since died.

Co. A.—Killed—J. Etly.

Wounded.—Lieut. W. W. Lany, P. Higgins, H. Hennant, P. Setger, P. Mahon, G. Rogers.

Co. C.—Killed—Capt. H. Decatur.

Wounded.—P. Donley, J. Trotter.

Co. D.—Killed—C. F. Covy.

Wounded.—J. McDowel, J. W. Smith.

Co. F.—Wounded—James Bush.

Co. H.—Killed—P. W. Mills.

Wounded.—J. B. Carnwell, D. J. Hill, W. A. Honey, John Spencer, H. L. Martin, T. Foster.

Co. L.—Killed—Jas. Brown, C. Schodt.

Wounded.—Smith Sims, F. Nichols, J. Coffee. Total killed, 6; wounded, 22.

SEVEN PINES.

Co. C.—Wounded—H. Smith.

Co. E.—Killed—D. D. Davis. Wounded.—J. C. R. Malay.

Co. K.—Wounded—Barney McNilly.

Co. L.—Wounded—J. W. Brown, W. A. Shelton. Total killed, 1; wounded, 5.

GAINES' FARM.

STAFF.—Wounded—Colonel Rainey.

Co. A.—Wounded—Serg't Jno. R. Crawford, J. R. Wright, M. Jacobi.

Co. B.—Killed—Lieut. W. B. Shotwell, Serg't J. Crobert.

Wounded.—Corp'l J. M. Canterbury, F. M. Carr, M. A. Dunnam, W. McDonald, W. O. Pankey.

Co. C.—Wounded—Serg't M. J. Giles, Serg't O. G. Armstrong, James Wriun.

Co. D.—Wounded—A. Dennis, M. W. Murry, D. P. Simms.

Co. E.—Killed—Sergeant J. A. Samson.

Wounded.—Serg't J. W. Smith, W. C. Scott, Wm. Campbell.

Co. F.—Killed—W. A. Allen, Jno Ambrose, ______. Hollaman, D. D. McMillen.

Wounded.—Lieut. Henry Snow, L. S. Jones, Robt. Hooker, H. Harville, Thos. Eskridge, Chas. Hicks.

Co. G.—Wounded—Lieut. E. S. Jamison, Charles Woodhouse, R. C. McKnight.

Co. H.—Killed—P. B. Hanks, Levil Lee, J. M. Doherty, J. J. Foster. Wounded.—George Hollingsworth, F. M. Embry, J. S. Rudd, A. J. Fry.

Co. I.—Killed—W. G. Morris, L. W. Maning, O. H. Boykin.

Wounded.—Lieut. J. L. Sheridan, Lieut. W. B. Wall, Sergeant J. H. Foster, C. O. Wagnon, D. B. Bush, E. B. Andrews, D. H. Beavers, Jno. De Long, L. J. Fitts, J. O. Foster, W. J. L. Harris, Robert Montgomery, A. Montgomery, S. H. Oliphant, E. Daurty.

Co. K.—Killed—Captain B. F. Benton, Corp'l W. J. Chambers, L. J. Mays, J. W. Coe.

Wounded.—Serg't Thos. A. Artry, W. J. Curton, W. W. Gray, G. W. Menefee, A. J. Proseler, H. C. Powell, Lieut. Jas. Waterhouse.

Co. L.—Killed—Corp'l J. L. Townsend, J. Panpart.

Wounded.—James Nagle, S. D. Smith, H. Shulty, G. Hawkins, R. Jacoolf. Total killed, 20; wounded, 58.

MALVERN HILL.

Co. B.—Killed—J. E. McClannahan, T. McNaully, Z. Williams, J. T. Dortch.

Wounded.—R. Love, M. G. Lewis, J. W. Gamer, A. Trinkman.

Co. C.—Wounded—Serg't J. W. Trotter, T. J. Calhoun, G. W. McNew, H.F.M. Freeman.

Co. E.—Wounded— J. K. Norwood.

Co. F.—Killed— Jacob Benidict.

Wounded.—E. T. Steadman.

Co. I.—Wounded— J. M. Hanks, D. N. McLane, F. M. Williams, G. M. Weatherhead.

Co. K.—Killed—Jas. Lane. Wounded—Corp'l C. W. Finley, C. F. McMahan.

Co. L.—Wounded—Capt. W. A. Bedell, Corp'l R. S. Robinson. Total killed, 6; wounded, 18.

SECOND MANASSAS.

STAFF.—Killed—Sergeant-Major A. H. Morton.

Wounded.—Adjutant A. D. Forsyth.

Co. A.—Wounded— Hugh Dougherty, E. P. Derrick.

Co. B.—Wounded— J. P. Stevens.

Co. C.—Killed—Edward Ashley, W. H. Vinson.

Co. D.—Wounded—A. Miles.

Co. E.—Killed—Corp'l R. B. Stephens, D. M. Walker.

Wounded.—Serg't Thos. Steel, J. W. Webb.

Co. F.—Killed—Serg't A. M. West.

Wounded.— J. W. Pool, George Cryer.

Co. G.—Wounded—Corp'l Scin Black.

Co. H.—Killed— J. M. Steincipher, T. R. Oldham.

Wounded.—T. E. Lides, G. A. Graham, J. C. Hollingsworth, W. N. Haynes.

Co. I.—Killed— P. F. Renfro.

Wounded.— J. M. Corley.

Co. L.—Wounded—Lieut. J. M. Baldwin, Serg't W. P. Randall, E. C. McCorquodall.

Co. M.—Killed—Willis T. Redden. Total killed, 10; wounded, 18.

SHARPSBURG.

STAFF.—Killed— Major Matt. Dale.

Wounded— Adjutant W. Shropshire.

Co. A. Wounded.—Capt. G.T. Todd, Serg't J. C. Hill, C. D.

Jones, B. R. Lane, G. W. Armstrong, G. E. Brewer, Green Baker, E. P. Demick, C. J. Epperson, W. F. McLindon, J. R. Malone, W. Whitaker.

Co. B— Killed— M. B. Anderson, S. G. McGee.

Wounded— Lieut. W. B. Shotwell, Serg't L. W. Butler, G. W. Barefield, J. Victory, B. L. Bolling, R. R. Choote, G. H. Johnson, W. O. Pankey, S. J. Woodward.

Co. C.—Killed—Lieut. L. F. Hoffman.

Wounded— G. Gage, C. Watson, W. S. Stamper, G. McMannus.

Co. D.—Killed—E. B. Brown, W. C. Jackson, A. P. Thenell, W. R. Jackson.

Wounded—D. W. Bartlett, J. D. Dickson, J. P. Dunklin, H. C. McCoy, J. F. Miles, E. C. Powell, L. W. Thomas, J. P. Wood, W. A. T. Oliver.

Co. E. —Killed—Corp'l H. E. Perry, Lieut. C. Perry.

Wounded— Lieut. B. W. Webb, Charles Woodson, Serg't J. W. Smith, Serg't W. S. Brazill, J. D. Campbell, R. S. Clark, C. W. Fields, M. Gillett, G. F. Heard, J. H. Hendricks, R. J. Marshall, E. C. Perry, S. F. Perry, Y. W. Willingham, S. G. Watson.

Co. F.—Killed— Lieut. J. P. Runnels, O. Phelps.

Wounded—Capt. S. A. Wilson, Serg't J. E. Perryman, Serg't S. G. Hanks, Wm. Holmes, S. Engleking, Wm. Scott.

Co. G.—Killed—B. A. Hallum, C. K. McFarland, Smith Botterms, M. M. Files, R. Butler, A. J. Posey, A. M. Matthews.

Wounded.— Lieut. E. S. Jamison, J. M. Corder, T. J. Watts, T. J. Rose, M. J. Ashley, Z. A. Caully, James Ward, M. Knox, Jas. Matthews, S. D. Blackshere.

Co. H.—Killed—A. A. Terson, W. Hollingsworth, J. G. Teppens.

Wounded.— J. H. Marshall, J. A. Counts, G. W. Culpepper, C. S. Bolton, E. F. Ezell, L. L. Evans, J. R. Jones, W. G. Hickman, J. M. Harrington, A. C. Strother, W. L. Williams, J. C. Hollingsworth, J. C. King.

Co. I.— Killed— S. J. Cook, L. J. Fitts, W. M. Bayrue, A. A. Cangleton, D. H. Hale, F. M. Box.

Wounded.— Capt. R. W. Cotton, Serg't R. O. Mitchell, Serg't A. A. Aldrich, Corp'l W. D. Pritchard, W. A. Homes, J. Rudicil, H.C. Patrick, M. Youngblood, J.S. Harwell, M. Reeves, T.A. Boone,

M. M. Berryman, J. A. Sheridan.

Co. K—Killed—Lieut. James Waterhouse, Lieut. S. F. Patton, J. M. Hail.

Wounded.—Capt. J. M. Massey, H. E. Mosley, O. C. Hanks, W. W. Gray, S. M. Dury, J. C. Nobb, E. G. Miller, W. O. Quinn, J. M. Ruddle.

Co. L.—Killed—Lieut. J. C. S. Thomson, J. Frank.

Wounded.—Capt. W. A. Bedell, Serg't S. A. Carpenter, Corp'l W. Zimmer, R. Jacobef, J. Hanson, J. T. Blessing, H. Cohen, P. Gillis, W. Hoskins, A. Jones, C. B. Halleck, C. H. Kingsley, J. Rouke, F. Schwarting, J. M. Smith, H. Schultz, J. Albrook, W. Leach, James Nagle, W. Young, —— Welch.

Co. M.—Killed—Serg't S. D. Roach, T. J. Bowman, J. Boon, W. L. Sting.

Wounded.—Capt. H. Ballenger, Lieut. T. P. Samford, J. E. Stewart, J. T. Evans, A. Walters, James Bass, E. Pope, O. Mc Bride, R. O. Bennett, James Day, Wm. Townes, E. B. Earnes, W. C. Earnes, C. Murry, A. Carlton, M. A. Dunnan, John Lancaster, H. Sweet. Number killed, 38; wounded, 136; missing 9.

Aggregate of men in battle on the 17th of August, - - 226
" " " uninjured, - - - - - - - - - - - - - - 43
" " " killed in all the battles, - - - - - - 74
" " " wounded " " " - - - - - - - - - 257

List of Casualties in the 5th Texas Regiment in the different engagements of the Campaign, as furnished by order of Colonel J. B. Robertson.

GAINES' FARM.

FIELD AND STAFF.—Wounded—Colonel J. B. Robertson, Color-Sergeant, G. Onderdonk.

Co. A.—Killed—Lieut. J. A. Clute, George Delesdenier.

Wounded—J. Bailey, J. Robertson.

Co. B.—Killed—J. R. Gaines.

Wounded—P. Murphy, J. Carroll, E. Besch, John O'Neil, John Smith, J. R. Ratigan, A. H. Coster, C. Lynch, Jacob Hohn.

Co. C.—Killed—W. K. Williams.

Wounded.—M. T. Welsh, S. L. Wallace, E. H. Bristor, S. W. Iroin, Z. Y. Dezell.

Co. D.—Killed—A. D. Alston.

Wounded.—George Grant.

Co. E.—Killed—R. W. Pearson, Moses Cooper, R. M. Ringgold.

Wounded.—Lt. T. Nash. Serg't Norwood B. Smith, T. Coffield, J. T. Dulaney, B. Eldridge, Jesse Lott, W. C. McCallister, P. Meadows, D. D. Patrick, S. Watson, D. Batte.

Co. F.—Killed—W. S. Hall, G. A. Woods.

Wounded.—J. V. Sloan, J. C. Ross, B. C. Brashear, E. R. Moody, E. T. Tucker, G. W. Knapp.

Co. G.—Killed—J. J. Lawrence, Charles Ward.

Wounded.—T. E. Bracken, D. H. Carson, W. V. L. Cooper, J. A. Hoffman, J. H. Hawkins, C. J. Jackson, D. H. Mays, R. Nance, J. Pool, J. Webb, Lieut. John Smith.

Co. &.—Wounded—H. Rose, T. Fitzgerald.

Co. I.—Wounded—Capt. Clay, W. Waters, L. Wells, J. Hallum, R. J. Haynes.

Co. K.—J. T. Baker, R. B. Collins, J. P. Smith, J. W. Peoples, L. W. Waldrop. Total killed, 12; wounded, 62.

MALVERN HILL.

Co. B.—Killed—F. Keopke.

Co. D.—Wounded—Thomas Scott, H. R. Brown.

Co. E.—Killed—Joseph Sherman.

Wounded.—D. Batte, James Farmer.

Co. F.—Wounded—J. C. Tutt, John Muldoon, James Johnston.

Co. G.—Killed—S. W. Sharp.

Wounded.—R. Griffin.

Co. I.—Wounded—J. T. Cross. Total killed, 3; wounded, 9.

SECOND MANASSAS.

FIELD AND STAFF.—Killed—Lieut. Col. J. C. Upton.

Wounded.—Col. J. B. Robertson, Capt. Bryant, Acting Major; Lieut. C. Wood, Acting Adjutant.

Co. A.—Wounded—1st St. E. A. Nobles, St. McMurtry, C'l B. O. Simpson, Corp'l J. H. Bell, John Heff, J. R. Patton, S. Bailey, D. W. Walker, J. B. Young, A. Angel, O. D. Mallory, John Delesdenier, William Kelley, John Massenburg, S. D. Hewes, R. Campbell, C. B. Gardner, James Stanger, John Morris, John Liverton

Wolf, John Garrison, T. W. Fitzgerald.

Co. B—Wounded—Capt. J. D. Roberdeau, Lieut. Benjamin Baker, J.B. Wall, Corp'l J. H. Whitehead, Corp'l J. S. Miller, Corp'l W. Pinchback, Corp'l A. V. L. Carter, E. Besche, J. S. Bruce, P. Collins, J. Currigan, M. Doggett, M. Flannigan, R. I. Humphrey, J. W. Johnston, W. F. Nelms, W. T. Snell, W. Sheppard, John Smith, John Freanor, J. P. Umborgn, P. Woodhouse, P. Lundy.

Co. C.—Wounded—Capt. J. J. McBride, Lieut. J. E. Anderson, Lieut. J. Shew, Serg't J. F. Borden, Serg't J. C. Cox, Corp'l J. T. Atkinson, J. W. Anderson, R. Allen, R. W. Bristoe, H. B. Dunn, H. P. Driscol, J. E. Ellis, J. B. Farris, J. E. Lacy, J. A. Green, B.D. Nunnery, T.R. Pistole, P. G. Philips, J.G. Ross, J.W. Wallace.

Co. D.—Wounded—1st Serg't D. P. Caldwell, Serg't W. B. Campbell, Serg't I. M. Robinson, Serg't O. M. Hinson, Corp'l R. A. Brankey, Corp'l Leroy Mitchell, Copr'l W. O. Smith, B. P. Estell, W. F. Spiney, S. T. Ross, J. C. Burton, J. P. Harris, W. P. Powell, W. M. Nelms, M.A. Lampkin, K. J. Page, F. C. Hume, A. F. Golden, M. Douglass, W. A. Keenan, J.W. Cotton, S. B. Randall, R. Stooton, R. Leals, R. H. Griffin, F. Lochman, W. Coleman, J. C. Hill.

Killed—W. D. Wynne, Lewis Moss.

Co. E.–Killed–1st Serg't V. E. Petty, C. Moncreiff, N.N. Mullins.

Wounded—Capt. T. Baber, Lieut. Thomas Nash, F. M. Williamson, Serg't J. C. Buster, Corp'l J. J. Smith, Corp'l W. M. Gray, I. M. Cortwell, S.H. Dean, F. Eldridge, M.M. Felder, F. Fanquhar, J. Gee, L. Gee, J. R. Goodwin, J. H. Hutcheson, L. L. Holliday, B. T. Kavenaugh, J. M. Lott, J. Lockett, B. M. McPherson, P. H. Mullins, B.O. Patrick, M. Marshall, J. A. Randall, William Lensabough, J. W. Span, B.T. Toland, George B. Williams, J. Wallace, Thomas Witherby.

Co. F.—Killed—Corp'l H. B. Johnson, A. G. Dugat.

Wounded—Lieut Williams, Serg't G. W. Starns, Serg't J. M. Dillon, Serg't J.F. Church, Corp'l C. McCally, J.K. Bryan, E.R. Bouch, T. J. Chaison, H. Griffith, J. Little, C. J. Fortesene, P. J. Buxton, P. Mallory, R. Sweany, J. W. Pemberton, J. C. Noble, F. Whittington, E. D. McCarty, Jas. Booth, R. H. Leonard, H. C. Spencer, W. A. Fletcher.

Co. G.—Killed—F. M. Bolinger, C. G. Adams, R. A. Roy, Y. B. Roy.

Wounded.—Serg't W. H. Tarver, J. Waller, A. J. Sperrill, C. Shelton, J. M. Stidham, Ed. Williams, J. E. Bryant, D. R. Beal, L. W. Caldwell, M. G. Garrett, G. T. Lony, R. B. Mays, E. McDonald, E. Pool, S. Richardson, S. W. Walker, H. H. Wroe, J. Moore.

Co. H.—Killed— _____. Baines, _____. Parnell, _____. Hall.

Wounded.—Captain J. S. Cleveland, Lieut. Robertson, Lieutenant Stanley, Lieut. Spratt, Serg't Woodhace, Serg't Ross, Serg't Osborne, Corp'l House, Corp'l Gorce, _____. Bass, _____. Barber, _____ Bell, _____ Curry, _____ Hemphill, _____ Korgin, _____ Lee, _____ Walters, _____ Shields, _____ Freeman, B. Grace, J. W. Grace, _____ Stone, _____ Stevenson.

Co. I. —Wounded—Lieut. B. J. Franklin, Lieut. C. A. Graham, 1st Serg't J. P. Drake, Corp'l W. D. Morgan, Corporal E. H. McKnight, D. B. Allen, W. G. Baldwin, W. R. Barlow, T. Bates, F. Bettiss, J. W. Dallis, S. Driscoe, J. Dick, R. Flemming, T. D. Harris, W. Haley, W. R. McRee, W. V. Royston, D. H. Robertson, J. Short, E. F. Spence, W. F. Thomas, C. D. Leonard, Wm. Short.

Co. K—Killed—Lieut. B. W. Henry.

Wounded.—Capt. John Turner, Lieut. Hubert, Lieut. Hurt, Serg't Joe Turner, Serg't McKinnon, Serg't Meece, Corp'l Dates, Corp'l Green, Corp'l Smith, _____ Brarwell, F. Baker, A. Dunn, L. B. Dorch, A. J. Easterling, J. P. Kale, J. T. McKee, J. M. Bowen, J. Rone, D. A. Rowe, Wiley Stewart, W. J. Ward, T. C. Matthews, W. J. McCoy. Total killed, 15; wounded, 240.

FREEMAN'S FORD.

FIELD OFFICERS—Wounded—Major Whaley; died next day.

Co. B.—Wounded—F. Matthias, F. R. Harris, D. Horley, T. Roberts.

Co. C.—Wounded—John Haley.

Co. H.—Wounded—L. B. Hicks.

Co. I.—Wounded—J. McRee.

Co. K.—Wounded—J. Wilson, John Beard.

Total wounded, 10.

SHARPSBURG, MD.

Co. A.—Wounded—D. Dyer, Frank Kosse, A. Wolfe, E. Gregory, N. Stewart.

Co. B.—Wounded—A. H. Baker, W. J. Darden, D. M. McNillis,

J. Kolbow, John Moviessey, W. Hoffman, W. Cherry, W. Rhodes.

Co. C.—Wounded—Lieut. New, Lieut. Boyd, Serg't Stewart, Serg't Cox, Corporal Shilling, J. W. Neighbors, E. M. Dizzell, R. Turner, B. Nunnery, J. M. Copeland, Z. Y. Dizzell.

Co. D.—Killed—S. Putle, T. J. Edwards.

Wounded—F. M. Ridgeway, P. G. Williamson, J. W. Ewing, J. Gilbert, A. Murry.

Co. E.—Killed—R. Toland, J. Hunt.

Wounded—H. Allen, Thomas Mullins, John Henderson, William Legrand, Lieutenant Norwood, F. M. Williamson, Thomas Maddox.

Co. F.—Wounded—Lieut. Strickland, T. Taylor, H. Taylor, M. H. Johnson, P. Buxton, Charles McCally, T. McCall, Thomas Spencer.

Co. G—Wounded—T. Walker, Jas. Pool, J. A. Jolley, J. Small, H. Sharp, L. Miller, J. Monroe, W. Smith, Lieutenant Smith.

Co. H.—Killed—William House.

Wounded.—D. McDonald, J. Shields, Wm. Wood, J. Hemphill, N. McCormick, M. M. Templeman, M. Ross, D. G. Martin.

Co. I.—Wounded.—Lieut. Drake, D. Morgan, Serg't Park, G. Newman, R. Howl, John Howl, B. Baker, Ed. Dunn.

Co. K.—Wounded—Lieutenant Alexander, R. B. Collins, Joe Turner, W. D. C. Henly, H. C. Hirams, B. C. Hurbert, W. B. Sandal, W. Walker, J. W. Stevens. Total killed, 5; wounded, 78.

Grand total killed, 35; wounded, 399

HEADQUARTERS 4TH TEXAS REGIMENT,
October 7th, 1862.

Orderly Sergeants will make out for Chaplain N. A. Davis, complete Muster Rolls of their Companies, showing the different engagements, in which each man has participated.

By order of

LIEUT. COL. B. F. CARTER,
Commanding Reg't.

F. L. PRICE, Adjutant.

KEY TO THE TABLE.—"p," present—"a," absent with leave—"*a," absent without leave—"s," sick—"w," wounded—"k," killed on the field—"d," died—"*d," discharged—"m," missing—"r," recruit. The letter "r" is omitted in some of the lists—but the blank will show them to be recruits. Those noted "a," and some of them several times, were usually absent from disability, either from wounds or were on detached service. [109]

MUSTER ROLL OF THE FOURTH REG'T TEXAS VOLS.

NAMES.	ELTHAM'S LANDING.	SEVEN PINES.	GAINES' FARM.	MALVERN HILL.	FREEMAN'S FORD	MANASSAS, 1862.	BOONSBORO GAP, MD.	SHARPSBURG, MD.	REMARKS.
Col. J. B. Hood, - - - - - - -	p	p	p	p	p	p	p	p	Pro'd Brig. Gen. Mar. 3d, '62. " Maj. Gen. October, 1862.
Lt. Col. John Marshall, - - - -	p	p	k						" Col. March 3d, 1862.
Maj B. Warwick,- - - - - - - -	p	p	w						" Lt. Col. March 3d, '62.
Capt. J. C. G. Key, - - - - - -	a	p	w	a			p	p	" Maj. March 3d, Col. July 7th, 1862.
Capt. B. F. Carter, - - - - - -	p	p	s	s	p	p	p	p	" Lieut. Col. July 7th, '62.
Capt. W. P. Townsend,- - - - -	p	p	p	p	p	w	a	a	" Major July 7th, 1862.
Capt. T. Owen, - - - - - - - -	p	p	w						Died August 3d, 1862.
Capt. Wade, - - - - - - - - - -			p						
Adj't Bassett, - - - - - - - - -	p	p	p	p	p	p	p	p	Captain Co. G, June 28,'62.
CO. A.									
Capt. J. C. G. Key, - - - - - -	a	p	w	a	a	a	p	p	
1st Lt. S. H. Darden, - - - - -	p	p	p	p	p	p	p	p	Prom'd Capt. 20th May, '62.
2d " A. J. McKean, - - - - -	p	p	p	p	a	a	p	w	Pro'd 1st Lt. 20th May '62.
2d " jr. R. M. Boman, - - - -	p	p	s	s	p	p	s	s	Prom'd May 20, 1862.
1st Serg't H. Marchant,- - - - -	p	p	s	s		s	p	p	Elec'd 2d Lt. 20th May, '62.
2d " A. P. Brown, - - - -	p	p	w	s	a				
3d " W. W. Brown, - - - -	a	p	p	p	a	p	p	p	Resigned May 29th, 1862.
4th " G. E. Lynch, - - - -	p	p	s	s	p	w	s	s	App'd 1st Serg't May 29, '62.
5th " T. J. Thomas, - - - -	p	p	p	p	p	w	s	d	App'd 2d " July 30th, '62.
1st C'l R. Thomas, - - - - - -	p	p	s	s	s	p	s	s	App'd 5th " " " "
2d " A. D. Chadoin,- - - - -	p	p	s	s	s	p	s	s	
3d " D. M. Martindale - - - -	p	p	s	s	p	p	p	w	App'd 3d Srg't 29th May, '62.
4th " A. N. Poteat, - - - - -	p	p	s	s	p	p	p	w	

Allis, M. H.,	a	a	a	a	a	a	a	a	On detached service.
Adams, John,	r	p	w	s	d				
Baker, S. H.,	r	s	s	s	s	s	s	s	
Bostwick, R. F.,	r	s	s	s	s	s	s	s	Discharged Sept. 15th, 1862.
Burton, A. J.,	r	p	k						
Chadoin, B. P.,	p	p	s	s	p	p	p	w	Missing since Sept. 17th, '62.
Cavett, W. C.,	r	p	p	p	p	p	p	p	
Caldwell, J. M.,	r	p	p	p	p	p	p	p	
Clark, John,	r	s	s	s	p	p	s	s	
Cox, L. C.,	r	s	s	s	d				
Deel, John,	p	p	w	s	s	s	s	s	
Deel, Pete,	p	p	p	p	a	a	a	s	
Doyle, R. D.,	r	s	s	s	d				
Doyle, M. C.,	p	s	s	s	s	s	p	p	
Dixon, J. T.,	p	s	p	p	s	s	p	p	
Davis, Frank,	p	p	p	p	p	p	p	w	
Derrington, R. G.,	r	p	p	p	p	p	p	p	
Drennan, Joe,	r	s	p	p	s	s	p	s	
Drennan, S. A.,	r	s	s	s	s	s	p	p	
Eldridge, Wesley,	p	p	w	s	s	s	s	s	Leg amputated 28th June.
Francis, E. D.,	p	p	p	p	p	w	s	s	Color-Sergeant.
Francis, W. C.,	p	s	p	p	s	s	s	s	
Fields, John,	p	s	p	p	s	a	a	a	
Finlay, Frank,	p	p	p	p	s	s	s	s	
Futch, G. A.	s	p	s	s	s	s	p	w	
Futch, John,	s	s	s	s	a	a	a	a	
Freestone, B. J.,	s	s	s	s	d				
Fletcher, George,	s	s	s	s	s	s	s	s	
Garth, V. A.,	p	p	p	p	p	p	p	w	App'd 4th Serg't May 29th,
Gunn, Henry,	p	p	p	p	p	p	p	p	1862.
Goldsticker, J. A.,	s	s	s	s	s	a	a	a	
Gross, P. H.,	p	p	p	p	p	p	p	w	
Grundy, J. H.,	r	p	s	s	p	a	a	a	
Haggerty, J. M.,	a	p	a	a	a	p	*d		
Haggerty, John,	a	p	s	s	p	p	p	p	
Harrison, Robt.,	r	s	s	s	s	s	s	s	
Hines, Joe,	r	s	s	s	*d				
Hopkins, J. M.,	r	s	p	p	p	w	s	s	
Hite, Walter,	p	p	a	a	p	s	a	a	
Hilliard, Alex.,	r	p	w	s	s	s	s	s	
Hall, Wm. A.,	p	p	p	p	p	p	p	w	
Holcomb,______,	r	p	p	p	p	s	s	s	
Jones, J. S.,	p	p	p	p	s	s	a	a	
Jones, R. H.	p	p	s	s					Transfer'd to Co. D, August
Johnson, Wm.,	p	p	s	s	s	p	s	s	15, 1862.
Key, Henry,	r	p	s	s	s	s	p	s	
Key, John,	r	p	w	s	s	s	s	s	
King, Henry,	p	p	a	a	a	a	*d		Detached service.
Lyle, Fount,	p	p	w	d					
Langford, O. H.,	a	a	p	p	s	s	p	w	Taken prisoner 17th September,
Lockridge, R. B.,	p	p	w	s	s	a	a	a	1862.
Munford, T. H.,	a	s	s	s	p	p	s	s	
Melhorn, A. B.,	p	p	w	d					
Monty, C.,			w						
Mooney, Wm. D.,	p	s	p	p	p	p	p	p	
Miley, Daniel,	s	s	s	s	d				
Murphy, Jemy,	p	p	w	w	s	s	s	s	
McDonold, Dan,	p	p	w	s	s	s	s	s	
McCarty, A. J.,	p	p	w	p	p	p	a	p	
Martin, A. J.,	r	s	p	p	p	p	p	p	
Monce, Chas.,	r	s	w	s	s	s	s	s	
Nations, Robt.,	r	p	s	s	p	p	p	s	
Nations, F. M.,	r	p	s	s	p	p	p	w	Missing since Sept. 17, '62
Owens, G. H.,	p	p	s	s	p	p	p	p	
Pangle, H. L.,	r	s	s	s	s	s	s	s	
Pitman, Wm. H.,	r	s	s	s	p	p	s	s	
Simmons, S.,	r	s	s	s	s	s	s	s	

Name									Remarks
Simpson, Joe,	s	s	s	s	p	p	s	s	
Strong, N. A.,	p	p	s	s	p	p	p	w	App'd corp'l Aug. 15th, '62
Stanfield, T. B.,	s	s	p	p	p	w	s	s	
Stanfield, W. H.,	p	p	w	s	s	s	s	s	
Stanfield, A. M.,	p	p	s	p	p	p	p	w	Taken prisoner Sept. 17, '62
Scanlan, E. R.,	r	s	p	p	p	p	p	w	
Stringfield, J. M.,	p	p	p	p	p	p	p	p	
Stamps, P. R.,	p	p	p	p	a	a	a	a	
Sandifer, John,	p	s	p	p	p	p	p	p	
Stevens, Geo.,	r	s	s	s	s	s	s	s	
Scheidle, C.,	r	s	s	s	d				
Surrett, J. C.,			w						
Thompson, J. E.,	a	a	s	s	p	p	s	s	
Thompson, Perry,	p	s	s	s	s	a	a	a	
Terrill, B. S.,	p	p	s	s	p	p	p	w	
Tebbs, A. S.,	r	s	s	s	s	s	s	s	
Vann, Thos.,	a	s	p	p	p	w	s	s	
Vann, Quint,	r	s	s	s	p	w	s	s	
Watkins, J.,	p	p	p	p	p	s	p	a	
Walker, P. H.,	p	p	s	s	p	p	p	w	
Walker, Wm. B.,	p	p	s	p	p	p	p	p	
Walker, E. R.,	s	s	s	s	p	w	s	s	
Woods, J. A.,	r	p	w	s	s	s	s	*d	
Wallace, T. S.,	p	p	p	p	p	p	p	p	Taken prisoner Sept. 17, '62.
Demitt, James,	*d								August 30th, 1861.
Campbe ll, Jessie,	*d								November 1st, 1861.
Kerr, George,	*d								" " "
Happle, James,	*d								" " "
Kelly, Peter,	*d								" " "
Mason, J. S.,	*d								July, 1862.
McLarin, J. H.,	*d								September, 1861.
McCatheron,______,	*d								November, "
McLaine, Dan,	*d								December, "
McEachem, L. E.,	*d								" "
O'Brien, Henry,	*d								June, 1862.
Rogers, John,	*d								December, "
Sterfell, Henry,	*d								October, "
Ward, Martin,	*d								November, 1861.
McAllister,_____,	a	a	a	s	a	a	a	a	
Alford, Julius,	d								October, "
Brown, L. M.,	d								December, "
Harrison,_____,	d								" "
Hardeman, T. M.,	d								August, "
Jones, Allen,	d								March, 1862.
Jones, S.,	d								November, 1861.
Minter, Frank,	d								" "
Michel, S.,	d								March, 1862.
Mooney, James,	d								November, 1861.
Landsdown, J. J.,	d								" "
Stanfield, E. C.	d								" "
Stiffler, Henry,	d								Drowned August, 1861.

CO. B.

Name									Remarks
Capt. B. F. Carter,	p	p	s	s	p	p	p	p	Prom'd Lt.-Col. July 10th, '62
1st Lt. W. C. Walsh,	p	s	w	a	a	a	a	a	Prom'd Capt. July 10th, '62.
2nd " J. T. McLaurin	p	a	p	p	p	p	p	w	Prom'd 1st. Lt. July 10th, '62.
3d " R. J. Lambert,	a	p	w						Died July 5th, 1862.
1st Serg't F. L. Price,	p	p	p	p	p	p	p	p	Prom'd Adj't. July 24th, '62.
2d " O. Flusser,	p	p	p	p	p	p	p	m	
3d St. C. W. McAnnelly	p	p	p	p	a	w			Died of Wounds.
4th St. T. W. Masterson	p	p	p	p	p	p	p	a	Prom'd 3d Lt. Aug. 15th, '62.
5th St. J. T. Price,	a	p	w	p	p	p	a	a	Prom'd 2d Lt. Aug. 15th, '62.
1st C'l N. Fawcitt,	p	p	w	a	p	k			
2d " M. T. Norris,	p	p	p	p	p	p	p	p	
3d " S. H. Burnham,	a	a	a	a	p	w			Died Sept. 22d, 1862.
4th " R. H. Clements,	p	p	p	p	a	a	a	a	

Adam, A. M., - - - - - - - - - -	a	a	a	a					Discharged July 11th, 1862.
Black, L., - - - - - - - - -	s	s	s	s	s	s	s	s	
Blakey, H. G., - - - - - - - - -	p	p	s	s	s	s	p	k	
Bonner, J. O., - - - - - - - - -	p	s	s	s	p	p	s	s	
Bonner, J. W., - - - - - - - - -	p	s	s	s	s	s	s	s	
Burdett, T. P., - - - - - - - - -	p	p	p	p	a	a	a	a	
Burditt, W. B., - - - - - - - - -	p	s	s	s	p	p	p	w	
Burnham, F. M., - - - - - - - -	p	p	p	p	p	p	p	a	
Burke, J., - - - - - - - - -	p	p	p	p	p	p	p	p	
Calhoun, W. C.,- - - - - - - - -	p	p	s	s	p	w			
Campbell, A. G., - - - - - - - -		p	s	s	p	w			
Carpenter, W. G., - - - - - - - -	p	p	a	a	a	a	a	a	
Cater, T. E., - - - - - - - - - -	p	p	p	p	p	p	p	p	
Caton, H. W., - - - - - - - - -	p	p	w						
Chandler, W. M., - - - - - - - -		p	s	s	p	w			
Colvin, G., - - - - - - - - - -	p	p	w	a	a	a	p	p	
Cooper, S., - - - - - - - - -		p	a	p	p	p	p	p	
Callahan, Jr., - - - - - - - - -				w					
Cook, J., - - - - - - - - -									Died May 27th, 1862.
Cox, L. B., - - - - - - - - -		a	a	a	p	p	p	a	
Crozier, G. H., - - - - - - - - -	p	p	w	a	a	a	a	a	
Davidge, R. A.,- - - - - - - - -	p	p	p	p	p	p	*a	p	
Dearing, J. H.,- - - - - - - - -	a	a	a	a	a	a	a	a	Regimental Teamster.
Dohme, C. A., - - - - - - - - -	p	p	a	a	a	a	a	a	
Dunkin, G. W., - - - - - - - - -		a	a	a	p	w			Died Sept. 22d, 1862.
Dunson, J. K. P., - - - - - - - -	p	s	s	s	s	s	s	s	
Durfee, A. A., - - - - - - - - -	p	a	a	a	a	a	a	a	
Falls, J., - - - - - - - - -	p	p	p	p	s	s	s	s	
Flanikin, W. J.,- - - - - - - - -	p	p	p	p	a	p	a	a	
Ford, W. F., - - - - - - - - - -	s	p	s	s	p	p	p	p	
Foster, W. K., - - - - - - - - -	a	p	a	a	a	a	a	a	
Freeman, C. L., - - - - - - - -	p	a	*a	p	p	p	p	p	
Giles, V. C., - - - - - - - - - -	p	p	p	a	p	p	a	a	
Glascock, T. A., - - - - - - - -	p	p	p	p	p	p	a	w	
Gould, U., - - - - - - - - -		p	a	a	p	p	p	w	
Griffith, J., - - - - - - - - -	p	p	w	a	p	p	p	w	
Grumbles, P. B., - - - - - - - -	p	a	p	p	p	p	a	a	
Hamby, R. W., - - - - - - - - -	p	p	p	p	p	p	a	a	
Hamilton, H.,- - - - - - - - - -		p	a						Died in July.
Hamilton, S. W., - - - - - - - -	p	p	p	a	a	a	a	a	
Haralson, C. L., - - - - - - - -	p	p	a	a	p	p	a	a	
Hathorn, A. J., - - - - - - - - -	p	p	*a	a	a	a	p	w	
Haynes, J. J., - - - - - - - - -	p	p	p	p	a	a	a	a	Litter bearer Aug. 20th, '6
Henderson, J. B., - - - - - - - -	p	a	a	a	a	a	a	a	
Hill, L. D., - - - - - - - - - -	a	a	a	a	a	a	a	a	On Detached service.
Heffler, G. W., - - - - - - - - -	p	a	p	p	a	a	p	w	
Holden, D. W., - - - - - - - - -	p	p	w	p	a	a	a	a	
Hopson, B. W., - - - - - - - - -	a	a	a	a	p	w	p	w	
Horton, W. H., - - - - - - - - -	p	p	w	a	p	p	p	a	
Howard, A. J., - - - - - - - - -	p	p	w	a	p	p	p	p	
Hughes, J. J., - - - - - - - - -		p	w	a	p	p	a	a	
Jones, A. C., - - - - - - - - -	p	s	s	s	s				Discharged Aug. –, 1862.
Jones, E., - - - - - - - - -	p	p	w	a	a	a	a	a	
Jones, J. E., - - - - - - - - - -	p	p	w	p	p	p	p	d	
Jones, J. K. P., - - - - - - - -	p	a	p	p	p	p	p	p	
Keller, W. A., - - - - - - - - -	p	p	w	a					Discharged Sept. –, 1862.
Keller, J. H.,- - - - - - - - - -		p	w	a	a	a	a	a	
Lessing, W. H.,- - - - - - - - -	p	p	p	p	a	a	p	w	
Lightfoot, W. H., - - - - - - - -	p	p	a	a	a	a	a	a	On detached service.
Luckett, A. T., - - - - - - - - -	a	p	p	p	p	p	a	a	
Maier, H., - - - - - - - - -	p	p	a	p	p	p	p	k	
Marckman, R., - - - - - - - - -	a	a	w	a	a	a	a	a	
Mayfield, N. W., - - - - - - - -	a	p	w	a	p	w	a	a	
McGehee, J. F., - - - - - - - -	p	p	a	a	p	w	p	w	
McMath, M. W., - - - - - - - - -	a	a	a	a	a	a	a	a	
McMullen, B., - - - - - - - - -	a	a	a	a	a	a	a	a	
McPhall, C. M.,- - - - - - - - -		s	p	p	p	p	*a	*a	Litter bearer.

Millican, E. B.,	p	p	p	a	p	p	a	a	
Morris, C. L.,	p	p	w	*a	p	a	a	a	
Mosely, S. E.,	p	p	w	p	p	p	s	p	
Moss, W. V.,	a	a	*a	*a	*a	*a	*a	*a	
Nenendorff, M.,	s	s	s	s					Discharged Aug.—, 1862.
Nichols, A. W.,	s	w	a	p	p	p	p	p	
Nichols, G. R.,	p	p	w	a	p	p			Colonel's orderly, Sept. 7th.
Piper, W. L.,	p	p	w	a	a	a	p	w	
Plagge, C.,	p	p	a	a					Discharged Sept.—, 1862.
Puckett, L.,	p	p	a	a	a	a	a	a	
Puryear, W. E.,	s	s	s	a	a	p	p	p	Deserted from the field.
Railey, J. D.,	*a	*a	w	a	*a	*a	*a	*a	
Rice, A. R.,	p	s	s	s	a	a	a	p	
Roberts, A. S.,	a	a	a	a	p	w			
Robertson, G. L.,	p	p	p	p	p	p	p	w	
Robertson, R. R.,		p	p	p	p	p	p	p	
Rose, G. W.,	p	p	s	s	a	a	a	a	Discharged.
Rushton, C. H.,	p	p	w	p	p	p	p	p	
Rust, R. S.,	p	p	p	p	p	p	p	w	
Schuler, J.,		p	w	a	a	a	a	a	
Simmons, E.,	p	p	p	a					Discharged.
Stanley, A. E.,		s	s	s	s	s	s	s	
Stein, I.,	p	a	p	p	p	w	a	a	
Stone, S. T. C.,	p	s	s	a	p	p	a	a	
Strohmer, F.,	p	s	s	a	a	a	a	a	
Summers, J. S.,	a	p	k						
Tannehill, W. J.,	a	a	a	a	a	a	a	a	
Tatum, J. M.,	p	s	p	a	p	p	p	p	
Taylor, S. O.,	s	s	s	s	*d				Discharged Aug. 16th, 1862.
Teague, S. P.,	p	p	a	a	p	p	*a	*a	
Thomas, J. H.,	p	s	p	p	p	k			
Thomas, M.,	p	p	w	a	a	a	a	a	
Todd, D. A.,	p	a	a	a	p	a	a	a	
Walker, G. W.,		s	s	s	s	a	a	a	
Wheeler, J. E.,		s	s	a	p	p	a	a	
White, J. A.,	p	a	a	a	a	a	a	a	
Whitesides, H.,	s	p	p	p	p	p	p	p	
Wilson, S. C.,	p	p	s	s	p	p	p	a	
Wright, P. A.,		p	a	a					Died July —, 1862.
Wright, J. A.,	a	a	a	a	a	a	a	a	Discharged Oct. 3d., 1862.
Buchner, C. A.,	a	a	a	a	a	a	a	a	Musician.
Horn, P.,	a	a	a	a	a	a	a	a	Musician.

CO. C.

Capt. W. P. Townsend	p	p	p	p	p	w			Promoted Major.
1st Lt. D. U. Barzeza,	p	p	p	p	p	w			" Captain 27th June.
2d " B. F. Turner,	p	p	s	s					Resigned.
3d " P. S. Wood,	p	p	w						Died from wounds.
1st Serg't J. P. Grizzle,	p	p	p	p	p	p	p	p	Prom'd Lieut. 27th June, '62.
2d " H. W. Davis,	p	p	w						
3d " J. C. Roberts,	s	s	w						
4th " J. J. Galloway,	p	p	w		p	w			
5th " J. H. Simmons,	p	p	w						
1st C'l A. P. Streetman	p	p	k						
2d C'l M. Livingston	p	s	s	s	p	p	p	p	Prom'd Lieut. 27th June, '62.
3d " J. W. M. P. Hill,	p	s	w						
4th " J. O. Adams,	p	p	k						
Adam, J. M.,	p	p	p	p	s	p	p	a	
Acruse, P.	p	p	s	s	s	s	s	s	
Alexander, J.,	s	s	s	s	p	p	p	w	
Andrews, A.,									Ambulance driver.
Barton, J.,	p	s	s	s	p	p	p	w	
Barton, L.,	p	s	s	s	p	p	p	w	
Barton, F.,	p	p	w						

Beavers, T. B.,	p	p	w						
Beavers, M.,	p	s	s	p	s	s	a	a	
Boyd, J. B.,			w						
Barzeża, P. J.,						p			Agent Texas Depot
Burns, J.,	s	p	s	s	s	s	s	s	
Bailey, W. L.,	s	p	w						
Blackburn, G. P.,					s				Litter bearer.
Brown, P. A.,	p	p	k						
Chambers, G. J.,	s	s	s	p	p	p	s		
Coe, E. N.,	s	s	s	p	s	s	s	s	
Cooley, W.,	p	p	k						
Drenman, J. H.,	p	p	w						
Drake, J. H.,	*a	p	p	p	p	p	p	p	
Davis, L.,	p	s	s	s	s	s	s	s	
Davidson, R.,	p	p	p	p	p	p	p	w	Left on battle field.
Elder, G.,	p	p	p	a	s	s	s	s	
Easten, M. L.,	p	p	w		p	p	p	p	
Eddington, H. F.,	p	p	w						
Foster, R.,	p	p	w						
Foster, H.,	p	p	w						
Frost, H.,	s	p	p	p	p	p	p	p	Ambulance driver.
Fields, F. L.,	s	s	s	s	p	p	p	w	
Gear, W. E.,	p	p	p	s	p	p	s	s	
Goodman, J.,	p	p	s	s	p	p	s	s	
Griffin, J. H.,	s	s	s	s	s	p			Taken prisoner at Manassas.
Garey, W.,	p	s	s	s	s	s	s	s	
Garrett, J. M.,	p	p	s	s	d				
Hearn, W.,	p	p	s	s	p	p	p	p	Discharged 1st August, '62.
Henderson, J. S.,	p	p	k						
Hammon, W. H.,						p			Prom'd Orderly Sergeant.
Hixson, G. M.,	p	p	w						
Herndon, J.,	s	p	w	p	p	p	p	p	
Herndon, E.,									Musician.
Herndon, A.,	p	s	s	s	p	k			
Hunter, W. R.,	p	p	k						
Jones, J. J.,	p	p	p	p	s	s	s	s	
Jones, W. A.,	p	p	p	p					Subsistence-Sergeant.
Jones, D. C.,	p	s							Assistant Surgeon 7th Ten .
Kirk, W. S.,	p	p	s	s	p	w			
Kinsey, D.,	p	p	p	p	p	p	a	a	
Keith, L. D.,	p	p	s	s	p	p	a	a	
Livingston, J.,	s	s	s	s	p	w			
Moore, R. E.,	p	s	p	p					Litter bearer.
Moore, M. C.,	p	p	s	s	s	s	s	s	
Marsh, J. E.,	s	s	s	s					Discharged.
McVoyman, B. F.,	p	p	w	w	s	p	p	p	
Marshal, W. W.	p	p	w						
Marshal, B. W.,	p								Musician.
Marshal, W. H.,	p	p	*a	*a	p	*a	*a	*a	
Mitchell, S. J.,	p	p	p	p	s	s	s	s	
Norwood, A.,	s	p	s	s	s	s	s	s	
Norton, W.,	s	p	p	p	s	s	s	s	
Olive, J.,	p	p	w	s	p	p	p		
Rimes, R. W.,	p	p	p	p	p	p	s	s	Left sick in Maryland.
Riece, W.,	p	p	s	s	s	s	s	s	
Robertson, J. R.,	p	p	k						
Roberts, J. C.,			w						Died 29th June.
Smiley, J. R.,	p	p	k						
Smiley, W. J.,	p	p	k						
Smiley, J.,	p	p	p	*a	p	p	a	a	
Sneed, J.,	p	p	w						
Smith, J. A.,	s	p	s	s	s	s	p	p	
Steel, W. C.,	p	p	p	p	p	p	p	p	
Tindall, O.,	p	p	s	s	s	p	*a	*a	
Talbot, Y. O.,	p	s	s	s	p	k			
Vaughn, T. H.,	a	a	a	a	a	a			Taken prisoner Boonsboro, Md.
Van Dusen, H.,	s	s	s	s	p	w			

Name									Remarks
Wood, B.,	p	p	w		p	p	s	s	
Wood, E. O.,	p	p	p	p	p	w			
Wood, J.,	p	p	p	p	s	s	s	s	
Webster, E.,	p	p	p	p					Litter bearer.
Wilson, F. M.,	s	p	s	s	p	p			
Wilkins, S.,	p	p	w						
Whiddon, W. G.,	p	s	s	s	p	k			

CO. D.

Name									Remarks
Capt. J. P. Bane,	p	p	w	a	a	a	a	a	
1st Lieut. C. Reich,	a	a	w						
2d Lt. T. H. Holaman,	p	s	k						
3d Lieut. E. Duggan,	p	p	s	s	p	p	p	s	
1st Serg't R. W. Davis,	p	s	s	s	*d				
2d Serg't A. D. Jeffries,	p	p	p	p	p	w	a	a	
3d Serg't C. L. Dibrell,	p	p	s	s	*a	*a	*a	*a	
4th S't McClaugherty,	p	p	p	p	p	p	p	p	
5th Serg't C. Wiprecht,	p	p	s	p	s	s	p	p	
1st Corp'l J. Patterson	p	p	p	p	p	p	p	p	
2d Cor. A. E. Wilson	p	p	s	s	p	p	p	s	
3d Corp'l J. L. Gett,	p	p	p	p	s	s	s	s	
4th Corp'l W. P. Smith,	p	p	p	p	s	s	s	s	
Mitcheal, R.,	p	a	a	a	a	a	a	a	Musician.
Anderson, C. W.,	p	s	s	s	s	s	s	s	
Aiken, Wm.	a	p	s		s	s	s	s	
Armstrong, D. H.,	s	p	s	s	s	s	s	s	
Baker, John,	a	a	a	a	a	a	a	a	Detached Service.
Baker, Joseph,	r	s	s						
Butler, Jas.,	p	s	s	s	s	s	s	s	
Buttler, George,	p	p	k						
Burges, W. H.,	p	s	s	s	p	p	p	w	
Burges, R. J.,	p	s	p	p	p	w			
Burges, R. A.,	p	p	p	p	s	s	p	p	
Burges, Gideon,	r		s	p	s	s	s	s	
Calvert, W. L.,	p	p	w	p	a	d			
Courtney, S. G.,	s	p	w	a	a	a	a	a	
Campbell, Jas.,	r		s	s	p	p	s	s	
Cox, Thomas,	p	p	p	p	p	w			
Cody, E. J.,	r		s	s	s	s	a	a	
Dunn, M. S.,	p	p	p	p	p	p	a	a	Taken prisoner at Manassas.
Daniall, J. S.,	p	p	s	s	p	p	p	p	Litter bearer.
Dimmit, Alamo,	p	p	p	p	p	p	p	s	
Dimmitt, Nap.,	r		w	a	a	a	a	a	
Dimmitt, Jas.,	r		w	a	a	a	a	a	
Davis, W. J.,	p	p	s	s	p	p	p	k	
Davidson, J. J.,	r		k						
Dougherty, G. W.,	r		s	s	d				
Douave, A. W.,	r		k						
Eweing, T. J.,	p	p	w	a	a	a	a	a	
Eweing, F. Z.,	a	a	a	a	a	a	a	a	
Erskin, A. N.,	r		p	p	p	p	p	k	
Erskin, A. M.,	r		w	a	p	p	p	w	
Eringhause, W. F.,	r		p	p	s	s	s	s	
Fennel, J. H.,	p	p	w	a	a	a	a	a	
Franks, R. H.,	p	p	s	s	p	p	p	w	
Flores, W. D.,	s	s	a	p	p	p	p	p	Missing at Sharpsburg.
Green, A. G.,	s	p	w	a	p	s	p	a	
Green, W. S.,	s	p	w	a	a	a	a	a	
Gregory, J. B.,	a	a	a	a	a	a	a	a	Detached Service.
Glasier, F. H.,	p	s	s	s	p	p	p	w	
Glasier, Julius,	p	p	w	a	a	a	a	a	
Gordon, A. H.,	r		w	a	a	d			
Harris, W. A.,	a	a	a	a	a	a	a	a	Detached Service.
Hoomes, J. F.,	s	p	p	p	p	p	p	s	
Harman, Z. J.,	p	s	p	*a	a	a	a	a	

Name	1	2	3	4	5	6	7	8	Remarks
Harman, W. H., - - - - - - - - -	p	s	p	a	p	p	p	a	
Huggins, George, - - - - - - - -	s	p	a	a	p	p	p	s	
Herron, A. C., - - - - - - - - -	r	n	p	p	p	s	s	s	
Hogges, G. A., - - - - - - - - -	r		p	p	p	s	p	p	
Henry, A. W., - - - - - - - - - -	r		p	p	p	p	p	w	
Jones, R. A., - - - - - - - - -					p	w			Transferred.
Jones S. A., - - - - - - - - - -	p	p	w	a	a	a	a	a	
Johnston, T. I., - - - - - - - - -	a	a	p	p	p	k			
Jordon, P.E., - - - - - - - - - -	p	p	a	a	a	a	a	a	
Jefferson, T. J., - - - - - - - -	a	a	a	a	a	a	a	a	
Jefferson, R. T., - - - - - - - -	p	s	s	s	s	s	p	p	
Knight, G. N., - - - - - - - - -	p	s	s	s	p	p	p	p	Sergeant Major. ·geant Major.
King, John, - - - - - - - - -	r		a	a	a	*d			
King, James, - - - - - - - - - -	r		a	a	a	d			
Lackey, J. R., - - - - - - - - -	p	p	w	a	d				
Little, B. F., - - - - - - - - - -	r		w	a	a	a	a	a	
Longstreet, George, - - - - - - -	r		p	p	p	p	p	p	
Leonard, Aug., - - - - - - - - -	r		w	a	a	a	a	a	
Mays, J. N., - - - - - - - - - -	p	s	s	s	p	p	p	p	
Maning, S. M., - - - - - - - - -	p	p	a	a	p	s	s	s	
Meriwether, Thomas, - - - - - - -	r		a	a	a	a	a	a	
McNeely, J. D., - - - - - - - - -	r		a	a	a	a	a	a	Detached Service.
Millett, Treoidas, - - - - - - - -	p	p	k						
Miller, M. E., - - - - - - - - - -	r		w	a	a	a	a	a	
Park, J. E., - - - - - - - - - -	p	p	a	a	*d				Doctor.
Pierce, A. L., - - - - - - - - -	p	p	k						
Park, Thomas, - - - - - - - - -	p	p	w	a	d				
Parent, E. J., - - - - - - - - - -	r		p	p	s	s	p	p	
Roggers, John, - - - - - - - - -	a	a	a	a	a	a	p	p	
Roggers, M., - - - - - - - - - -	a	a	a	a	p	p	s	s	Detached Service.
Readus, Wm., - - - - - - - - - -	p	s	s	s	a	a	p	p	
Rutledge, A. H., - - - - - - - -	p	p	*a	*a	*a	*a	*a	*a	
Reeves, J. T., - - - - - - - - -	r		a	a	s	p	s	s	
Rhoades, R. A., - - - - - - - - -	r		a	a	p	w	a	a	
Saunders, Frank, - - - - - - - -	p	p	w	a	p	w	s	s	
Smith, J. D., - - - - - - - - - -	p	p	p	p	s	s	s	s	Litter bearer.
Smith, W. R., - - - - - - - - - -	p	p	p	a	a	a	a	a	
Smith, Paris, - - - - - - - - - -	p	p	w	a	a	a	s	s	
Smith, E. H., - - - - - - - - - -	r	p	a	a	a	a	p	w	
Smith, Thomas, - - - - - - - - -	p	a	a	a	a	d			
Shumate, Wm., - - - - - - - - -	r		w	a	a	a	a	a	
Singletary, J. W., - - - - - - - -	r		p	s	s	s	s	p	
Schmidt, B., - - - - - - - - - -	p	p	p	p	a	a	a	a	Detached Service.
Smith, M. V., - - - - - - - - - -	p	p	a	a	p	p	p	p	
J. M. White, - - - - - - - - - -	p	p	w	a	a	a	a	a	
J. M. White, jun., - - - - - - - -	a	a	p	s	a	*d			
F. C. White, - - - - - - - - - -	r		a	a	a	a	s	s	
Whitehead, Jas., - - - - - - - -	p	p	p	p	p	k			
Wilson, W. W., - - - - - - - - -	p	p	w						
Watson, T. W., - - - - - - - - -	p	p	a	a	p	p	p	p	
Wood, A. H., - - - - - - - - - -	p	p	s	s	p	p	p	p	
Young, J. T., - - - - - - - - - -	p	p	w	a	d				

CO. E.

Name	1	2	3	4	5	6	7	8	Remarks
Capt. E. D. Ryan, - - - - - - - -	p	p	w	d					Died July 4th, 1862.
1st Lt. J. M. Brandon, - - - - - -	a	p	w	a	a	a	a	a	
2nd " D. L. Sublett, - - - - - - -	p	p							Aid-de-Camp.
3rd " J. C. Billingsly, - - - - - -	p	p	p	p	p	p	p	w	
1st Serg't Killingworth, - - - - -	a	p	p	p	p	p	p	p	
2nd Serg't J. C. Smith, - - - - - -	p	p	a	a	p	p	a	p	
3rd " P. M. Ripley, - - - - - - -	p	p	a	a	p	w	p	w	
4th " W.W. Dunklin, - - - - - - -	p	p	p	p	a	a	a	a	
5th " R.S. Dean, - - - - - - - -	p	p	a	p	a	k			Sublett, Dunklin,
1st. Corp'l J. B. Majors, - - - - -	p	p	w	a	p	p	p	p	
2nd " S. Young, - - - - - - - -	p	p	w						Died July 10th, '62. 10th, '62

3rd Corp'l A. J. Wallars, - - - -	p	p	a	a	a	a	a	a	
4th " J. H. Long, - - - - - - - -	p	p	p	p	p	p	p	k	
Ashmead, G. L., - - - - - - - -	p	p	p	a	a	a	a	a	
Aycock, B. L., - - - - - - - - -	p	p	w	a	a	a	a	a	
Blocker, J. C., - - - - - - - - -	p	p	a	a	a	a	a	a	
Billingsley, S. J., - - - - - - - -	a	p	p	p	p	a	a	a	
Bible, Noah, - - - - - - - - - -	p	p	w	a	a	a	a	a	
Bible, Phil, C., - - - - - - - - -	p	p	a	a	p	k			
Burton, W. H. P., - - - - - - - -	p	p	a	a	p	p	p	p	
Clark, J. E., - - - - - - - - - -	p	p	a	a	a	k			
Clarke, J. D., - - - - - - - -		i	a	a	a	a	a	a	
Cowden, W. B., - - - - - - - - -	a								Died May 21, '62.
Chenault, G. N., - - - - - - - -	p	p	a	a	a	a	a	a	
Creed, Geo., - - - - - - - - - -	a	p	p	a	a	a	*a	*a	
Chambers, S. H., - - - - - - - -	a	p	p	p	a	a	a	a	
Charman, J. B., - - - - - - - - -	p	a	p	p	p	a	a	a	
Dunklin, T. L., - - - - - - - - -	p	p	a	p	p	k			
Duncan, W. E., - - - - - - - - -									Courier to Gen. Hood.
Donnally, H. M., - - - - - - - -	p	p	p	p	a	a	p	w	
Decherd, A. P., - - - - - - - - -	r	a	a	*d					
Decherd, D. M., - - - - - - - - -	p	p	a	a	p	a	a	a	
Delk, W. G., - - - - - - - - - -	p	p	p	a	p	p	p	w	
Edwards, B. G., - - - - - - - - -		p	a	a	p	w	d		
Fitzhugh, D. C., - - - - - - - -	p	p	a						Detached Service.
Freeman, R. L., - - - - - - - - -	p	p	w	d					Died of wounds Aug. 2d, '62.
Fossett, S., - - - - - - - - - -		a	a	a	p	p	p	p	
Good, D. J., - - - - - - - - - -									Musician.
Hunt, J. F., - - - - - - - - - -	p	p	p						Detached Service.
Holloway, L. D., - - - - - - - -	p	p	w	a	a	a	a	a	
Hirst, T. D., - - - - - - - - - -									Musician.
Hughes, Josiah, - - - - - - - - -	p	p	a	a	a	a	a	a	
Herrington, J. A., - - - - - - - -	p	p	p	p	a	a	a	a	
Harrison, G. H., - - - - - - - - -	p	p	w	a	p	p	p	a	
Hicks, W. M., - - - - - - - - - -	p	a	a	a	p	p	p	a	
Hicks, H. K., - - - - - - - - - -		a	a	a	d				Died in Hospital July 12th, 1862.
Holden, J. W., - - - - - - - - -		a	p	p	a	a	a	*d	
Hannah, W., - - - - - - - - - -	a	d							
Hill, Eldon, - - - - - - - - - -	p	p	a	a	p	w	*d		
Johnston, J. W., - - - - - - - - -	p	a	p	p	p	p	p	a	
Johnson, Jno., - - - - - - - - -		r	a	a					Detached.
Jones, R. M., - - - - - - - - - -	a	a	a	a	p	w	a	a	
Lehmann, Joe, - - - - - - - - -	p	p	a	p	p	p	p	w	
Kirvin, W. H., - - - - - - - - -	a	p	p	p	p	p	p	w	
Loyd, W. J., - - - - - - - - - -	p	a	a	a	p	a	a	a	
Leonard, R. H., - - - - - - - - -									Field Hospital Steward.
Manahan, J. H., - - - - - - - - -	p	a	a	a	p	p	a	a	
Makung, T. M., - - - - - - - - -	p	p	a	p	a	a	p	a	
Miller, J. D., - - - - - - - - - -	p	a	p	p	a	p	p	p	
Mullens, T. M., - - - - - - - - -	a	p	p	p	a	a	a	a	
Mullens, W. T., - - - - - - - - -	p	p	a	a					Detached Service.
Morgan, A. B. - - - - - - - - -									Hospital Attendant.
Madden, C. P., - - - - - - - - -	p	p	w	a	a	a	a	a	
Moore, N. P., - - - - - - - - - -	p	p	w	a	a	a	a	a	
McGee, Greene, - - - - - - - - -		a	p	a	p	p	a	a	
Norwood, T. L., - - - - - - - - -	p	p	a	p	p	a	a	a	
Pamplin, W. A., - - - - - - - - -		*p	p	p	p	w	a	a	
Peters, L. C., - - - - - - - - -	a	a	a	a	p	w	a	a	
Ross, W. M., - - - - - - - - - -	a	p	p	p	p	a	a	w	
Robinson, J. A., - - - - - - - -			a	a	a	a	a	a	
Robinson, S. A., - - - - - - - -	p	p	p	p	a	a	p	w	
Robinson, James, - - - - - - - -	a								Detached Service.
Robinson, W. S., - - - - - - - -	a	p	a	a	p	w	p	w	
Reed, J. C., - - - - - - - - - -	p	p	p	a	p	a	p	w	
Rogers, W. D., - - - - - - - - -	a	p	w	a	a	a	a	a	
Rogers, H. B., - - - - - - - - -	p	p	p	p	p	p	p	p	
Rogers, J. L., - - - - - - - - -	p	p	p	p	p	w	a	a	
Roberts, Abner, - - - - - - - - -	a	p	k						

Ragsdale, J. B., - - - - - - - -	p	p	p	p	p	a			Detached.
Rotan, W. T.,- - - - - - - - - -	p	a	p	a	a	a	a	a	
Ramsey, , - - - - - - - -									Litter Bearer.
Ripley, N. N., - - - - - - - - -	p	p	a	a	a	a	a	a	
Selman, T. J., - - - - - - - - -	p	p	p	p	a	a	a	a	
Sandefer, L. G., - - - - - - - -	p								Detached Service.
Smith, Jno. S., - - - - - - - - -	p	p							Courier to Gen. Hood.
Smith, Jas. S., - - - - - - - - -	p	p	w	d					Died of wounds, July 8th,
Sharp, F. C., - - - - - - - - - -	p	p	w	a	a	a	a	a	1862.
Taylor, G. M., - - - - - - - - -	a	p	w	a	a	a	a	a	
Terry, J. C., - - - - - - - - - -	p	p	p	p	p	p	p	a	
Tilly, Ed., - - - - - - - - - - -	p	p	a	a	a	a	p	w	
Umberson, R. W., - - - - - - - -	p	a	a	a	a	a	a	a	
Wideman, C. A. - - - - - - - - -	a	a	a	a	p	m	a	a	
Williams, T. D., - - - - - - - -	p	p	a	a	p	p	p	p	
Willis, J. B., - - - - - - - - - -	p	p	a	p	a	a	a	a	
Walland, A., - - - - - - - - - -	p	p	a	a	a	a	a	a	
Worsham, E. L., - - - - - - - -	p	p	w	a	a	a	a	a	
Worsham, J. N., - - - - - - - -	p	p							Transferred.
Wor sham, C. G., - - - - - - - -	p	p	a	a	p	a	p	p	
Wilson, G. H., - - - - - - - - -	p	p	a	p	a	a	a	a	
Way, C. B,, - - - - - - - - - -	p								Detached Service.
Whitehead, C. M., - - - - - - - -	p	p	a	p	p	w	a	a	
Young, T. H., - - - - - - - - - -	a	a	d						Died June 14th, 1892.

CO. F.

Capt. E. Cunningham - - - - -	p	p	p	p	p	p	p	p	
1st Lieut. J. F. Brooks - - - -	p	p	w	s	s	s	s	s	
2d Lieut. L. P. Hughes - - - -	a	p	p	p	p	p	p	w	
3d " L. P. Lyons, - - - - -	p	p	k						
1st Serg't H. Brahan, - - - - -	p	p	p	p	p	p	p	p	
2d " C. S. Brown - - - - -	p	p	p	p	p	s	p	w	
3d " J. D. Murray - - - - -	p	s	s	s	p	p	p	w	
4th " Eli Park, - - - - - - - -	p	p	p	p	p	p	p	m	
5th " W. A. Bennett - - - - -	p	p	p	p	s	s	s	s	
1st C'l R. H. Skinner - - - - -	p	p	p	s	p	s	s	s	
2d " D. M. McAlister - - - - -	p	p	k						
3d " E. T. Kindred - - - - -	a	p	p	p	a	a	a	a	
4th " C. A. McAlister - - - -	p	p	w	s	s	p	p	p	
Adams, T. J., - - - - - - - - -	r	s	s	s	p	s	p	w	
Alford, James, - - - - - - - - -	p	s	s	p	p	w	s	s	
Allen, George - - - - - - - - -	p	p	s	p	p	p	p	p	
Aylmer, G. G., - - - - - - - - -	r	p	w	s	s	s	s	s	
Bedell, A. M., - - - - - - - - -	r	a	a	a	a	a	a	a	Left sick on the march from
Brantley, J. L.,- - - - - - - - -	p	p	p	*a	p	s	*a	*a	Yorktown, not heard from since.
Brieger, J. G., - - - - - - - - -	r	p	s	s	s	s	s	s	
Buchanan, L., - - - - - - - - -	p	p	s	s	s	s	s	s	
Brooks, C., - - - - - - - - - -	r	p	p	p	p	s	p	p	
Camp, T. P., - - - - - - - - - -	r	s	s	s	s	s	s	s	
Cohen, A. T., - - - - - - - - -	r	p	p	p	p	p	p	*a	
Cook, John, - - - - - - - - - -	p	p	p	p	p	w	s	s	
Copeland, Solomon, - - - - - -	p	p	s	p	p	s	s	s	
Crigler, R. T., - - - - - - - - -	r	p	w	s	p	p	p	p	
Clark, Joseph - - - - - - - - -	r	s	s	d					
Cunningham, J. T., - - - - - -	a	a	k						
Campbell, J. M., - - - - - - - -	r	p	p	p	s	s	s	s	
Crockett, E. R., - - - - - - - -	p	p	w	p	p	p	p	m	
Currie, J. B., - - - - - - - - -	p	p	p	p	p	p	p	p	
Dansby, H., - - - - - - - - - -	p	p	p	p	p	p	p	w	
Dial, A. A., - - - - - - - - - -	r	p	w	s	s	s	s	s	
Dollery, Davis, - - - - - - - - -	r	s	s	s	s	s	s	s	
Downing, Edward, - - - - - - - -	r	p	k						
Dreyer, Henry, - - - - - - - - -	r	p	s	s	p	p	p	w	Left in Maryland.
Dunn, W. H., - - - - - - - - - -	p	p	s	s	p	p	s	s	
Fishburn, J. A., - - - - - - - -	s	s	s	s	s	s	s	s	

Floyd, W. F.,	p	p	s	p	p	w	p	w	
Gabbert, H.	p	p	s	s	p	p	p	w	
Givens, W. M.,	p	p	p	p	p	s	p	s	
Goodloe, Calvin,	s	s	*d						
Goodloe, William	s	s	s	*d					
Goodwin, Benjamin,	r	p	a	a	s	s	s	*d	
Graham, J. C.,	r	s	s	s	s	s	s	s	
Green, W. A.,	p	p	w	s	s	s	s	s	
Hahn, John,	s	p	p	p	s	s	s	s	
Harbour, C.	r	s	s	s	s	s	s	s	
Hardoin, A.,	r	s	s	d					
Hardoin, S.,	r	p	p	p	p	a	a	a	
Henry, W. R.	r	s	s	d					
Harwell, J. R.,	r	s	w	s	s	s	s	s	
Henderson, B. G.,	r	p	s	s	p	p	p	m	
Henderson, C. F.,	r	p	k						
Hollander, W. M.,	p	p	p	p	p	p	p	w	
Houston, Russell,	p	p	s	s	s	s	p	p	
Howard, William,	r	p	s	p	p	s	s	s	
Johnson, W. C.,	p	s	w	s	s	s	p	p	
Johnson, J. N.,	p	p	p	s	p	s	s	s	
Jones, A. R.,	p	a	a	a	p	p	p	p	
Jones, William,	s	s	s	s	*d				
Kahr, N.,	p	p	k						
Kindred, J. B.,	r	p	w	s	p	p	p	w	Left at Bunker's Hill, Va.
Kindred, J. H.,	r	s	p	p	p	p	p	w	Left in Maryland.
Kindred, J. P.,	r	p	w	s	p	p	a	a	
Kindred, J. S.,	r	s	k						
Koolbeck, G.,	p	p	w	s	s	s	s	s	
Love, J. P.,	r	s	p	p	p	p	p	m	
Maisine, Edward,	p	p	p	p	d				
Mans, Peter,	p	p	w	s	p	p	p	m	
McCann, T. J.,	p	p	w	s	s	s	s	s	
Menefee, O. M.,	s	s	s	s	p	p	p	w	Left in Maryland.
Menger, Oscar,		r	w	s	s	s	s	s	
Morris, William,	p	p	w	s	s	s	s	s	
Murray, J. C.,	r	p	s	s	p	p	p	p	
Murray, R. W.,	p	p	s	s	p	p	p	w	
Pengra, M. M.,	p	p	w	p	s	s	s	s	
Penn, P. J.,	p	p	p	p	p	p	s	s	
Pickett, M.,	r	p	w	s	p	p	s	s	
Pogue, L. S.,	r	s	a	p	p	s	s	s	
Polley, J. B.,	p	p	w	s	a	p	a	a	
Quick, Jacob,	r	s	p	p	p	p	p	w	
Riggs, John,	p	p	s	s	s	s	p	w	Left at Shepardstown, V.
Roberts, John,	a	a	a	a	s	s	s	s	
Rumley, J. J.,	r	s	s	s	s	s	s	s	
Sampson, Edward J.,	p	p	k						
Schweeir, George,	p	p	s	p	p	p	p	w	Left in Maryland.
Self, M. M.,	r	s	s	s	d				
Sergeant, A. H.	r	s	s	s	p	p	p	p	
Smith, Henry,	p	s	s	p	p	p	p	w	
Sneed, Albert,	p	p	s	s	p	w	s	s	
Sullivan, R. A.,	s	p	k						
Summerville, James,	r	p	s	s	p	p	s	p	
Sutherland, Jack,	p	p	s	s	p	p	s	s	
Thornton, H. G.,	p	p	s	s	s	s	s	s	
Waber, Simon,	p	p	p	p	p	p	s	s	
Wallace, E. F.,	p	s	s	s	s	s	m	[illegible]	
Weir, Henry,	p	p	p	p	p	p	s	s	
Wiseman, J. O.,	p	s	p	s	p	s	s	s	
Wolff, Simon,	p	p	p	p	p	k			
Wood, G. W.,	r	s	s	s	p	p	p	w	
Dockstadear, Osaar,									Musician.
Warner, Charles,									"
Foster, B. H.,									"
Veal, Frank,									"
Naurath, William									"

CO. G.

Capt. J. W. Hutcheson,	p	p	k						
1st. Lieut. J. Dunham,	a	a	a						Resigned June 10th, 1862.
2nd " J. R. Kennard,									" Sept., 1861.
3rd " R. H. Bassett,	a	p	p	p	p	p	p	p	
1st Serg't J. L. Gould,	p	p	w	a	a	a	a	a	
2nd " J. M. Bookman,	p	p	p	p	p	p	p	p	Jr. 2d Lt. July, 1862.
3rd " R. H. Wood,	a	p	p	a	*d				Discharged Aug't 7th, 1862.
4th " D. L. Butts,	a	p	k						Jr. 2nd Lt. Oct. 1861.
5th " T. N. Baines,									Died in Hospital, Nov. 6, '61.
1st Corp'l J. W. Baker,	p	*a	p						Lt. Sept. '61, res'd Jy 20, '62
2nd " J. J. Blarkshear,	p	p	a	a	p	p	p	w	5th Serg't January, 1862.
3rd " J. J. Atkinson,	p	p	p	p	p	p	a	p	1st Serg't July, 1862.
4th " W. McClunny,	a	p	p	p	p	a	p	p	
Arnett, David,	p	p	p	p	p	p	p	p	
Beecher, R. A.,	p	p	p	p	p	p	m	m	5th Serg't Sept. '62.
Baines, W. M.,	p	p	w	a	a	a	a	a	
Barnes, J. T.,									Died in Hospital, Dec. 1861.
Buffington, T. C.,	p	p	p	p	m				Jr. 2d Lt. June, 1862.
Barry, W. E.,	p	p	w	p	p	p	p	m	
Barker, J. C.,	p	p	a	p	a	a	a	a	
Boozer, H. D.,	p	p	p	p	p	p	p	p	2d Corporal, Sept., 1862.
Brietz, A. C.,	p	p	p	p					Ordinance Sergeant.
Barry, Jno. D.,	p	p	a	a	p	p	p	w	
Carley, M. F.,	p	p	a	a	p	p	a	a	
Cotton, H.,									Died in March.
Collins, D.,									Chief Bugler, Oct. 1st, 1861.
Dance, J. T.,	p	a	w	a	a	a	a	a	
Duke, J. G.,	p	p	p	p	p	p	a	a	
Dawkins, F. A.,									Died in Hospital, Nov. 1861.
Dunn, Frank,	a	a	a	a	p	p	p	m	
Ferrel, S. D.,	p	p	w	a	a		a	a	
Finley, J. K.,									Died in Hospital.
Field, D. H.,	p	a	*d						Discharged, June 21, 1862.
Floyd, C. E.,	a	p	a	a	p	p	p	p	
Floyd, Wm.,	p	a	a	a	a	p	a	a	
Flournoy, J. J.,	p	p	w	a	a	a	a	a	
Guy, G. A.,	p	p	w	a	a	a	a	a	
Giles, P. L.,									Died in Hospital.
Giles, J. J.,									" " "
Giles, E. D.,									" " "
Griffin, D. C.,	p	p	w	a	a	a	a	a	
Grissett, W. J.,	p	p	a	p	p	p	p	p	
Helm, E. G.,									Died in Hospital.
Hadden, M. E.,	p	a	p	p	p	k			
Harrison, M. M.,	a	a	a	a	a	a	a	a	
Hubbell, N. L.,									Died in Quarters.
Hassen, Robt.,	p	a	a	a	a	a	a	a	
Hyman, Geo. W.,	p	p	p	p	p	p	p	m	
Jackson, J.,	*d								Discharged in February,
Jackson, Job,	p	p	p	p	p	w	p	w	
Jones, Geo. W.,	p	p	p	p	a	a	a	a	
Jones, J. N.,	a	p	a	a	a	a	a	a	
Kelly, B. F.,	p	p	w	a	p	p	p	w	
Kelly, S. P.,	p	a	a	a	p	a	p	p	
Kennard, A. D.,									Died In Hospital.
Kendall, J. L.,									" " "
Lawrence, G.,	p	p	p	p	p	p	p	w	Corporal Oct. '62.
Mooring, J. S.,	p	p	a	a	p	p	p	p	Medical Orderly.
Muldrow, J. T.,	a	a	a	a	p	p	p	p	
Martin, W. A.,	p	p	p	p	p	p	a	a	
Martin, Jno. F.,	p	p	a	a	p	p	a	a	
Mays, J. W. T.,	p	p	p	a	p	w	a	a	
Montgomery, J. W.,	p	p	w	a	p	w	a	a	
Muse, J. T.,	p	a	w	a	p	p	p	a	

Midkiffe, J. A.,									Medical Teamster.
Moss, Geo. T.,									Discharged.
Nix, J. L.,	p	p	p	p	a	a	a	a	
Nelms, E. P.,	a	p	w	a	p	p	a	a	
Neetles, J. H.,	p	a	a	a	a	a	a	a	
Neal, F.,	a	a	a	a	a	a	a	a	
Pearce, B. W.,	p	p	a	a	a	a	a	w	
Pearce, E. W.,	p	p	w	a	a	a	a	a	
Pinckney, Jno. M.,	p	p	p	p	p	p	p	w	
Pinckney, R.,	p	p	p	p	p	p	p	p	
Peteet, W. B.,	p	p	w	a	p	p	p	a	
Peteet, J. M.,	p	p	w	a	a	a	a	a	
Parnel, J. C.,	p	p	p	p	p	a	a	a	
Plasters, J. H.,	p	p	w	a	p	p	p	p	
Rogerson, Jno.,	p	p	k						
Robinson, Jno.,	p	p	p	*a	p	p	p	p	
Roco, A. C.,	p	p	p	p	p	p	a	a	
Roach, Jno.,	p	p	p	p	p	p	p	w	Jr. 2d Lt., July, '62.
Stewart, A. J.,	p	a	a	a	p	p	a	a	
Silverbaugh, D.,	p	p	w	a	p	a	a	a	
Stucy, W. A.,	p	p	w	a	a	a	a	a	
Shaffer, H. E.,									Field and Staff Teamster.
Schults, W. J.,									Hospital Steward.
Scott, G.,	p	p	p	p	p	p	p	k	
Thomas, J. W.,	p	p	p	p	p	p	w	a	
Terrell, E. T.,	p	p	a	p	p	p	p	p	Hospital Attendant.
Terrell, W. H.,									Died in Hospital.
Turner, J.,									Died in Quarters.
Turner, W.,	*d								Discharged in October, 1861.
Trunt, Jno.,	p	p	w	a	p	p	p	k	
Walton, A. E.,	p	p	p	p	a	a	a	a	
Whitehurst, J. K.,	p	a	a	a	a	a	a	a	
White, M. D.,									Died in Quarters.
White, Caleb,	p	p	k						
Whitelock, A. T.,									Brigade Teamster.
Whitesides, A. H.,	p	p	p	p	p	p	p	p	
Williams, J. J.,	p	p	w	a	a	a	a	a	
Wood, D. A.,	p	p	p	p	p	p	p	m	
Ward, Chas. H.,									Died in Hospital.
Womack, M. S.,	p	a	a	p	p	p	a	a	
Barry, L. H.,	p	p	p	p	p	p	p	w	

Recruits Enlisted in March and April, '62.

Adams, Sam'l H.,	p	a	a	*d					Discharged in July.
Allen, W. J.,	p	a	a	a	a	a	a	a	
Aikens, James O.,	p	a	a	a	a	a	a	a	
Bassett, Noah,					p	p	a	a	Arrived July 10, 1862.
Bowen, Allen,	a	*a	a	a	a	a	a	a	
Blackshear, R. D.,	p	p	p	p	p	p	p	w	
Chambers, G. C.,	a	p	a	a	a	a	p	k	
Churchwell, Thos.	a	a	a	a	a	a	a	a	
Chatham, W. L.,	p	p	a	a	a	a	a	a	
Cruse, A. J.,	a	p	k						Arrived May 10th, 1862.
Class, T. O.,	p	a	a	a	p	p	a	a	
Davis, E. C.,	p	p	p	a	p	p	p	p	
Daffin, L. A.,	a	p	a	a	p	p	p	p	Arrived May 10th, 1862.
Davis, Jno. A.,	p	p	p	a	a	a	p	p	
Ekelis, W. R. A.,	p	a	a	a	a	a	a	a	
Green, Jno. H.	p	p	a	a	p	p	p	a	
Hughes, W. T.,	p	p	a	a					Died in July.
Hiett, J. W.,	p	*a	*a	*a	*a	*a	*a	*a	
Hadden, J. J.,	p	a	a	a	a	a	a	a	
Jones, W. S.,	a	p	k						Arrived May 10th, 1862.
Jones, N. B.,	a	a	a	a	a	a	a	a	" " " "
Kay, Eli,	p	a	a	a	p	p	p	p	

Name									Remarks
King, Jno. H.,	p	a	a	a	a	a	a	a	
Livingston, A.,	p	a	a	a	*d				Discharged in August.
Loggins, J. C.,	p	a	a	a	p	p	p	p	
Moaring, Chas. G.,	p	p	a	a	a	a	p	p	
McCowen, Jos.,	p	p	p	p	p	p	p	p	Corporal, October, 1862.
Midkiffe, E. P.,	a	p	a	a	p	p	p	p	
McGregor, W. B.,	a	a	a	a	a	a	a	a	
McDaniel, B. H.,	a	p	*d						Discharged in June.
Patterson, W. R.,	p	a							Died in Hospital.
Quarles, Geo. S.,	p	a	a	a	a	a	a	a	
Reynolds, J. S.,	p	p	a	a	p	p	a	a	
Rowe, H. T.,	a	a	a	a	p	p	p	p	
Stacy, Jno. J.,	a	a	a	a	p	p	p	p	Arrived May 10th, 1862.
Smith, W. H.,	a	a	a	a	a	a	a	a	
Spencer, C. W.,	w	a							Died in Hospital.
Tidwell, W. C.,	p	p	p	p	a	a	a	a	
Wilson, Walter	p	a	a	a	a	w	a	a	
Wallingford, T. G.,	p	p	p	p	p	p	p	p	
Williams, H. F.,	p	a	p	a	a	a	a	a	
Webb, F. X.,	p	a	a	a	a	a	a	a	
Scott, J. B.,	p	p	k						

CO. H.

Name									Remarks
Capt. J. J. Porter	p	p	w						Died from wounds at Gaines' Farm.
1st Lieut. J. T. Hunter,	p	p	p	p	p	w			
2d " B. Randolph,	p	p	w						
Lieut. C. E. Jones,	a	p	s	s	p	k			
" M. C. Holmes,	p	p	s	s	p	w			Leg amputated.
" Ben. Reynolds,	p	p	s	s	s	s	s	s	Elected Lieut. Oct. 7th, '62.
1st Serg't N. A. Myer,	a	p	k						
2d " T. O. Wilkes,	p	p	k						
3d " G. A. Wynne,	s	s	w	a	a	a	p	m	
5th " R. L. Tyler,	p	p	k						
1st Cop'l C. M. Conrow,	p	p	k						
2d " H. T. Sapp,	w								
3d " Zach. Landrum,	p	s	s	a	a	a	a	a	
4th " F. H. Wade,	p	p	a	a	p	p	a	a	
2d Serg't G. W. Kipps,	p	p	p	p	p	p	p	p	
3d " R. J. Tedford,	p	s	a	a	p	p	p	p	
4th " J. G. Cartwright,	p	p	p	p	p	p	p	m	
5th " Thomas Dillard,	r	p	a	a	p	p	p	p	
1st Corp'l B. F. Bulloch,	p	p	p	p	p	w			
2d " W. C. Kerr,	p	p	p	p	p	p	a	a	
3d " J. I. Smith,	r	p	a	a	p	p	p	w	
4th " J. Connally,	p	s	a	a	p	w			
Allen, B. H,	p	s	k						
Anders, B.,	r	a	a	a	p	p	p	*a	
Barzo, H.,	p	p	k						
Brent, T. A.,	a	a	a	a	p	k			
Bryant, ,	r	p	k						
McDaniel, Y. L.,	p	a	a	a	*a				
Jett, J. R. P.,	p	p	p	p	p	p	p	p	Musician.
Bell, O. W.,	a	a	a	a	*d				
Copeland, W. E.,	p	p	w						
Cartwright, L. C.,	r	s	a	a	p	p	p	p	
Chilton, F. B.,	p	a	a	*a					
Clepper, L.,	r	a	a	a	a	a	a	a	
Coode, Wm.,	r	p	a	a	p	p	p	a	
Dawson, R. C.,	p	p	a	p	p	w			Dead.
Dale, G. W.,	r	a	a	a	a	a	a	a	
Dowdy, C.,	r	p	a	a	p	p	a	a	
Ellis, J.,	r	a	a	a	a	a	a	a	
Fox, R.,	r	p	a	a	p	a	a	a	
Faulkner, A.,	r	p	p	p	p	p	p	m	
Farrow, S. W.,	r	a	a	a	a	a	a	a	

Name									Remarks
Fisher, W.,	p	p	w						
Griggs, G.,	p	p	a	a	a	a	a	a	
Hopkins, J. C.,	p	p	s	a	p	p	p	p	
Harrison, D.,	p	a	a	a	a	a	a	a	
Hahn, A.,	a	a	w	a	p	p	p	p	
Hall, J. H.,	p	a	a	a	p	m			
Jeffers, M. S.,	r	p	p	a	p	a	a	a	
King, S. P.,	p	a	a	a	p	w			
King, F. G.,	p	a	a	a	p	p	p	p	
Keyser, H.,	r	p	a	a	p	p	a	a	
Kerby, B.,	r	a	w						
Lewis, J. L.,	p	p	a	a	p	p	p	m	
Lemon, J. W.,	p	p	p	p	p	p	p	a	
Landrum, W. J.,	*a	p	a	a	p	p	*a		
Lewis, C. A.,	p	s	w						
Lowns, J.,	r	p	w						
Lavantuer, L.,	r	a	a	a	p	w			
Long, J.,	a	p	w						
Mitchell, ______,	r	p	a	a	p	a	a		
May, W. C.,	p	p	w	a	p	w			
May, R. M.,	p	p	w	a	a	a	a	a	
Collier, A.,	r	a	p	p	s	s	s	s	Musician.
May, Thomas,	p	p	p	p	p	a	a	a	
May, D. G.,	p	p	w						
McCowan, A. J.,	p	p	p	p	p	p	a	a	
Myers, M. F.,	p	a	a	a	a	a	a	a	
Parker, W. A.,	a	a	a	a	p	p	p	w	
Petty, Thomas,	p	a	w						
Rankin, R.,	r	a	a	p	a	a	a	a	
Sharp, J. H.,	p	p	a	a	p	w			
Savage, Ed.,	p	p	a	a	a	a	a	a	
Seay, A. B.,	a	a	p	a	a	a	a	a	
Seargeant, Thomas,	p	p	a	a	a	a	a	a	
Seargeant, James,	r	p	w						
Stewart, R. H.,	p	a	a	a	a	a	a	a	
Stewart, J. E.,	p	p	p	p	p	p	w		
Smith, John,	r	p	w						
Stratton, R. R.,	p	p	w						
Stucy, Matt,	r	p	w						
Stucey, J.,	r	a	a	a	a	a	a	a	
Spivey, J. S.,	p	p	w						
Tucker, D. J.,	p	p	a	a	a	a	a	a	
Talliaferro, J.,	p	p	p	s	p	a	a	a	
Taylor, C. L.,	r	a	s	s	s	s	s	s	
Taylor, Alexander,	p	p	a	a	a	a	a	a	
Talley, R.,	r	p	p	p	p	p	p	p	
Talley, J. C.,	r	s	a	a	p	p	a	a	
Travis, H.,	p	p	w						
Watson, W. A.,	p	p	p	p	a	a	a	a	
Watson, H. C.,	r	p	s	s	p	k			
Waltrip, C. M.,	p	a	a	a	a	a	a	a	
Wynne, S. W.,	r	p	p	p	p	k			
Wynne, T. A.,	r	a	p	p	p	p	w	a	
Wilkes, B. B.,	r	a	a	a	p	w			
Martin, W.,	a	a	k						
Ransom, R. W.,	a	p	a	a	p	k			
Gillam, J. H.,	p	p	k						
Nevils, D. E.,	a	a	a	a	*d				
Gafford, R.,	r	d							
Sanders, C. B.,	r	a	a	a	*d				
Lewis, William,	r	a	a	a	*d				
Holt, A. C.,	s	s	s	s	*d				
Quigley, R.,	r	p	k						
Edmondson, T. J.,	p	a	a	a	d				Died 1st July, 1862.
Myers, T. J.,	r	a	s	s	d				
Leach, ______,	r								
Cathey, B. H.,	r	a	a	a	a	a	a	a	

Name									Remarks
Hatch, L. B., - - - - - - - - - -	d								Date of the following deaths not remembered.
Morris, A., - - - - - - - - - - -	d								
Howard, C.,- - - - - - - - - - -	d								
Howard, N.,- - - - - - - - - - -	d								
Seward, J., - - - - - - - - - - -	d								
Bascomb, G. F.,- - - - - - - - -	d								
Farrow, D.,- - - - - - - - - - -	d								
Rogers, J. P.,- - - - - - - - - -	d								
Wallace, J.,- - - - - - - - - - -	*d								Date of the following discharges not remembered.
Sanderlin, J., - - - - - - - - - -	*d								
Mathews, T. R.,- - - - - - - - -	*d								
Thigpen, Ed, - - - - - - - - - -	*d								
Thigpen, G., - - - - - - - - - -	*d								
Keyser, G. W., - - - - - - - - -	*d								
Walker, Jno., - - - - - - - - - -	*d								
Wynne, A. J., - - - - - - - - - -	*d								
Lackland, S. M.,- - - - - - - - -	*d								
Millican, Wm.,- - - - - - - - - -	*d								
McGraw, Wm., - - - - - - - - - -	*d								
Thomas, J.,- - - - - - - - - - -	a	p	a	a	a	a	p	a	Detached March, 1862.
Finley, Howard,- - - - - - - - -									Detached Service.
Beck, Jacob, - - - - - - - - - -									Detached Service.
Peacock, William, - - - - - - - -									Detached Service.

CO. I

Name									Remarks
Capt. C. M. Winkler, - - - - - -	a	p	p	p	p	p	p	p	
1st Lt. J. Loughridge - - - - -	p	p	w	a	a	a	a	a	
2d "Mat Beasley, - - - - - -	p	p	w	a	a	a	a	a	
2d " N. J. Mills,- - - - - - -	p	p	p	p	p	p	p	w	
1st Serg't. J. W. Duren,- - - - -	p	p	s	s	s	s	p	p	
2d " S. M. Riggs,- - - - -	p	p	p	p	p	p	p	p	
3d " T. R. Morris, - - - -	a	p	p	w	p	w	a	a	
4th " S. B. Terrell - - - -	a	s	s	s	s	s	s	s	
5th " J. D. Caddell - - - -	p	p	p	p	p	p	p	p	
1st C'l J. B. Lanham, - - - - -	p	p	p	a	s	s	p	w	
2d " R. G. Hollaway- - - - -	s	s	p	s	p	p	p	p	
3d C'l Jas Hamilton,- - - - - -	s	s	s	s	*d				
4th " J. A. Foster,- - - - - -	p	p	s	s	p	w	a	a	
Astin, J. H., - - - - - - - - -	p	p	w	a	a	a	a	a	
Armstrong, R. C., - - - - - - -	s	s	s	s	p	p	*a	*a	
Allen, W. B., - - - - - - - - -	r	s	p	p	p	p	p	p	
Beasley, J. R., - - - - - - - -	s	p	p	s	p	k			
Barry, M., - - - - - - - - - -	p	a	p	*a	p	a	*a	*a	
Barry, A.,- - - - - - - - - - - -	a	a	p	*a	*a	*a	p	m	
Brewster, A. J.,- - - - - - - -	p	p	p	s	a	a	a	a	
Bales, W. H., - - - - - - - - -	s	s	s	s	s	s	s	s	
Boynton, G. S., - - - - - - - -	p	s	s	s	s	s	s	s	Discharged 22d Sept.
Byas, A. J., - - - - - - - - -	r	s	s	s	s	s	s	s	
Black, J. R., - - - - - - - - -	r	p	s	s	s	s	s	s	
Black, H. F., - - - - - - - - -	r	s	s	s	p	w	a	a	
Crabb, E. S., - - - - - - - - -	p	p	s	s	p	w	a	a	
Crabtree, J. W., - - - - - - - -	p	p	p	w	p	w	p	p	
Crawford, R. W.,- - - - - - - -	p	p	p	a	p	m	a	*a	Taken prisoner at Manassas.
Carroll, W. E., - - - - - - - -	r	p	w	a	a	a	a	a	
Childress, B. F., - - - - - - - -	s	s	s	s	s	p	s	s	
Dillard, F. P., - - - - - - - -	p	s	s	s	p	p	p	w	
Foster, G. W.,- - - - - - - - -	p	p	s	s	p	w	a	a	
Faster, M. L.,- - - - - - - - -	s	s	s	s	p	*a	*a	*a	
Franklin, James, - - - - - - -	s	p	w	a	a	a	a	a	
Fagan, J. G., - - - - - - - - -	p	p	p	*a	*a	*a	*a	*a	
Fuller, W. W., - - - - - - - - -	p	s	p	s	p	p	p	*a	
Fuller, J. L., - - - - - - - - -	r	s	s	s	s	s	s	s	
Fondren, W. A., - - - - - - - -	p	p	k						
Fortsan, J. R., - - - - - - - -	r	p	p	s	a	a	a	a	
Garner, E. M.,- - - - - - - - -	p	p	w	a	p	p	p	m	
Green, J. T., - - - - - - - - -	a	a	a	a	p	p	p	*a	

Name									Remarks
Green, John,	s	d							
Gregory, R.,	r	s	a	a	a	a	a	a	
Gregory, John	r	p	w	a	a	a	a	a	
Harrison, H. H.,	p	p	p	s	*a				
Harrison, J. J.,	p	p	s	s	s	s	s	s	
Hill, Jack,	s	s	w	a	a	p	a	a	
Hill, J. H.,	p	p	w	a	a	a	p	w	
Holdaman, J. W.,	p	p	p	p	s	s	s	s	
Hagle, James,	s	s	s	s	p	p	*a		
Herbert, J. H.,	p	p	p	p	p	w	a	a	
Henderson, G. W.,	p	p	p	p	p	p	p	p	
Harris, J. Q.,	p	p	p	p	s	s	s	s	
Hamilton, J. L.,	r	s	s	s	s	s	s	s	
Jackson, W. G.,	p	m	*a	*a	s	s	s	s	Taken prisoner Seven Pines.
Jefferson, W. R.,	p	p	s	s	p	p	s	s	
Jordan, J. C.,	p	s	s	s	p	*a			
Killian, H. L. W.,	p	p	p	p	p	p	p	w	
Kennedy, Thomas,	p	p	s	s	p	w	a	a	
Lemmon, A. M.,	p	p	w	a	a	a	a	a	
Lummons, J. M.,	s	s	p	p	p	w	a	a	
Miller, R. S.,	p	p	p	s	p	w	a	a	
Massey, J. H.,	p	w	a	a	a	a	a	a	
Melton, J. E.,	s	p	p	p	p	p	p	p	
McMorris, J. M.,	p	p	p	p	p	k			
Platt, W. G.,	p	p	w	a	a	a	a	a	
Pickett, John,	p	p	w	a	a	a	a	a	
Polk, J. M.,	a	p	w	a	a	a	p	p	
Orendoff, J. H.,	r	s	p	p	p	p	p	p	
Rice, L. W.,	p	p	s	s	s	s	s	s	
Rice, R. N.,	p	p	s	s	p	k			
Rice, J. L.,	r	s	s	s	d				
Ruskin, M. D. L.,	r	p	s	s	p	p	p	p	
Simmons, J. W.,	p	p	p	p	p	p	s	s	
Smith, P.,	p	p	p	p	p	p	p	p	
Smith, W. T.,	p	s	s	s	p	w	a	a	
Smith, W. G.,	s	*a							
Spence, W. P.,	a	s	s	s	p	w	d		
Sessions, E. G.,	p	s	s	s	s	s	s	s	
Shaw, J. R.,	r	p	w	a	a	a	a	a	
Templeton, William,	p		p	s	s	s	s	s	
Templeton, M. B.,	r	s	s	s	s	s	s	s	
Treadwell, J. H.,	p	p	w	a	a	a	a	a	
Utzman, J. L.,	p	p	a	a	a	a	a	a	
Wade, R. H.,	p	p	w	a	a	a	a	a	
Weil, S.,	a	p	a	a	a	a	a	a	
Welch, J. C.,	p	p	w	a	a	a	a	a	
Walker, J. C.,	p	p	p	a	s	s	s	s	
Walker, H. E.,	s	s	p	a	a	a	a	a	
Waters, Ezekiel,	r	s	w	a	a	a		a	
Warren, B.,	r	s	s	s	s	s			

CO. K.

Name									Remarks
Capt. Wm. H. Marin,	p	p	p	p	p	p	p	p	
1st Lt. John F. Burress,	a	p	w	a	a	a	a	a	
2d " M. O. Clanahan,	p	a	w	a	a	a	a	a	
3d " W. D. Rounsavall,	p	p	w	a	a	a	a	a	
Anding, John	r	p	d						Died in Hospital.
Allen, J. M.,	r				p	p	p	p	
Allen, J. W.,	r								Died in Hospital.
Antle, Milton,	r		p		p	p	p	p	
Ball, B. L.,	r				p	p	a	p	
Barham, C. J.,									Died of wounds received at Yorktown.
Boles, Axom,	p								
Bradley, J. F. T.,	p	a	p	p	p	p	p	p	
Baker, Joseph	a	a	p	p	a	a	a	a	
Boyd, James	p								Pioneer.
Banks, T. C.,	p	p	p	p	p	p	a	a	
Brown, W. B.,	r	p	s	a	a	a	a	a	

Name									Remarks
Carguilo, W. A.,	a	a	p	w	s	a	a	a	
Cox, B. M.,	p	p	k						
Champion, L. D.,	a	a	w	a	a	a	*a	*a	
Campbell, A.,	a	a	a	a					
Campbell, J. E.,	a	p	p	p	a	a	a	a	
Campbell, J. M.,	p	p	w	a	p	p	a	a	
Clanahan, W. R.,	r	a	a	a	p	p	p	w	
Chapman, M.,	r	p	p	p	p	p	p	p	Litter bearer.
Chapman, J.,	r	p	a	a	p	p	a	a	
Carter, Hugh,	a	p	p	p	p	w	a	a	
Derden, W. L.,	p	a	p	p	p	p	p	p	
Elledge, H. D.,	r	p	k						
Elledge, J. F.,	r	p	p	a	p	p	p	p	
Edwards, W. L.,	r	p	w						Died of wounds received
Forester, Joel,	p	p	a	p	p	p	p	a	at Gaines' Farm.
Forester, Thomas,	r	a							Died in Hospital.
Green, J. J.,	p	a	a	a	a	a	a	a	
Green, D. N.,	a	a	a	a	a	a	a	a	
Guthrie, L. J.,	p	p	a	a	p	p	a	a	
Gibbon, J. F.,									Litter bearer.
Guiger, John B.,									Musician.
Godwin, Wesley,	r	a	a	a					Died in Hospital.
Hodge, M. H.,	p	a	a	a	p	w	a	a	Detached service.
Hobgood, T. J.,	p	w	a	a	a	a	a	a	
Hight, F. M.,	p	p	k						
Heard, J. D.,	a	a	w	a	a	a	a	a	
Hamby, John,	p	a	a	a	p	p	p	p	
Hilliard, E. C.,	a	p	k						
Holland, F. M.,	r	p	a	a	a	a	a	a	
Isaacks, William S.,	a	a	w	a	a	a	a	a	
Kimbrough, J. H.,	p	a	p	p	p	a	a	a	
Loop, G. R.,	p	p	a	a	p	p	a	a	
Larue, A. J.,	p	p	p	p	p	p	p	a	
Lemox, A. C.,	r	p	a	a					Died in Hospital.
McCall, J. C.,	p	p	p	p	p	p	a	a	
McNeeley, T. G.,	p	p	w	a	a	a	a	a	
Martin, R. B.,	a	p	p	p	p	p	p	p	
Martin, Alfred,	r	p	a	a	p	p	a	a	
Martin, Henry	p	p	p	p	p	k			
Norvell, Robert,	r	p	p	a	p	p	p	p	
Owen, S. T.,	p	p	p	a	a	a	a	a	
Owen, J. D.,	a	p	p	a	p	p	p	p	
Owen, S. Trice,	p	p	w						Died of wounds received
Paul, R. B.,	p	p	a	a	p	p	p	m	at Gaines' Farm.
Patillo, B. A.,	a	a	p	p	p	p	p	p	
Pickering, James,	r	a	a	a	p	p	a	a	
Price, Russell,	r	p	a	a	p	p	w	a	
Price, W. B.,	r	p	a	a	p	p	p	p	
Phillips, H.,	r	p	a	p	p	p	a	a	
Pairr, W. R.,	r	p	a	a	a	m			
Richardson, W. E.,									Ambulance driver.
Rice, John,	p	p	a	a	p	p	p	m	
Rounsavall, James A.,	p	p	w						Died of wounds received
Rounsavall, I. M.,	p	p	p	a	a	p	p	p	at Gaines' Farm.
Rogers, A. H.,	p	p	w	a	p	p	p	p	
Rogers, S. S.,	a	p	p	p	p	p	p	p	
Rushing, J. H.,	r	a	*d						
Ross, C. C.,	r	a	p	p	p	p	p	p	
Redmon, R.,	r	a	a	a	a	a	a	a	
Swindle, J. M.,	a	p	w	a	a	a	a	a	
Smith, F. J.,	p	w	a	a	a	a	a	a	
Tubbs, Robert,	p	p	p	a	p	p	a	a	
Wilton, W. T.,	p	p	w	a	a	a	a	a	
Weisensee, C. P.,	r	p	p	p	p	w	a	a	
Whitaker, W. F.,	r	p	p	p	p	k			
Williams, E. J.,	p	p	k						
Wiggington, William,	r	p	a						Died in Hospital.
Total killed			46			22		8	Killed in all engagements, 76
wounded	2	4	198	4		77	4	85	Wounded in all " 374

NOTES

NOTES

CHAPLAIN DAVIS AND HOOD'S TEXAS BRIGADE

Introduction

[1]Unless otherwise indicated, all quotations and source material in the Introduction come from the Nicholas A. Davis Diary (1861-1862). The diary and Davis' papers are in the possession of his grandson, Frank C. Davis, jr., San Antonio, Texas, who permitted microreproductions to be deposited in the George Storch Memorial Library, Trinity University. Mr. Davis obtained these materials from his aunt, the late Mrs. Floyd McGown, only surviving daughter of Nicholas A. Davis.

[2]Dr. Brown purchased the influential *Central Presbyterian* from Dr. Moses D. Hoge and Dr. Thomas V. Moore, pastor of the First Presbyterian Church of Richmond, in 1859. Peyton H. Hoge, *Moses Drury Hoge; His Life and Letters* (Richmond, 1899), 118, 166.

[3]There were no Poles in the short-lived Polish Brigade, the 3rd Louisiana Battalion, which was raised by one G. Tochman, native of Poland. Richmond *Dispatch,* November 6, 1861.

[4]"Jerusalem!" exclaimed a Texan to a division administratress of Chimborazo, "Why, you's as pretty as a pair of red shoes with green strings." Phoebe Yates Pember, *A Southern Woman's Story* (New York, 1879), 11.

[5]Richmond *Enquirer,* September 25, 1861. A letter signed by Davis did not appear, but a complaint of tailor charges published on October 1 may have been written anonymously by the chaplain. Davis' completed uniform did not conform to his expectations, a possible explanation of the discrepancy in the number of rows of buttons.

[6]*Ibid.,* September 17, 1861; Richmond *Dispatch,* September 18, October 7, November 11, 13, 29, 30, 1861.

[7]Address of Gov. Edward Clark, November 1, 1861, *War of the Rebellion: Official Records of the Union and Confederate Armies,* 128 vols. (Washington, 1880-1901), Ser. 4, I, 717. Cited hereafter as *O. R.*

[8]*Ibid.,* 595.

[9]Despite this natural interference, a U. S. navy fleet under Admiral Samuel Francis du Pont participated in the capture of Port Royal, S. C., on November 7. Clement Eaton, *A History of the Southern Confederacy* (New York, 1954), 179.

[10]A photograph of the mess of Captain C. M. Winkler near Dumfries, except for the tent roof, is very similar to the one described. Mrs. Angelina V. Winkler, *The Confederate Capital and Hood's Texas Brigade* (Austin, 1894), 97. For a contemporary description of Dumfries, see Richmond *Dispatch,* October 21, 1861.

[11]Hood was baptized during the Atlanta campaign at Dalton, Ga. in May, 1864, by Bishop-General Leonidas Polk. William M. Polk (ed.), *Leonidas Polk, Bishop and General,* 2 vols. (New York, 1894), II, 329.

[12]Joseph B. Polley, *Hood's Texas Brigade: Its Marches, Its Battles, Its Achievements* (New York, 1910), 17-18. This volume is useful if the reader recalls the caution of a reviewer of Civil War books, "one suspects that some of the participants' accounts, put in print several [nearly fifty in this instance] years later, grew with retelling." Wendell Holmes Stephenson, "Civil War,

Cold War, Modern War: Thirty Volumes in Review," *Journal of Southern History,* XXV (August, 1959), 302.

[13]A more generous gift to the Tom Green Rifles from Austin (Co. B) on January 9, 1862, included "over four thousand dollars worth of clothing, blankets, &c." from the ladies of Travis county. Richmond *Dispatch,* January 17, 1862. Contributions received by the Texans in Virginia from their home state totaled $87,800 as of March 11, 1862. Howard Swiggett (ed.), J. B. Jones, *A Rebel War Clerk's Diary at the Confederate States Capital,* 2 vols. (New York, 1935), I, 114.

[14]Captain Wise of the "Richmond Blues" died of wounds received in the Battle of Roanoke Island. He had been an editor of the Richmond *Enquirer.*

[15]Richmond *Dispatch,* February 22, 1862.

[16]Francis R. Lubbock to Judah P. Benjamin, March 7, 1862, *O. R.*, Ser. 4, I, 978.

[17]Samuel A. Roberts to Samuel Cooper, March 12, 1862, *ibid.*, 991-92. Roberts, a classmate of Jefferson Davis at West Point, had previously served the Republic of Texas as secretary of state under Mirabeau B. Lamar. Walter P. Webb (ed.), *The Handbook of Texas,* 2 vols. (Austin, 1952), II, 485.

[18]Lubbock to Benjamin, March 13, 1862, *O. R.*, Ser. 4, I, 995.

[19]Both of Co. B, Tom Green Rifles. William C. Walsh, permanently disabled at Gaines' Mill, later served eight years as Commissioner of the General Land Office. Sometime editor and wit Robert A. Davidge, following his capture in Maryland, wrote of his "death" to his mess mate, Bill Calhoun, in a letter which arrived with a flag of truce message! Polley, *Hood's Texas Brigade,* 317; Frank B. Chilton, *Unveiling and Dedication of Monument to Hood's Texas Brigade . . .* (Houston, 1911), 289. For another amusing episode involving Davidge and Calhoun, see Polley, *A Soldier's Letters to Charming Nellie* (New York, 1908), 71-74.

[20]Winkler, *The Confederate Capital and Hood's Texas Brigade,* 36-37.

[21]Frank Brown, "Annals of Travis County," 13 vols. and appendix, VIII, 51. Typescript in possession of Dr. Frances K. Hendricks, his granddaughter, of San Antonio.

[22]E. B. Cushing, "Edward Hopkins Cushing: An Appreciation by His Son," *Southwestern Historical Quarterly,* XXI (April, 1922), 266, 268.

[23]Houston *Tri-Weekly Telegraph,* August 17, 1863.

[24]*Ibid.*

[25]*Ibid.*

[26]*Ibid.*, May 26, 1863.

[27]United States Census Reports, Seventh Census, Schedule I, Free Inhabitants in the County of Limestone, State of Alabama, 1850, p. 145; *ibid.*, Eighth Census, Schedule I, Free Inhabitants in the Town of Bastrop, County of Bastrop, State of Texas, 1860, p. 11. Microfilm copies of all census reports in the Barker Texas History Center, University of Texas.

[28]Willis Brewer, *Alabama: Her History, Resources, War Record, Public Men. From 1540 to 1872* (Montgomery, 1872), 326-27. Although he did not accept encouragement to run for the United States Senate, the elder Davis did serve as a presidential elector. William Garrett, *Reminiscenses of Public Men in Alabama, for Thirty Years* (Atlanta, 1872), 233-34.

[29]Dr. L. A. Johnson, "Rev. Nicholas A. Davis," Nashville *Cumberland Presbyterian*, January 17, 24, 1895.

[30]United States Census Reports, Eighth Census, Schedule II, Slave Inhabitants in the Town of Bastrop, County of Bastrop, State of Texas, 1860, p. 4.

[31]Nicholas A. Davis Papers.

[32]United States Census Reports, Ninth Census, Schedule I, Free Inhabitants in the Town of Hemphill, County of Sabine, State of Texas, 1870, p. 12.

[33]Nicholas A. Davis Papers.

[34]Frank W. Johnson and Eugene C. Barker (eds.), *A History of Texas and Texans*, 5 vols. (Chicago, 1916), IV, 1860.

[35]Hattie J. Roach, *The Hills of Cherokee: Historical Sketches of Life in Cherokee County, Texas* (Rusk, Tex., 1952), 70, 124.

[36]Johnson, "Nicholas A. Davis," Nashville *Cumberland Presbyterian*, January 24, 1895; photostat of unidentified newspaper clipping in possession of Frank C. Davis, jr.

[37]Johnson, "Nicholas A. Davis," Nashville *Cumberland Presbyterian*, January 24, 1895.

[38]George W. West to John B. Hood, May 28, 1867, Nicholas A. Davis Papers.

[39]San Antonio *Express*, November 21, 1894.

[40]Johnson, "Nicholas A. Davis," Nashville *Cumberland Presbyterian*, January 24, 1895.

THE CAMPAIGN FROM TEXAS TO MARYLAND

[1]Although the Convention reassembled on that date, it was not until two days later that secession was effected. Rupert N. Richardson, *Texas: The Lone Star State* (Englewood Cliffs, 1958), 186. On March 2, however, the Congress of the Confederate States passed an act to admit Texas to the Confederacy. *O. R.*, Ser. 4, I, 120.

[2]General Tom Green of Austin commanded the troops at Camp Clark, named for the governor. Colonel R. T. P. Allen, superintendent of the Bastrop Military Academy, drilled the troops. The men remained there only about three weeks instead of the expected forty days. Brown, "Annals of Travis County," VIII, 53, 56-58.

[3]See *ibid.* for a description of the gala departure from Austin of the Tom Green Rifles.

[4]Nicholas A. Davis, *The Campaign from Texas to Maryland* (Houston, 1863), 4. Cited henceforth as Houston edition.

[5]A lengthy letter published in the Richmond *Enquirer*, September 21, 1861, supported Davis' description of the ordeals of the journey.

[6]"We were thus contending eleven days with the rain above us, the mud and water below us, and billions upon billions of the largest and fiercest *mosquitoes* in the world around us . . . . When I reflect, that in Texas, most of us almost live, move, and have our being upon horseback; and that none of us ever *walk* there any distance at all, it seems almost incredible to me, that we have walked 150 miles . . . And when I reflect that we have not only *walked*, but *waded* that distance, I feel almost afraid to publish the statement." *Ibid.* Shortly thereafter the Terry Rangers experienced similar conditions

between Niblett's Bluff and New Iberia. Margaret Bell Jones (comp.), *Bastrop: A Compilation of Material Relating to the History of the Town of Bastrop with Letters Written by Terry Rangers* (Bastrop, Tex., 1936), 41.

[7]Diary of Nicholas A. Davis, September 12, 1861. Cited henceforth as Diary.

[8]*Ibid.*

[9]*Ibid.*, September 17, 1861.

[10]*Ibid.*, September 27, 1861.

[11]Houston edition, 10.

[12]Diary, October 8, 1861.

[13]Houston edition, 11.

[14]*Ibid.*

[15]Diary, October 21, 1861.

[16]*Ibid.*, November 7, 1861.

[17]Houston edition, 12.

[18]*Ibid.*

[19]Diary, November 12, 1861.

[20]Later in the war Texas soldiers learned to march light, but they "could not reduce the weight to be carried to less than thirty-six pounds. A gun weighed about ten pounds, the cartridge box, cap-box, bayonet and the belts and straps to which these hung, another ten, and the roll of blanket and tent, or oil-cloth still another ten. Add to these the weight of the haversack, in which not only provisions but under-clothing and many other necessities were carried—often went a little beyond forty [pounds]. A canteen full of water weighed at least three pounds." Polley, *Hood's Texas Brigade*, 73.

[21]Diary, November 14, 1861.

[22]Houston edition, 13.

[23]Diary, November 29, 1861.

[24]*Ibid.*

[25]Polley, nearly fifty years later, blamed Wigfall rather than Archer. "General Wigfall's imagination was too often quickened by deep potations to be reliable. The colder the night and the more metallic the rustling of the pine tops above his quarters, the more plainly he could hear the rattling of oars in the oar-locks of boats transporting Federal troops across the Potomac." Polley, *Hood's Texas Brigade*, 15-16.

[26]Houston edition, 14; Richmond *Dispatch*, February 3, 6, 1862.

[27]See Richmond *Enquirer*, February 13, 1862, for a similar account.

[28]Houston edition, 14.

[29]Davis departed nearly two weeks later.

[30]Prior to Christmas, measles and pneumonia restricted the activities of the men. "Diarrhea led the way to the more fatal complaints. At one time there were not exceeding twenty-five men fit for duty in the Fifth Texas, although it had in camp fully eight hundred men." Polley, *Hood's Texas Brigade*, 17.

[31]There had been public speculation as to these movements. See Richmond *Dispatch*, March 12, 1862.

[32]"Assign Brig. Gen. J. B. Hood to the command of the Texas Brigade (late Wigfall's)." Samuel Cooper, Adjutant General, to Maj. Gen. Theophilus H. Holmes, March 12, 1862, *O. R.*, Ser. 1, V, 1097.

[33]Reported in Fredericksburg *Herald*, quoted in Richmond *Dispatch*, March 24, 1862.

[34]Of the Yorktown assignment, Hood later stated that there he continued the training of the brigade. "I had so effectually aroused the pride of this splendid body of men, as to entertain little fear in regard to their action on the field of battle." John B. Hood, *Advance and Retreat*: *Personal Experiences in the United States and Confederate Armies* (New Orleans, 1880), 20. According to Hood's biographer, "By the first of May the Confederates had achieved their purpose on the peninsula. They had delayed McClellan for a month and were now ready to withdraw to previously prepared positions closer to Richmond." This was a "voluntary strategic retirement," according to John P. Dyer, *The Gallant Hood* (Indianapolis, 1950), 66. Biographer Dyer noted that "Hood's own book, written largely as a defense of himself, is biased and at times inaccurate, but it also contains valuable information." *Ibid.*, 368.

[35]Hood's Brigade numbered 1,922 and that of E. M. Law's, 2,398. *O. R.*, Ser. 1, XI, 50.

[36]Houston edition, 18.

[37]"We were marched to the corn crib like horses." Diary, May 6, 1862.

[38]"John Deal & Doak Sater fired & both balls took effect." *Ibid.*, May 7, 1861. Subsequent historians of the brigade did not mention Sater either.

[39]Houston edition, 20.

[40]For further comments see Report No. 10 of Maj. Gen. Gustavus W. Smith, May 12, 1862, *O. R.*, Ser. 1, XI, Pt. 1, 627-28. Maj. Gen. D. H. Hill reported that the enemy's "experience gained with the Texans had been ample and satisfactory." *Ibid.*, 605. Also see Hood's and Whiting's reports, *ibid.*, 629-32.

A general engagement was not intended. General Joseph E. Johnston reportedly stated: " 'General Hood, have you given an illustration of the Texas idea of feeling an enemy gently and falling back? What would your Texans have done, sir, if I had ordered them to charge and drive back the enemy?' " Hood allegedly replied: " 'I suppose, General, they would have driven them into the river, and tried to swim out and capture the gun-boats.' " Shelby Foote, *The Civil War*: *A Narrative, Fort Sumter to Perryville* (New York. 1958), 412.

[41]Diary, May 8, 1862.

[42]*Ibid.*, n.d.

[43]*Ibid.*, May 31, 1862.

[44]*Ibid.*

[45]*Ibid.*

[46]*Ibid.*, June 3, 1862. For a description of the field after the battle, see Richmond *Enquirer*, July 7, 1862.

[47]Diary, June 1, 1862.

[48]Of this skirmish a Texan wrote that it was not their purpose "*to dig* trenches—that's not our style," but to scour the woods "in front of our line and the Nine Mile Road . . . and to drive them out if possible." With the command,

"'Forward boys! Give them h-ll!' The Texas warhoop rose on the air, and a thousand Yankees rose like dark spirits through the gloom of the forest. The voices of their officers could be heard through the din of battle urging their men to stand, but it was in vain they assayed to stop our fast advancing line. They fired one volley and took [to] their heels." Richmond *Dispatch*, June 11, 1862. This incident led to another Texas brag. "When 'the fight' takes place the *Texas Brigade* will kill more Yankees, storm more batteries, and capture fewer prisoners than any other brigade in the service." *Ibid.* Following this episode there were complaints in the Richmond press from Texans that their action was slighted in favor of news printed of Virginia regiments.

[49]Robert E. Lee commanded the Army of Northern Virginia after the Battle of Seven Pines. "His first move was to send General Whiting's Division to Staunton, as a ruse, to join General Jaskson; to order the latter then to march toward Richmond" and eventually "with his united forces to make a general assault upon the Federals." Hood, *Advance and Retreat*, 24-25.

[50]Another anecdote, possibly apocryphal, emphasized Hood's efforts to speed up the march. "There were many stills in the secluded nooks of the Blue Ridge, and by 9 a. m. [June 16] many of the boys were in good humor, more than a few were staggering, and apple-jack brandy could be had out of dozens of canteens. To prevent any straggling for the purpose of replenishing empty canteens, Hood authorized the statement, which was industriously circulated and really belived, that small-pox was raging among the citizens living along our route. Riding by himself, half a mile in rear of the brigade, he discovered, lying in the middle of the road and obviously very drunk a member of the Fourth Texas." When other stragglers went to assist the drunk he warned: " 'Don't you fellers that ain't been vaccinated come near me—I've got the small-pox—that's wha's the masser with me.' " Polley, *Hood's Texas Brigade*, 35-36.

[51]Houston edition, 25.

[52]*Ibid.*, 26.

[53]Known variously as Gaines' Farm, Gaines' Mill, Cold Harbor, or Coal Harbor. The 1860 census listed William F. Gaines, age 56, as "M.D. & Farmer." His real estate was valued at $69,000 and personal property at more than $54,000. United States Census Reports, Eight Census, Schedule I, Free Inhabitants in St. Paul's Parish in the County of Hanover, State of Virginia, 1860, Vol. 11, p. 51. Living in a large dwelling six miles ENE of Richmond, "rampant secessionist" Dr. Gaines was kept under house guard during the fight. Joel Cook, *The Siege of Richmond: A Narrative of the Military Operations of Major-General George B. McClellan During the Months of May and June, 1862* (Philadelphia, 1862), 1701-71. For the relationship of the fighting at Gaines' Farm and Coal Harbor to the east, part of the same engegement, see Frank E. Vandiver, *Mighty Stonewall* (New York, 1957), 304-309. To answer Bruce Catton's Federal officer in *A Stillness at Appomattox* (New York, 1955), 149, "who visited the place [and] wondered how it had ever got its name. There was no harbor within miles, and the place was far from cold—was, in fact . . . very much like a bake oven," a contemporary newspaper notice explained in part. "There is some misapprehension in regard to the name of the locality of one of the most important of the series of battles lately fought and won

in the neighborhood of this city. A misapprehension not only in regard to the origin of the name, but to the name itself. Some of our contemporaries speak of the battle of 'Cold Harbor.' This name will be news to the readers of the 'Enquirer,' but Coal Harbor has been familiar to them, as a voting place, ever since the establishment of precinct elections, and long before the birthday of the greater number of soldiers who distinguished themselves in the battle of Friday evening. Coal Harbor is the name, but we do not know its origin." Richmond *Enquirer,* July 12, 1862. While Coal Harbor was the name place in the Richmond press, in Cook's, *Siege of Richmond,* 123, and in Edward A. Pollard, *The First Year of the War* (Richmond, 1862), 329-31, twentieth century historians have used the corrupted spelling, Cold Harbor, found in official reports and memoirs.

[54]Houston edition, 29.

[55]The chaplain might have quoted a lengthy statement of the 4th Texas' role at Gaines' Mill printed in the Richmond *Enquirer,* July 4, 1862. Other source materials for the 4th Texas in this engagement may be found in Hood's report, *O. R.,* Ser. 1, XI, Pt. 2, 568-69; Jackson's report, *ibid.,* 555-56; and Whiting's report, *ibid.,* 563-64. A 4th Texas casualty list was reported by Adjutant W. E. Bassett to the Richmond *Enquirer,* July 10, 1862. Captain D. U. Barziza, in a private letter not published until war's end, described the battle in some detail. Houston *Tri-Weekly Telegraph,* April 3, 1865.

[56]Houston edition, 32.

[57]*Ibid.*

[58]*Ibid.*

[59]Officers of the 6th New Jersey surrendered their swords to Lt. Col. John C. Upton of the 5th Texas, reportedly naked with the exception of a woolen overshirt, a sword trailing at his side, and a long-handled frying pan in his hand. Polley, *Hood's Texas Brigade,* 68-69.

[60]Diary, June 27, 1862.

[61]It was on this oft-recalled occasion that Tom Owens, just before the battle opened, waved his sword above his head and quoted the lines from Scott's "Marmion." " 'Charge, Chester, charge! On, Stanley, on!' Were the last words of Marmion." Polley, *Hood's Texas Brigade,* 57-58. Warwick had left his sick bed against his physician's orders. *Ibid.,* 50.

[62]Houston edition, 33-34.

[63]The White House was "a very fine plantation belonging to Mrs. Gen. Lee. It was the residence of Mrs. Custis when she was married to Washington." George B. McClellan, *McClellan's Own Story . . .* (New York, 1887), 60. A more detailed description may be found in Cook, *The Siege of Richmond,* 168-70.

[64]Diary, n.d.

[65]After their successes in the seven days fighting around Richmond, the Texans drew crowds of onlookers when they were in the city. Swiggett (ed.), Jones, *A Rebel War Clerk's Diary at the Confederate States Capitol,* II, 37. Even prouder were the people back home. "Texians, save your choicest honors and your brightest laurels for the Texas Brigade. Hereafter, let whoever was in that great battle [Gaines' Mill] be welcomed to your homes, and be made to feel that for the fame he has gained for Texas, a greatful [*sic*] people will

never cease to feel proud." Houston *Tri-Weekly Telegraph,* August 13, 1862. Accounts of costly victories were not without humor; although a Texas soldier cautioned a newspaper editor not to repeat his "original" anecdote, it was published forthwith.

"One of the Yankee prisoners talking to me, said: 'The grand army will be on hand in a few days.'

'Oh no,' I remarked; 'that will be prevented.'

'What's in his road?' asked the Yankee.

'Why, in the first place, I don't think he can pass our 'Pickett'; and if he does, he will have *rough* 'Rhodes' to travel on; and after that a *mighty* 'Longstreet' to travel through; then two *terrible* 'Hills' to pass over; and, lastly, an impassable barrier in the shape of a 'Stonewall'—these are impediments which no Yankee army could make way with.' " *Ibid.*, July 25, 1862.

[66]Casualty reports from division and brigade headquarters varied slightly. See *O. R.*, Ser. 1, XI, Pt. 2, 503-569. Regimental losses of the 4th Texas included 44 killed, 208 wounded, and 1 missing. William F. Fox, *Regimental Losses in the American Civil War, 1861-1865* (Albany, 1889), 556-58.

[67]Diary, July 13-15, 1862. A description of the sad conditions of the hospitals, and a special plea for attention to the Chimborazo Hospital, appeared in the Richmond *Enquirer*, July 11, 1862. The Confederate Congress debated and there were letters to the editor of the *Enquirer* on this subject throughout September and October. A soldier wrote home, "Ah, my dear friend, you know, in Texas, nothing of the horrors of this war. If you could see the poor, sick and wounded soldiers in the Hospitals, and along the streets of this city, your heart would sink within you. But I will not 'harrow up your soul' by describing them. May God have mercy on them and us." Houston *Tri-Weekly Telegraph,* October 1, 1862. For a later and more favorable report, see Dr. J. R. Gildersleeve, "History of Chimborazo Hospital, C. S. A.," *Southern Historical Society Papers,* 49 vols. (Richmond, 1876-1943), XXXVI, 86 ff.

[68]Diary, July 14, 1862.

[69]*Ibid.*

[70]The month-long rest on the Mechanicsville Road, three miles outside Richmond, was overdue. "To the Texans at this place came long-delayed letters . . . a great deal of much needed clothing, and with the latter, that pest of the soldier, the body louse. Up to this time we had no acquaintance with the animal—thenceforward to the close of the war, he remained with us." Polley, *Hood's Texas Brigade,* 72.

[71]According to a Company F private writing just prior to the Seven Days battles, a planned Texas hospital in connection with the Infirmary of St. Francis de Sales failed when a "loud mouthed" Methodist chaplain insisted on holding a service there without the permission of the nuns. The same individual reported that Mrs. Mollie J. Young had "succeeded in raising thirty thousand dollars in gold" for a Texas hospital. Polley, *A Soldier's Letters to Charming Nellie,* 49. The editor seriously doubts the authenticity of this statement. Chaplain Davis, generous in his praise to those who assisted him, did not mention Mrs. Young nor such a sum of money in his diary or publications; his hospital, an adjunct to St. Francis de Sales, cost only $758.47. It

was true that the Sisters of Mercy at the Catholic hospital had nursed the Texans, who appreciated the superior, Sister Juliana, for her "patience, fortitude, and sensible oversight of her charges." Winkler, *Confederate Capital and Hood's Texas Brigade,* 88. In reference to the chaplain and his hospital, Mrs. Winkler stated that this "God-fearing man did a grand work here, when, it will be remembered, he took many of the men from empty box-cars, and gave them comfortable quarters." *Ibid.,* 87. The establishment of the hospital also received the attention of the Houston *Tri-Weekly Telegraph,* September 24, 1862.

[72]Lee ordered Hood on August 13 to report to Longstreet at Gordonsville. *O. R.,* Ser. 1, XI, Pt. 3, 928.

[73]Davis clearly stated that the cornfield episode took place after the battle, but nearly fifty years later Polley recalled the cornfield episode as the cause of the fight at Freeman's Ford. "Faulty memories play tricks on the pen-men," according to Stephenson, "Civil War, Cold War, Modern War," *Journal of Southern History,* XXV (August, 1959), 295.

[74]At 2:00 a. m. the fatigued men were awakened when a barrel rolled downhill into their midst. This excited a regimental favorite, "the old grey mare," to break away "loaded with kettles, tin cups and frying pans." Startled out of their sleep, the men ran "before they awoke sufficiently to recover their wits." Thus, the brigade song, "The old Gray Mare came tearing out o' the Wilderness," originated according to Hood, *Advance and Retreat,* 32-33.

[75]The Texans advanced "up the Warrenton Turnpike, 'the light of battle in our eyes, I reckon'—one recalled—'and fear of it in our hearts, I know.' " Foote, *The Civil War,* 634.

[76]Hood later declared, "The gallant Upton was, indeed, preeminent in his sphere as an outpost officer." Hood, *Advance and Retreat,* 33.

[77]Houston edition, 45.

[78]Reportedly, "one of Hood's men became strangely homesick at the sight of the dead Zouaves strewn about in their gaudy clothes. According to him, they gave the western slope of the little knoll 'the appearance of a Texas hillside when carpeted in the spring by wild flowers of many hues and tints.' " Foote, *The Civil War,* 639.

[79]Houston edition, 45.

[80]For a lengthy description of their participation in the battle "From the Note Book of the Rev. Penfield Dell, Chaplain of [the] 18th Ga. Reg., Tex. Brigade," see Richmond *Enquirer,* November 3, 1862. Dell described the Hampton Legion as "a sword in the enemy's side," and the 5th Texas as a "flame of terror."

[81]The term "skedaddle," used frequently by Davis, was of Yankee origin according to the Richmond *Dispatch,* July 26, 1862, and a "Western slang term," according to [Sallie A. Putnam], *Richmond During the War; Four Years of Personal Observataion* (New York, 1867), 169.

[82]A phrase used by McClellan during the seven days battles around Richmond and later repeated derisively by Confederate troops.

[83]An "Eye Witness" account of the Texas Brigade in the battle was printed in the Richmond *Enquirer,* September 13, 1862.

[84]Houston edition, 51.

[85]"I . . . ordered the Texas Brigade, Col. W. T. Wofford commanding, and the Third Brigade, Col. E. M. Law commanding, to move forward with bayonets fixed, which they did with their usual gallantry, driving the enemy and regaining all our lost ground, when night came on and further pursuit ceased." Report No. 248 of Hood, September 27, 1862, *O. R.*, Ser. 1, XIX, Pt. 1, 922.

[86]Houston edition, 51.

[87]Lee's order was dated September 14, 1862, *O. R.*, Ser. 1, XIX, Pt. 2, 609.

[88]Houston edition, 51-52. Hood later gave his own account of his arrest in *Advance and Retreat,* 38-40.

[89]Houston edition, 52.

[90]*Ibid.*, 52-53. The loss of 82.3% of their men at Antietam, placed the 1st Texas first in percentage of losses by Confederate regiments in a particular engagement. Fox, *Regimental Losses in the American Civil War, 1861-1865,* p. 556. Ranking third in percentage losses in any one battle, the Texas Brigade lost 64.1% at Antietam. *Ibid.*, 558.

[91]*Ibid.*, 53.

[92]Lt. Col. B. F. Carter led only about two hundred of the 4th Texas into battle, of whom ten were killed and ninety-seven wounded. *O. R.*, Ser. 1, XIX, Pt. 1, 811. The entire brigade "went into the action numbering 843 and lost, in killed, wounded, and missing, 560—over one-half." *Ibid.*, 929. Referring to the 4th Texas, Carter reported: "I cannot speak in too high terms of the conduct of both officers and men of my command. Exposed to a tremendous fire from superior numbers, in a position which it was apparent to all we could not hold, they fought on without flinching until the order to fall back was given. These men, too, were half clad, many of them barefooted, and had been only half fed for days before. The courage, constancy, and patience of our men is beyond all praise." *Ibid.*, 936.

[93]Houston edition, 54-55.

[94]Dr. Fennell, of Seguin, had arrived during the summer to work with Chaplain Davis in setting up the Texas hospital. Houston *Tri-Weekly Telegraph,* September 24, 1862.

[95]Houston edition, 58. For her account of the social life in Richmond during this period, see Mrs. D. Giraud [Louise Wigfall] Wright, *A Southern Girl in '61* (New York, 1905).

[96]*Ibid.*, 59. An earlier flag at the Texas camp, near Dumfries, had been made of her mother's wedding dress. It bore "the emblem of the 'Lone Star' and this is of pure white silk, set in blue background; the folds are purple and white. The hearts of all are riveted to it. It never will be given up." Austin *Gazette,* quoted in Richmond *Enquirer,* December 17, 1861.

[97]Chaplain Davis was less critical of Hood during this phase of the campaign than some of his contemporaries. Lee criticized Hood for the prevalence of smallpox and his failure to keep the camp clean. Lee to Longstreet, October 28, 1862, *O. R.*, Ser. 1, XIX, Pt. 2, 686. Shortly thereafter an inspection revealed Hood's lack of discipline and supervision of the 4th Texas, "two thirds badly clad and shod, 60 barefooted; camp in bad order, and the regiment showing inexcusable neglect and attention to duty on the

part of its officers." R. H. Chilton to Hood, November 14, 1862, *ibid.*, 719. See also Chilton to General Samuel Cooper, *ibid.*, 721. Pigs, fence rails, and chickens disappeared when the Texans were about. Lee admonished their leader, " 'Ah, General Hood, when you Texans come about the chickens have to roost mighty high.' " Hood, *Advance and Retreat*, 51. Nearly two years later, Lee described Hood as "a good fighter, very industrious on the battlefield, careless off." Lee to Jefferson Davis, July 2, 1864, quoted in Douglas Southall Freeman (ed.), *Lee's Dispatches* (New York, 1915), 283. A similar appraisal can be found in Freeman, *Lee's Lieutenants: A Study in Command*, 2 vols. (New York, 1943), I, 297. These accusations were supported by Hood's biographer. "Carelessness was a fault which Hood possessed from his youth and which he never overcame. From the time he dated incorrectly the acceptance of his appointment to West Point to the end of his military career . . . he was never able to make himself a capable administrator with a proper regard for details." Dyer, *The Gallant Hood*, 146. However, the chaplain's failure to criticize his general may be explained in part through biographer Dyer's estimate of Hood's leadership. "These Texans Hood understood, and they, in turn, understood him. Save for the almost fanatical response of Forrest's brigade to the leadership of 'Old Bedford' there appears to have been no brigade in the Confederacy in which there were greater *esprit* and more mutual understanding between men and their leader than in Hood's Texas Brigade. Part of this respect on the part of the men doubtless arose out of the fact that their tall powerful colonel could whip any one of them in a fist fight and would not hesitate to do so if it became necessary. But more important than this seems to have been the fact that Hood treated his men as men and not as automatons whose only duty was to do and die. The Texan proved on many a Virginia battlefield that he could and would die if necessary, but he was individualist enough to want to know why. Hood never commanded his men. He led them." *Ibid.*, 55-56.

[98]Houston edition, 63.

[99]*Ibid.*

[100]Clement L. Vallandigham, former Ohio congressman, was outspoken against the Republican administration.

[101]Houston edition, 65.

[102]*I should have taken great pleasure in giving a Lithograph of Colonel M., as well as a more extended biography had it been in my power, but not having his likeness, nor the data, I have furnished all that I could under the circumstances. THE AUTHOR

[103]Houston edition, 75-80.

[104]*Ibid.*, 81-82.

[105]Reportedly the seats of their pants were worn out from playing cards while seated on the ground, and Hood informed visiting British Colonel Garnet Wolseley: "Never mind their raggedness, Colonel—the enemy never see the backs of my Texans." Polley, *Hood's Texas Brigade*, 239.

[106]An identical letter was published in the Richmond *Enquirer*, November 29, 1862.

[107]Houston edition, 83-85.

[108]*Ibid.*, 87.

[109]Duty status corrections on the Muster Roll have not been made according to the information in Davis' letter to the Houston *Telegraph*, May 26, 1863. See pp. 19-20. The reader should keep in mind the many variations in the spelling of proper names.

INDEX